## THE TEAM

YOSEF KENET, the Israeli who led the group that relentlessly tracked Eichmann down.

SHALOM DANI, the famous artist whose talents at forgery played a crucial role.

DINA RON, the attractive agent who acted the role of Dani's mistress in the house where Eichmann was held captive.

ISSER HAREL himself, the cool, dedicated professional on whom everything hinged.

# THE HOUSE ON GARIBALDI STREET

# THE
# HOUSE
# ON
# GARIBALDI
# STREET

---

## Isser Harel

BANTAM BOOKS · TORONTO · NEW YORK · LONDON

THE HOUSE ON GARIBALDI STREET
*A Bantam Book*

PRINTING HISTORY

*Viking edition published June 1975*

*Book Digest condensation published
July & August 1975*

*Literary Guild Club edition published July 1975*

*Commentary Library edition July 1975*

SATURDAY REVIEW *edition August 1975*

*Bantam edition | June 1976*

ISBN 0–553–02501–5

*Published simultaneously in the United States and Canada*

---

---

PRINTED IN THE UNITED STATES OF AMERICA

# Foreword

Isser Harel was born in Russia in 1912, the son of a prosperous family which was ruined after the Revolution when the family business was nationalized. The family retreated to Latvia in 1923, but Isser, at the age of seventeen, followed his older sister, who had gone to Palestine a few months before. An idealistic young Zionist, he arrived there determined to dedicate himself to work on a kibbutz. Five years later he and his young wife left the kibbutz because of their urgent need for money to bring their families to Palestine from Hitler-threatened Europe.

Isser Harel's first intelligence work was against the Germans as a member of the *Hagana* (the underground force of the Jewish community in Palestine during the British mandate, which was controlled by the Jewish national institutions). From that he graduated to *Shai,* the intelligence service of the Resistance, which became that of the new nation when the State of Israel was proclaimed in May 1948. Isser Harel was appointed head of its department of internal security, *Shin Bet,* whose principal functions were to ferret out and destroy underground subversive movements and to direct counterespionage. He became directly responsible to the Prime Minister, and it was then that his close friendship with David Ben-Gurion began.

It was not until the years 1952 and 53 that Israel's secret services, internal, political, and military, acquired their permanent form. At that time Isser Harel was appointed head of the *Mossad,* the Central Bureau of Intelligence and Security, whose main functions were to gather intelligence abroad for all Israel's secret services and to direct special operations outside of Israel. Prime Minister Ben-Gurion insisted that Harel keep on supervising the department of internal security as well. Hence he created a new title for him—Chief Executive of the Secret Services. As head of the *Mossad,* Harel was also the chairman of the committee of the heads of the secret services. For all these functions, he was responsible personally to the Prime Minister.

This was a position of extraordinary power, and the history of other states has too often demonstrated that such power can corrupt. It is Israel's—and Isser Harel's—distinction that a scrupulous dedication to the legitimate purposes of a secret service was maintained, an achievement even more important than the many brilliant coups brought off during the fifteen years he remained in charge.

Isser Harel's resignation in April 1963 was the result of a serious disagreement on the issue of the German scientists who at that time were playing an extremely active role in Egypt's war effort against Israel. This did not prevent Ben-Gurion, two and a half years later, from affectionately inscribing a photograph to the "faithful guardian of the State's security, its honor and its secrets." Readers of *The House on Garibaldi Street* may be tempted to add "and its good sense," which, though it sounds less impressive, is certainly no less important. When a man who has been called "puritanical" in his regard for legality and morality made the decision to break international law in order to bring Adolf Eichmann to judgment in Israel, he carried that sober quality to the point of genius.

THE EDITORS

# *Preface*

The trial of Adolf Eichmann—the man an Israeli court convicted of committing millions of murders with the intention of "wiping an entire people off the face of the earth"—was held in the full glare of world-wide publicity. The extraordinary nature of the trial and the storm of emotions it unleashed drew to Jerusalem hundreds of journalists and radio and television personnel from dozens of countries. Each tried in his own way to capture the drama-laden atmosphere of the courtroom—the horror and repugnance of a people reliving the blackest years of their history.

The trial itself was followed by hundreds of millions of people, but details of the events preceding it —locating, capturing, and transporting Adolf Eichmann to Israel—were known to only a select few. Several books have been written on the subject, some wholly imaginary, some describing actual tracing efforts made by various parties. One or two of them even sought to link those vain attempts with the operation which finally led to the capture of Eichmann.

In this book I have given a faithful and factual account of this operation, which I was privileged to lead and whose crowning point was the handing over of Eichmann to the Israeli police. In order to reconstruct what happened without depending solely on my own memory, I talked with most of the participants— though for reasons I cannot enumerate I was unable to meet all of them, just as I did not have access to all the records. We recollected with pride the struggles and experiences of those days, trying to shed as much light as possible on each step of the complicated process.

In operations of this nature various details, important from the technical angle though secondary from the point of view of continuity of the narrative, must remain secret even after these many years. The same applies to the identity of the people who took part in the operation: they appear in the book under pseudonyms, and now and then I have even altered a detail or two in order to preserve their anonymity. Only one is presented under his real name—Shalom Dani, who, unfortunately, died in spring 1963 in the prime of life. I have tried to portray his wonderful character as it was revealed to me in the years we worked together, on this and other operations, until almost the day of his death.

The men who worked with me on Operation Eichmann were all motivated by an inner conviction that the capture of this loathsome criminal was a national and humane mission. There was no trace here of adventurism, no hint of the characteristics ascribed to special-services agents in fiction or suspense films. These were volunteers from the ranks of the Israeli special-actions agencies, where a man is above all a creature of flesh and blood, not a superman. He is devoted to his homeland, self-sacrificing, and resourceful; his prime weapon is his intelligence, and his success comes through patience and conscientiousness. If he has gained a world-wide reputation it is because he finds simple and human solutions to his problems: the reader will, I hope, concede that the solutions to the problems of Operation Eichmann were logical and far from spectacular.

Operation Eichmann had to be performed. The fact that it was necessary to take Eichmann out of Argentina caused us a great deal of inner conflict. My mind was by no means easy about the need to carry out a clandestine action in the sovereign territory of a friendly country, and the question of whether it was permissible to do so—from both the ethical and political points of view—had to be faced in all its gravity. The proper procedure would have been to advise the Argentine authorities of our suspicions that a German immigrant resident in a suburb of Buenos Aires was the war criminal Adolf Eichmann, and then to wait for the prolonged legalities entailed in extraditing him, either to Germany or to one of the other countries where he was wanted. But how could we know that Eichmann himself would wait? This was one consideration, and there was another: not much remained of the zeal that had sparked war trials in the years following the war. Sentences passed on some of the greatest criminals were commuted, while others waited many years and in the end were not brought to trial. There was every reason to fear that even a criminal of the caliber of Eichmann might benefit from the general atmosphere of clemency prevailing in Europe fifteen years after the perpetration of the crimes.

Israel was the only country in the world determined to leave no legal stone unturned and to judge Eichmann without evasions and political calculations. Israel was also—by the rules of law, logic, and historical justice—the state most competent to pass judgment on the man known to have been in charge of implementing the "Final Solution of the Jewish Problem."

In consultation with others, I came to the conclusion that there was no alternative but to capture Eichmann through an undercover operation and to transport him to Israel. I made the decision with a heavy heart, in view of the mutual respect and esteem between Israel and Argentina, but with a feeling of certainty that, once the court in Jerusalem had projected the image of the archmurderer in his true colors before the eyes of the world, our Argentine friends would appreciate our motives and agree that there had been no other course open to us.

Here, then, is everything that can now be told of the story of Operation Eichmann.

*Isser Harel*

Zahala, Israel, 1974

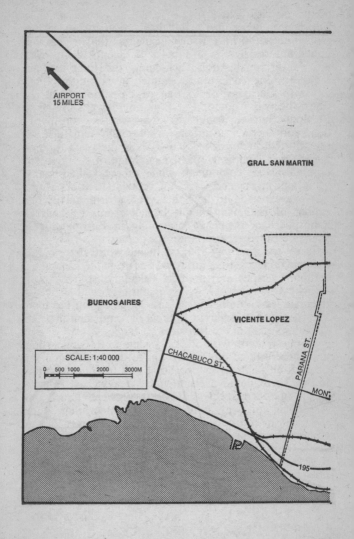

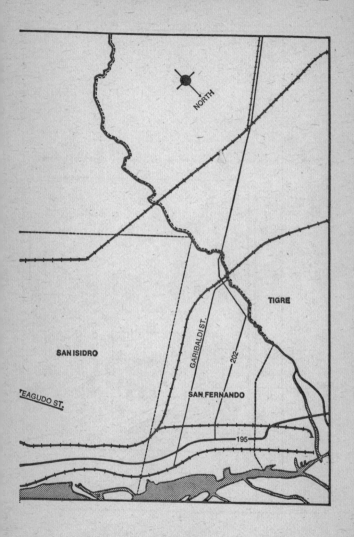

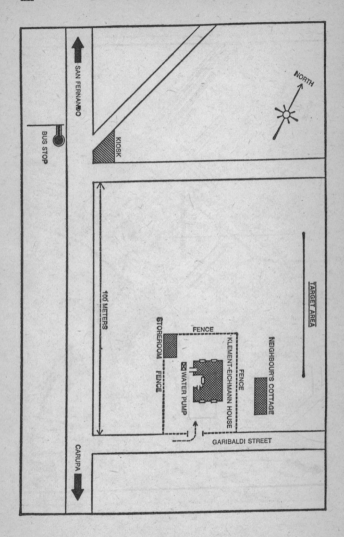

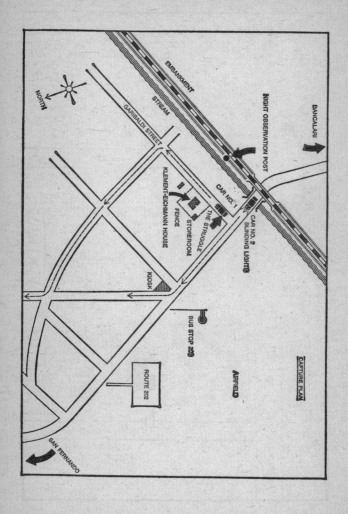

# *DRAMATIS PERSONAE*

## *1 / The Start of Operation Eichmann*

DR. WALTER EYTAN—Director-General of the Israeli Foreign Affairs Ministry; conveyed to Isser Harel the information from Germany about Eichmann's presence in Argentina.

DR. SHINAR—Head of the Reparations Mission in West Germany, who received the information about Eichmann in Argentina from Dr. Fritz Bauer, Public Prosecutor of the Province of Hesse.

DR. FRITZ BAUER—Public Prosecutor of the Province of Hesse in West Germany, who, by means of Dr. Shinar, passed on the information about Eichmann's presence in Argentina to the Israeli authorities.

SHAUL DAROM—Special agent of the Israeli Security Services, sent by Isser Harel as liaison with Dr. Fritz Bauer in the Eichmann affair.

## *2 / First Preliminary Investigation in Argentina, January 1958*

YOEL GOREN—Experienced operations man sent to Argentina in January 1958 to investigate the address

given by Dr. Bauer: 4261 Chacabuco Street, Olivos
(suburb of Buenos Aires).

MENASHE TALMI—An Israeli citizen working in
Argentina at the time, who was asked to assist Yoel
Goren. At a later stage he also assisted Ephraim Hofstaetter, another investigator. Afterward he was a member of the task force.

### 3 / Second Preliminary Investigation in Argentina, March 1958

LOTHAR HERMANN—Dr. Bauer's "source."

EFRAIM HOFSTAETTER—Police officer and crack
investigator of the Israeli Police Force, "borrowed" by
Isser Harel at the beginning of 1958 to approach
Lothar Hermann and check his reliability and credi-
bility.

KARL HUPPERT—German *nom de plume* adopted
by Efraim Hofstaetter for his contact with Lothar Hermann.

### 4 / Third Preliminary Investigation in Argentina, beginning of 1960

RICARDO KLEMENT—The name under which
Adolf Eichmann was living in Argentina, according to
Dr. Bauer.

YOSEF KENET—Senior investigator in the Israeli Secret Services, sent to Argentina at the end of February
1960 to locate Ricardo Klement and determine if he
and Adolf Eichmann were one and the same.

HAGGAI—Yosef Kenet's superior officer, himself a
survivor of Auschwitz.

DAVID and HEDDA KORNFELD—Residents of a
South American country (not Argentina). A young
married couple, he a successful architect and she a

graduate in psychology and languages. Both assisted Kenet.

LUBINSKY—Lawyer resident in South America. Assisted Kenet.

PRIMO—Student in the Faculty of Engineering, resident in South America. Assisted Kenet.

PEDRO—Hotel page, working at a large hotel in Buenos Aires; assisted Hedda Kornfeld, although unaware of the purpose of his errand.


## 5 / Preliminary Investigation in Europe

EZRA ESHET—Director of an operations unit investigating the families of Eichmann and his wife (whose maiden name was Vera Liebl) in Europe. At a later stage he was attached to the task force.

GAD ARMON—Participated in the investigations in Europe, together with Ezra Eshet.


## 6 / Organizational Team in Israel

HILLEL ANKOR—Chief of special unit for collecting material of the VIPs among the war criminals, and coordinator of the organizational team.

REUVEN HARPAZ—Security officer of the Reparations Mission in Germany, served as liaison with Dr. Fritz Bauer.

LEORA DOTAN—Administration, finance, and manpower expert, engaged in investigating ways of taking Eichmann out of Argentina and solving complicated organizational problems pertaining to the operation.

MOSHE VERED—Assistant to Hillel Ankor.

MIRIAM SAVYON—Specialist in cover and documentation. In the early stages of the operation she located persons who had known Eichmann and could identify him. Later she arranged the personal documentation for the task force.

NAHUM AMIR—The task force's "travel agent."

## 7 / Identification of Eichmann

DR. BENNO COHEN—Chairman of the German Zionist Organization from 1936 to 1938, in which capacity he had met Eichmann personally.

DR. HANS FRIEDENTHAL—Co-chairman of the German Zionist Organization from 1936 to 1938, in which capacity he had met Eichmann personally.

ELI ILAN—Israeli Police Force's expert in the comparison of photographs for identification purposes. He was given photographs of Eichmann from the SS period to compare with the operational shots taken by Kenet's team.

MOSHE AGAMI—Knew Eichmann, having been the Jewish Agency representative in Vienna in 1938. He was called to identify Eichmann after the latter was brought to Israel.

EFRAIM HOFSTAETTER—Police officer who met with Lothar Hermann at the outset of the operation. In his official capacity he dealt with the identification of Eichmann after the latter was brought to Israel.

## 8 / The Task Force

GABI ELDAD—Commander of the task force.

EHUD REVIVI—Second-in-command to Gabi Eldad; leader of the advance party.

MENASHE TALMI—Attached to the team because of his knowledge of local conditions. Participated in the preliminary investigations.

YOSEF KENET—Directed the investigation which concluded with the location of Ricardo Klement and his identification as Adolf Eichmann; attached to the advance party for positive identification and interrogation of Klement/Eichmann.

EZRA ESHET—Directed the preliminary investigations in Europe. Member of the advance party as co-ordinator of organizational matters.

ZEV KEREN—Member of the advance party, expert technician.

SHALOM DANI—Master of the art of documentation forgery.

ELI YUVAL—Versatile technician, expert in disguise by make-up, chosen to be the first to seize Eichmann because of his physical strength and fitness.

YITZHAK NESHER—Member of the advance party; attached to the task force because of his ability to assume varying cover identities.

DINA RON—Attached to the team to play the role of "girl friend" in the house where Eichmann would be held in custody after his capture, the purpose being to give the place a normal-looking "front."

THE DOCTOR—His part was to keep Eichmann drugged at various stages of the operation and to look after the general health of the team and the captive.

## 9 / Fortuitous Assistants in Buenos Aires

RAFAEL ARNON—Happened to be in Argentina by pure chance; he was set up as the victim of an alleged road accident in order to make it possible, in case of need, to take Eichmann out of Argentina with his documents.

MEIR LAVI and HIS WIFE—Assisted Isser Harel in an attempt to locate (for the purpose of capturing) the war criminal Dr. Mengele.

BINYAMIN and ADA EFRAT—Assisted Isser Harel in an attempt to locate (for the purpose of capturing) the war criminal Dr. Mengele.

## 10 / The Special Flight on Which Eichmann Was Smuggled Out of Argentina

ASHER KEDEM—Departmental director of an airline company, through whom Isser Harel made the first inquiries about the flight; he participated in all stages of the special flight.

MOSHE TADMOR—Deputy director of the airline; assisted in the organization of the special flight.

AHARON LAZAR—Manager of one of the airline's large overseas stations, who joined Asher Kedem in Buenos Aires. In his childhood he underwent all the horrors of the holocaust and was saved by a miracle.

YOAV MEGED—Captain of the special-flight aircraft.

GAD NISHRI—Co-pilot of the special flight.

DAN AVNER—Senior member of the airline's staff; during Asher Kedem's absence in Argentina he handled the Israeli angle of all the problems involved in the special flight. Later he joined the crew aboard the special aircraft.

ESTHER ROSEN—Senior employee of the airline, resident in Buenos Aires, where her husband was working; assisted in the handling of the special flight, though not aware of its secret aspect.

FRITZ SHEFER—Senior employee in the flight services department of the airline, attached to the flight at the special request of Captain Meged.

LEO BARKAI—Veteran steward of the company, attached to the special flight.

ZVI GUTMANN—The airline company's hangar foreman. When asked to select a mechanic for the special flight, he offered his own services. He was unaware of the real purpose of the flight and was bowled over when he encountered Eichmann on board. He then recollected the horrors he had experienced as a child in the holocaust.

NEGBI—Electrician in the company's maintenance department, attached to the special flight.

GILADI—Navigator on the special flight.

BRIGADIER ZOREA—Passenger on the special flight as a member of the Israeli delegation to the anniversary celebrations.

RABBI EFRATI—Chance passenger on the special flight to Argentina.

## 11 / Operations Agents on the Special Flight

YORAM GOLAN—Chosen to act as Eichmann's operational double. He wore flight-crew's uniform and traveled on the flight to Argentina under the name of Zichroni.

YOEL GOREN—Operations agent who had participated in the preliminary investigation at 4261 Chacabuco Street in 1958. He was to act as guard and escort for Eichmann on the flight back to Israel.

ELISHA NAOR—Operations agent who, with Goren, was to act as guard and escort for Eichmann during the flight to Israel.

## 12 / People Who Knew the Secret Purpose of the Flight

GENERAL LASKOV—Close personal friend of Isser Harel.

GIL—Isser Harel's closest associate for many years.

YITZHAK NAVON—Prime Minister David Ben Gurion's political secretary.

YOSEF NAHMIAS—Inspector General of the Israeli Police. When Eichmann was brought to Israel he was handed over to Nahmias, who was responsible for the prisoner.

YAKI—Isser Harel's loyal driver and confidant.

EFRAIM—Shalom Dani's immediate superior. Dani was the documentation expert of the task force.

## 13 / Police Officers Who Took Charge of Eichmann Immediately on His Arrival in Israel

MATITYAHU SELA—Head of the Investigations Department of the Israeli Police National Headquarters.
SHMUEL ROTH—Acting head of the Criminal Branch of the Israeli Police National Headquarters.

# THE
# HOUSE
# ON
# GARIBALDI
# STREET

# 1

It was late 1957 but it could have been yesterday, so clearly do I remember how the decision to capture Eichmann crystallized in my mind. Twelve and a half years had passed since the rout of the Nazi armies had ended the monstrous career of that mystery figure, the SS officer appointed to implement the total liquidation of the Jewish people.

The sharp ringing of the telephone on my desk heralded the start of it all: Walter Eytan, Director-General of the Ministry of Foreign Affairs was calling from Jerusalem. He had something for me, he said, and must see me as soon as possible. Eytan was a calm, restrained person, and I had always admired his pleasant manner and quiet, cultured way of speaking. But that day he sounded agitated, and I suspected that something quite out of the ordinary was in the wind. I asked no questions, expressed no surprise at this unaccustomed excitement; I understood he didn't want to discuss it on the telephone. He said he was on his way to Tel Aviv to attend a reception at one of the embassies, so we arranged to meet at a Ramat Gan café as soon as he arrived.

I could see at once that he was almost overcome with emotion. A message from Dr. Shinar, head of the Reparations Mission in West Germany, contained the astounding information that Adolf Eichmann was alive —and his address in Argentina was known.

We didn't talk for long. I thanked him for the in-

formation and assured him it would be investigated
thoroughly and without delay.

———

Anyone holding the sort of office entrusted to me at
that time soon learns from experience not to build too
many hopes on startling news of this kind. Throughout
the years that had passed since Eichmann disappeared
we kept getting tips about places where he was supposedly hiding, but in each case investigation ended in
disappointment—and what's more, we couldn't even
find definite proof that he was still alive. All trace of
him had been lost since the beginning of May 1945,
and we had never succeeded in verifying any of the
so-called reliable evidence of people who claimed to
have seen him thereafter.

I still don't know why I gave more credence to this
latest report than to any of its predecessors; perhaps
instinct told me that this time it was no rumor plucked
out of thin air, or perhaps I had caught some of
Walter Eytan's excitement. Anyway, I went straight
back to my office and asked our archivist to bring me all
the material available on Eichmann. I knew that he was
one of the chief Nazi criminals, and I also knew that his
principal function was the extermination of the Jews,
but I had never gone very deeply into his place in the
Nazi hierarchy or the decisive part he played in what
the Nazis called "the Final Solution of the Jewish Problem." This somber chapter in the history of the Jewish
people haunted me like a nightmare that had no place
in the world of reality—something going so far beyond
the known limits of dastardly crime, wanton cruelty,
and mortal hatred that no human being could plumb
the depths of its true significance.

That night I sat for hours reading the Eichmann
dossier, and in my mind's eye an image took shape, the
image of an archfiend whose vicious crimes were un-
precedented in the annals of humanity, a man on whose
shoulders rested the direct responsibility for the butch-
ery of millions.

I didn't know then what sort of man Eichmann was.
I didn't know with what morbid zeal he pursued his

murderous work nor how he went into the fray to destroy one miserable Jew with the same ardor he devoted to the annihilation of an entire community. I didn't know that he was capable of ordering the slaughter of babies—and depicting himself as a disciplined soldier; of directing outrages on women—and priding himself on his loyalty to an oath; or of sending helpless old men to their deaths—and classifying himself as an "idealist."

But I knew when I rose from my desk at dawn that in everything pertaining to the Jews he was the paramount authority and his were the hands that pulled the strings controlling manhunt and massacre. I knew that at all the Nuremberg trials of Nazi war criminals this man was pointed to as the head butcher. I knew that he was a past master in police methods, and that on the strength of his professional skill and in the light of his total lack of conscience, he would be an exceedingly dangerous quarry. I knew that when the war was over he had succeeded in blotting out all trace of himself with supreme expertise.

I knew that the blood-drenched earth which held the remains of his millions of victims was crying out for vengeance, but no agency in the entire world, no government, no police were looking for him to answer for his crimes. People were tired of atrocity stories; their one desire was to dismiss those unspeakable happenings from their minds; they maintained that, in any event, there was no punishment on earth to fit the perpetration of outrages of such magnitude; and they were reconciled to the violation of law and the perversion of justice.

That night I resolved that if Eichmann were alive, come hell or high water he'd be caught.

———

Shortly after my talk with Walter Eytan, Dr. Shinar came on a visit to Israel. He told me that the source of his information on Eichmann was Dr. Fritz Bauer, Public Prosecutor of the province of Hesse in West Germany.

Bauer, a Jew who came from a family of jurists, held

the position of a judge in Stuttgart till the Nazis came
to power. Afterward he was imprisoned for about a
year. In 1936 he emigrated to Denmark, but the Nazis
caught up with him there as well, and in 1940 he was
again arrested. This time he spent three years in prison
before he managed to escape and find refuge in Sweden.
After the war he returned to Germany, fully determined
to devote himself to bringing Nazi war criminals to
book.

Bauer was a long-standing member of the ruling
Social Democratic Party in the province of Hesse and a
man of eminence in the government. During his years
of service he had earned the reputation of being an eminent jurist and had won acclaim for the books he had
written on criminal law and jurisprudence.

Dr. Shinar told me that on September 19, 1957, while
on a visit to Frankfurt, Rabbi Lichtigfeld of the province of Hesse had informed him that Bauer wanted to
see him on an important issue. Rabbi Lichtigfeld did
not know the nature of the matter. It was arranged
that Bauer and Shinar should meet at the Metropol
Hotel, but as soon as Bauer arrived he requested that
they find more discreet surroundings. They drove to an
inn situated by the Cologne–Frankfurt highway.

"Eichmann has been traced," began Bauer without
any preliminaries.

"Adolf Eichmann?" exclaimed Shinar excitedly.

"Yes, Adolf Eichmann. He is in Argentina."

"And what do you intend to do?"

"I'll be perfectly frank with you," said Bauer. "I
don't know if we can altogether rely on the German
judiciary here, let alone on the German embassy staff in
Buenos Aires. That is why I was so interested in talking
to you. I see no other way but to turn to you. You are
known to be efficient people, and nobody could be
more interested than you in the capture of Eichmann.
Obviously, I wish to maintain contact with you in connection with this matter, but only provided strict secrecy is kept."

"Thank you from the bottom of my heart," replied
Shinar warmly, visibly moved, "for the great faith you

have shown in us. Israel will never forget what you have done. Naturally, I am prepared to assume full personal responsibility for keeping our contact secret. It won't be made public except with your express consent."

Dr. Shinar promised to make all necessary arrangements for the information to reach the proper quarters as soon as possible. As soon as the meeting was over, he hurried to his office in Cologne to transmit a full telegraphic report to the Director General of the Foreign Office in Jerusalem.

What Dr. Shinar told me about Fritz Bauer's personality impressed me a great deal. I promised Shinar that when he went back to Cologne I would send him a special representative to maintain contact with Bauer. The suitable man for this assignment was soon found: his name was Shaul Darom.

Shaul came of a traditionally observant family who emigrated from Germany to Israel (then Palestine, under British Mandate) in the early days of the Nazi regime. Unlike his brothers who chose academic careers, Shaul even as a young child showed a leaning toward art; he was always a bit of a dreamer and was the perfect example of the bourgeois's image of a bohemian. He went to France in 1947, when he was 26, to study art; there, quite by chance, he was drawn into *Hamossad La'aliya,* the secret organization engaged in bringing Jews to Israel without the knowledge of the British authorities. From then on he pursued both interests with equal enthusiasm and even found a way of combining the two: he painted pictures of the Jews he helped on their way to Israel.

When the State of Israel came into being he continued to paint, at the same time working as a representative of Israel's Security Services. He became renowned—not as a secret agent but as a painter—and some of his paintings still hang in countries hostile toward Israel.

He had a natural flair for intelligence work, so he was able to concentrate on his art, interrupting occasionally for his other assignments. His rich imagination and skill at improvisation, his command of several languages, and his knowledge of the culture and customs of many countries all helped to make him one of the most outstanding professionals in the Service.

At the time of my meeting with Dr. Shinar, Shaul was on a protracted mission in Europe. I wired him to come to Tel Aviv, and a few days later he was sitting in my office.

"I want to entrust you with certain inquiries relating to Eichmann," I said.

Shaken and excited, he took a little while to reply. He looked at me searchingly to see if I was indeed serious. Finally he asked, "Is Eichmann alive?"

I told him about Dr. Bauer and the information he had given Shinar.

Shaul's eyes lit up. He was doubly exhilarated—at the prospect of finding Eichmann and at the thought that he could play a part in the operation.

"Bauer," I continued, "is known to be a man of balanced judgment, and he treats the report with great seriousness. Our assignment is to investigate his information with the utmost thoroughness."

Shaul Darom arrived in Cologne on November 6, 1975, and immediately presented himself to Dr. Shinar. The next day they went to Bauer's home, where Shinar introduced them and then left them to themselves.

Shaul scrutinized the other man, thinking that an appropriate background for a painting of him would be a book and a sword. Bauer appeared to be an energetic and excitable man. He returned Shaul's gaze with a penetrating glance from his calm gray eyes.

"Before we start our talk," Shaul began, "permit me to tell you that we're grateful you came to us. I can assure you that we'll do all within our power to bring Eichmann to trial before a properly constituted court of justice."

"I should really be thanking you for your quick response," Bauer said. "I was sure that you were the only ones who would be ready and willing to act. I really think that this time we're on Eichmann's trail. Our information seems to be dependable."

Shaul said, "Actually, that was our first question: Can we rely on the source of your information?"

"It's a man who says he is half-Jewish, a German by birth, now living in Argentina. We won't reveal his name for the time being. I must admit I don't know him personally, only by letter. He initiated the correspondence when he wrote to the German authorities after reading in the newspapers that Adolf Eichmann's name was mentioned at the trial of another war criminal and it was reported that Eichmann had disappeared." Bauer went on, "I suspect that he knows more than he is prepared to divulge at this stage. He sent us Eichmann's address: 4261 Chacabuco Street, Olivos, Buenos Aires, but he hasn't told us what name he uses."

"Do you know anything about your man?" Shaul asked. "If you do, we may be able to find the key to his behavior."

"No, I know nothing beyond what he himself has offered. He may be afraid of reprisals, so perhaps he feels he is taking less of a risk by passing on only part of the information," Bauer replied. "In any event," he continued, "some of the items he sent correspond with known facts about Eichmann, such as certain particulars about the sons born before his disappearance, the alleged second marriage of his wife Vera, and so on. We have compared these details with the material available in Germany and found them to be correct."

Shaul said, "If I'm not mistaken, this isn't the first report of Eichmann's flight to South America."

"That's correct. Various sources of dubious reliability have stated that in 1947 or 1948 he arrived in Argentina and went to live somewhere in the south. The fact that this latest news tallies with previous reports is precisely what makes it seem encouraging. He probably managed to obtain Argentine papers and later decided to move to Buenos Aires."

"And what about his wife and sons?" Shaul asked.

"All we know about them is that they left Germany

after he did. There was a rumor early on that Vera
Eichmann met an American in Germany and married
him, but since then nothing has been heard about her.
Every effort to learn something from her family in
Europe has failed, and my guess is that the so-called
second husband is Adolf Eichmann himself. But," said
Dr. Bauer, "this is pure conjecture with no verification
whatsoever."

"Some other war criminal may have married Vera
after her husband left her, and this may be the man
living with her at the address you were given," Shaul
mused aloud.

"That's also a possibility we can't ignore," Bauer
said. "But as far as I can see, the prospects are that
we'll find Eichmann himself filling the role of Vera's
second husband."

As the conversation continued, Shaul gathered that
Bauer's plan was for us to take all necessary steps, using our own ways and means, to find out the name
and true identity of the man living at the address he'd
been given. If we succeeded, he would then send a man
to Argentina who knew Eichmann and would be able
to identify him. If this man confirmed the identification,
Bauer would press West Germany to demand that the
Argentine authorities extradite Eichmann. But he had
few illusions about the prospects of extradition. It was
his opinion that simultaneous pressure would have to
be brought by Israel and West Germany, and public
opinion would have to be mobilized—principally in the
United States—to persuade Argentina to extradite the
criminal.

The problem of extradition worried me as well, and
I had instructed Shaul to attempt to probe into Bauer's
attitude—but very carefully.

"It's quite likely," he said to Bauer, "that if we manage to prove that the man really is Eichmann we may
run into insurmountable difficulties in trying to get him
extradited, and in the end, instead of putting Eichmann
on trial we may be giving him the opportunity of van-
ishing again and covering his tracks even more efficiently than before."

"I too am worried about that," Bauer replied thoughtfully, "and I won't reject the idea of your getting him to Israel in your own way."

Darom was struck by the courage implicit in these words. Had he needed any further proof of Bauer's integrity, here it was. To hide his own emotions, he spoke crisply. "Well then, to begin with," he said, "we'll investigate the identity of the man in Argentina —not an easy matter. Only when that's done can we tackle the clarification of the legal position and the possibility of extradition. If we run into problems, we'll do all we can to make certain that Eichmann will be brought to trial. But the overriding consideration in everything we do is the sure knowledge that the minute he finds out he has been located—he'll run away again."

"I agree with you absolutely," Bauer said.

Shaul asked for copies of documents that might help him in the location and identification of Eichmann, and Bauer promised to let him have the material within two hours. He gave Shaul photostats of documents containing information about Eichmann's life; copies of rather blurred photographs of him and his wife taken in the late thirties or early forties; personal details about both of them, the date of their marriage and the dates of birth of the three sons born in Germany; and details of his career in the SS (*Schutzstaffel*, the Nazi military security police) up to 1944. The last document was accompanied by a slightly clearer photograph than the others. Bauer's final bit of information for Shaul was that Eichman had a strident voice and was known to be a lover of strong drink and women.

At the end of the conversation Shaul asked who else knew about their contact in this matter. Bauer replied that he had told only one man about his appeal to the Israelis, a man of standing and of high integrity.

Shaul remained in Europe after this meeting and reported to me in writing. About the personality of his host he wrote:

As for Fritz Bauer himself, all I can do is confirm Dr. Shinar's opinion and impression that he is

an honest man with a warm Jewish heart, whose
object in coming to us was that the matter not be
set aside or put off because the means or the
desire were lacking to become involved in a problem both difficult and delicate, even unpleasant
under prevailing political conditions in Germany.
I gather he is disappointed with present developments in Germany, and I have the feeling that he
is not at peace with himself for having decided to
resume his public activities in such a Germany.

# 2

It was now necessary to send an operator to Argentina.

Bauer's refusal to disclose his informant's name severely hampered our investigation. If it were possible to meet the man and form an impression of his good faith, to learn from him personally what he knew, and to test his conclusions, the prospects of success would be appreciably greater. But in the circumstances, all we could do was inspect 4261 Chacabuco Street, Olivos, Buenos Aires.

I gave the assignment to Yoel Goren, an experienced operations man who, before joining the Service, had spent quite a lot of time in the Latin American countries as the representative of a private company and still spoke some Spanish. In January 1958 he left for Buenos Aires. I had no illusions about the prospects of a lone man working in a strange place, with a limited knowledge of the language. Before he left I had to warn him not to make any move likely to attract attention to our interest in the house and its tenants. I knew that any careless step, any unwarranted activity around the house or its tenants, was liable to act as a warning signal to the wanted man.

To make Goren's difficult task a little easier, I told him he could try to enlist the help of Menashe Talmi, an Israeli who was doing research into the history of Jewish settlement in Argentina. Menashe had been born in one of the oldest settlements in Israel and for years had

11

dreamed of doing this kind of study; he earned a schol-
arship, which enabled him to take an extended leave
from the public institution where he was employed. A
skilled linguist, fluent in more than ten languages, Talmi
was completely at home in Spanish. He was familiar
with the customs of the country and, being very sociable, had made good connections in Buenos Aires.
I did, however, warn Goren that, while Talmi loved
holding long conversations and had an excellent sense
of humor, he was not the most practical of men. He unhesitatingly placed himself at Goren's disposal.

Olivos is a suburb just north of the city limits of
Buenos Aires. The way the area has developed, holiday
homes and luxury residences fill the area closest to the
Río de la Plata, and the farther from the river bank the
humbler the dwellings, mostly single-story houses with
small gardens. The quarter is linked to the center of the
city by the General Bartolomé Mitre railway line. Most
of the residents—many of whom are Germans, including some who came to Argentina after the war—are
workers who get up early in the morning to go to work
in Buenos Aires and come home late in the evening, so
perpetual quiet prevails in the streets. Relations among
the tenants are extremely close and neighborly, practically everybody knows everybody else, and they all
know each other's business.

Goren and Talmi reconnoitered several times in the
vicinity of 4261 Chacabuco Street, even photographing
it secretly. The house was surrounded by a low fence,
and several leafy trees in the yard cast their shade over
a wide area. The entrance to both house and grounds
was at the front right-hand corner, though they were unable to determine if the place had any other entrances.
The street wasn't paved, and in general the impression was one of shabbiness.

It somehow didn't make sense. At that time people
still thought that the Nazi criminals who had succeeded
in escaping from Germany had considerable financial
means. According to rumors which had been widely
circulating for many years, when the Third Reich began

to totter the leaders secreted valuables and large sums of money in various hiding places both inside and outside of Germany, and this treasure was being used to support them and to finance the activities of the Nazis who went underground. As for Eichmann, it was presumed that at the time of his flight he had managed to take with him a mint of money looted from the Jews of Europe. We knew that he was arrogant, boastful, and pleasure-loving. The poverty-stricken suburb of Olivos, the unpaved street, and the wretched little house could in no way be reconciled with our picture of the life of an SS officer of Eichmann's rank.

From his impressions of the place, Goren came to the conclusion that it was impossible for Adolf Eichmann to be living there, so he started making inquiries about the members of the German colony in Argentina in the hope that he might thus find out something about Eichmann. He and Talmi collected a great deal of important information on the subject, but there was nothing to help bring us nearer to our goal.

The report Goren made when he returned from Argentina was a great disappointment to me. The obvious conclusion was that the information passed on to us by Bauer was unfounded, but it was my belief that this wasn't so. Goren had seen a stout, slovenly woman in the yard, and although she was European-looking both he and Talmi refused to believe that this untidy female could be Eichmann's wife.

I still wasn't totally convinced that it was impossible for Eichmann and his family to be living in that Chacabuco Street house. I did feel, however, that without direct contact with Bauer's source we couldn't judge its validity. I hoped that when Bauer heard about the negative results of Goren's mission he would change his stand and yield to our request for a personal meeting with this informant.

Shaul Darom had almost completed his mission in Europe and was about to return to Israel, so I conveyed to him Goren's findings and my opinions and asked him to have another talk with Bauer.

They met in Frankfurt on January 21, 1958. Bauer

understood our situation perfectly and agreed to divulge his source. He also wrote a letter of introduction to be handed over by the person we sent. On a separate sheet he wrote the name and address of his informant: Lothar Hermann, Coronel Suárez, Province of Buenos Aires.

---

It was my opinion that we could avoid risk and save ourselves anxiety if our representative introduced himself not as an Israeli but as a messenger from Dr. Bauer. The candidate would have to be German-speaking and an expert in the technique of identification, as he would have to determine whether the man Lothar Hermann indicated was indeed Adolf Eichmann.

As luck would have it, I was told that the police were sending one of their crack investigators, Efraim Hofstaetter, to South America to conduct a criminal inquiry with Israeli connections. With the consent of the Inspector-General of the Israeli Police Force, I contacted Hofstaetter, explained what it was all about, and asked him if, at the end of his official investigation, he would undertake an assignment on my behalf. He agreed without hesitation. Hofstaetter was not particularly well versed in the history of the holocaust even though his parents and sister had been murdered by the Nazis, but he had heard of Eichmann and knew that this man was among those in charge of the extermination of European Jewry and one of the most wanted war criminals.

I provided him with all the material we had on Eichmann and gave him detailed instructions on the execution of his assignment. I told him that, first of all, his personal impressions of Lothar Hermann were of decisive importance. Is he an earnest man? Does he inspire confidence? Where did his information on Eichmann come from? What's his motive? And what else does he know? I stressed the necessity of obtaining any item likely to help in the indentification of Eichmann: personal data on him and his family, recent photographs, and so on. I added that fingerprints of the Eichmann-suspect would be an extremely valuable means of identification (I didn't know yet that there were no fingerprints of Eichmann on record, neither in Germany nor anywhere else).

Hofstaetter himself emphasized the need to proceed with extreme caution, since if the information was correct, and if Eichmann became aware that the hunt was on, he was liable to vanish without a trace. We assumed that after so many trouble-free years he was not liable to be particularly on the alert; all the same, nothing must be done to rouse him out of his complacency.

Hofstaetter took Dr. Bauer's letter of introduction to Hermann, and I reminded him to introduce himself as a representative of the German authorities who had been living abroad for some time—which would also account for his accent.

As I did not want Hofstaetter's family to know the nature of his mission, we arranged for his personal correspondence to go through a third country. Menashe Talmi was asked to assist Hofstaetter as he had assisted Goren. Before his departure I told Efraim that if he succeeded in making a positive identification of Eichmann he might get a second trip to Argentina.

# 3

Even in the most detailed briefing some important item may occasionally be forgotten. Hofstaetter found this out the moment he reached Buenos Aires after completing his official mission wearing winter clothes. Nobody had thought to warn him that he might be arriving at the height of the Argentine summer. In a bath of perspiration he went to meet Talmi, and it was only after Menashe had told him some of the jokes he kept in stock for new acquaintances that Efraim began to get over his bad temper.

Talmi told him that Coronel Suárez was a remote township situated a few hundred miles to the southwest of the capital, and any stranger turning up there would inevitably attract general attention. It would be better, therefore, if Hofstaetter were to invite Hermann to Buenos Aires. He sent Hermann a telegram in German, mentioning Bauer's name and explaining that he was on a short visit to Argentina and would like very much to see him. He suggested that Hermann come to the capital or any large town in the vicinity.

The reply came without delay: "I don't know you. If you want to speak to me you'll have to come to me." Hofstaetter wired back that he would come.

But now misgivings crept into his mind. Here he was, on the point of traveling to a strange and remote region of the country, to meet a man he knew nothing about. How could he know it wasn't a trap? Menashe shared his suspicions, and also believed it would be difficult for

Efraim to find his destination in such an out-of-the-way spot without knowing Spanish. They would go together to Coronel Suárez.

---

The early-evening train they set out in reminded them of something in an old American cowboy movie. After a tiring overnight journey, they reached Coronel Suárez at nine-thirty A.M. and made inquiries at the antiquated little railroad station about the return trip to the capital. There was only one passenger train a day on that line—it would leave in the afternoon.

Their plan was that Hofstaetter would go alone to Hermann's house, and two hours later Talmi would wait for him in a taxi somewhere near the house; if Efraim didn't reappear within a reasonable amount of time, Menashe would go look for him.

A long road led from the railway station, single-story houses on either side, and at first glance there appeared to be no other streets in the town. They hailed a taxi—an ancient American model—and gave the driver the address; they could easily have gone on foot, as it turned out to be only a three-minute drive from the station. Efraim got out, and Menashe continued on.

Everything in the town seemed to be old, including Hermann's house. Hofstaetter knocked at the door. A man of about fifty, short and thin, his hair sprinkled with gray, opened it. There was something odd about his whole appearance, his hesitant walk, his slow movements. A feeling of discomfort crept over Hofstaetter as he stood face to face with the man.

"Good morning. Is this Mr. Hermann's house?" he asked.

"Yes. I'm Lothar Hermann. What can I do for you?"

"My name is Karl Huppert," Hofstaetter said. "I sent you a telegram from Buenos Aires to tell you I was coming."

"Oh yes," said Hermann. "Please come in."

The living room was poorly and sparsely furnished: an old cupboard with a glass door, a table, and a few simple chairs. The trained senses of an experienced police officer told Hofstaetter that something was out of kilter in this house, though he could not immediately put his finger on it. Hermann invited him to sit down but made no attempt to hide his suspicions.

"Excuse me, Mr. Huppert," he said, "but I've never heard of you. Who in fact are you?"

"I spend most of my time in America and Canada as representative of the German authorities, and I've come to you on their behalf," Hofstaetter said.

"How am I to know if you are telling the truth? Anybody can make such claims. And besides, what have those authorities of yours got to do with me?"

"Mr. Hermann, for obvious reasons, I prefer not to say too much about the people who sent me. Allow me, however, to remind you of your correspondence with Dr. Fritz Bauer of Frankfurt, Public Prosecutor of the Province of Hesse, in connection with the Nazi war criminal Adolf Eichmann. Dr. Bauer wrote to you on January 21 to inform you that he would be sending someone to talk to you on his behalf. I have with me a letter of introduction from Dr. Bauer written on the same date. Here it is, as you see."

The letter in his outstretched hand remained dangling in midair. Hermann ignored it completely. Hofstaetter's discomfort increased.

Hermann suddenly raised his voice and called out in the direction of the door, "Come in, my dear, come in."

A middle-aged woman appeared in the doorway. "Yes, Lothar," she said.

"Mr. Huppert," said Hermann, "this is my wife. Meet Mr. Huppert, my dear. He's brought a letter from the Public Prosecutor in Frankfurt. Please take it and read it aloud."

He's blind, he didn't see my outstretched hand! flashed into Hofstaetter's mind, and his suspicions were immediately set at rest. He would have to be careful to conceal his surprise and relief. "Here's the letter, Mrs. Hermann," he said, rising and handing it to her.

"Do sit down, please," she said. "If you don't mind, I'll read the letter for my husband: 'The bearer of this letter is the person whose visit I advised you about in my letter of today's date. He will discuss with you the subject of our correspondence. Sincerely, Dr. Bauer.' "

Hofstaetter noticed a smile spreading over his host's face.

After a moment's pause, his wife added, "The signature is without doubt Dr. Bauer's." This was apparently a customary ritual between the two. Now the ice was broken.

"Bring us something to drink, my dear," said Lothar cheerfully. The woman went out, and he turned to Hofstaetter. "I also used to do investigations, when I was still a young lawyer. But when Hitler came to power everything changed. My parents were murdered by the Nazis, and I too had firsthand experience of the horrors of the concentration camps. I have Jewish blood in my veins, but my wife is German and our daughter has been brought up according to her mother's traditions."

At first Hofstaetter fancied that this was an attempt to sound out his reaction to the "Jewish angle." He decided not to comment at all.

Hermann continued. "Don't think that I started this Eichmann business through any desire to serve Germany. My only purpose is to even the score with the Nazi criminals who caused me and my family so much agony and suffering. Because of that, I don't even want any reward or any other sort of compensation for my efforts."

"How did you in fact get on to Eichmann's trail?" asked Hofstaetter.

"Let's say it was a combination of chance and analytical skill."

"Would you please be good enough to explain?"

"With pleasure," Hermann said. "I have a daughter, a charming girl—you'll meet her, she'll be home soon —a sensible and intelligent girl."

"And she has something to do with the matter?"

"Yes. Until eighteen months ago we lived in Buenos Aires, in the Olivos quarter. There she met a young man of twenty-one or twenty-two, named Nicolas Eichmann. He started taking her out and visited our house several times. Naturally, he didn't know that I have Jewish blood—or that my daughter does, of course. Since we've been in Argentina we've been accepted as German in every way. So Nicolas used to talk freely in our company. Once, when the conversation turned to the fate of the Jews in the Second World War, he said it would have been better if the Germans had finished their job of extermination. On another occasion, he said that his father was an officer in the German army during the war and did his duty for the fatherland. One day, when he happened to drop in, my wife asked him how it was that his German accent wasn't typical of any one region but reflected the influence of many dialects. He replied that during the war his father served in many different regions and the family went with him on his journeys, so they never stayed long enough in one place to become fluent in the local idiom."

Hofstaetter paused for a moment and then said, "I was told that the trial of a war criminal in Germany had something to do with your interest in this affair."

"Yes, that trial, I must say, started me thinking. One day my wife—or it may have been my daughter—read a report in the local paper about the trial of a war criminal in Frankfurt. At the trial a man by the name of Adolf Eichmann was mentioned as a central figure in the mass murders. When I heard the name a thought flashed through my mind: That Nicolas Eichmann, who's so sorry that the Nazis didn't manage to wipe out all the Jews, must be the son of Adolf Eichmann, the army officer in the war who, according to his son, 'did his duty for the fatherland.' Without any hesitation, I wrote to the Public Prosecutor in Frankfurt, voicing my suspicions. An exchange of letters followed, and he requested me to investigate the matter further. He even provided me with various details about Eichmann, including a personal description. Not long after, the Public Prosecutor of Hesse was transferred and Fritz Bauer took his place. I continued to correspond with him."

"And what investigations did you carry out to verify your suspicions?" asked Hofstaetter. The second part of the question he did not express aloud: And how could a blind man undertake such an investigation?

"At Bauer's request, I went back to Buenos Aires twice in an effort to discover where the Eichmann family lived and to meet the head of the family. My daughter accompanied me on both journeys. It was then that we recalled an episode to which we had not attributed any importance at the beginning: my daughter and Nicholas had been writing to each other since we moved here, but he never told her where he lived; he asked her to send her letters to the address of a mutual friend. This detail naturally heightened our suspicions."

A voice broke in. "Good morning, Dad!" An attractive young woman of about twenty entered the room with Mrs. Hermann, who carried a tray with two cups of tea on it.

"Mr. Huppert, this is my daughter," Hermann said, and turning to her he added, "I'm glad you came. Mr. Huppert is interested in the Eichmann family. Tell him how you found their house and whom you saw there. You can speak English." He turned back to Hofstaetter, saying, "In two months she's going to study at a university in America."

"Dad must have told you," the young woman began, "that Nick never let me know his address. When we went to Buenos Aires I asked a friend to help me find his house. I knocked at the door and it was opened by a woman. I asked her in German if this was the house of the Eichmann family. Her reply did not come immediately, and during the pause a middle-aged man wearing glasses came and stood beside her. I asked him if Nick was at home. He said no, Nick was working overtime. I asked if he was Mr. Eichmann. No reply. So I asked if he was Nick's father. He said he was, but only after long hesitation."

"Are you sure about the hesitation?" asked Hofstaetter. "And, incidentally, was there anything special about the way he spoke?"

"There's no doubt about the hesitation. And his voice was unpleasant and strident, just as the Public Prosecutor in Frankfurt described it in one of his letters."

Hofstaetter said, "So you may have been influenced by the letter, thinking his voice sounded strident?"

"No. I'm a hundred per cent sure it was an unbiased impression."

Hofstaetter was still not convinced. He continued pressing her with questions about the family. She said the Eichmanns had five children, three born in Germany and two in Argentina. She said—and her father confirmed it—that the ages of the three older boys tallied with the information given in the Public Prosecutor's letter. She gave a description of the house at 4261 Chacabuco Street which contributed nothing new.

"I must tell you," said Hermann, "that everything we're telling you now has been passed on to the Prosecutor in Frankfurt. I only asked him to cover the expense I have been put to because I'm in no position to bear it myself."

Mrs. Hermann interrupted for the first time. "This whole business frightens me enough already, and I don't think that we have to be out of pocket as well. As a mother, it was natural for me to be interested in finding out something about the young man who was courting my daughter. I never met his parents, but my heart tells me we have stumbled on the family of the criminal Adolf Eichmann. And take my word for it, Mr. Huppert, my mind's not easy about it."

"I don't expect any reward," her husband added, "but I think it would be fair for them to reimburse me the 120 or 150 dollars I spent on my trips to Buenos Aires. I've written to Frankfurt about it, as I said, but I haven't had any direct reply. All they told me was that someone would be coming to see me."

"That aspect of the problem is new to me, Mr. Hermann," Hofstaetter said. "I'll be in touch with my superiors to arrange the matter, but I'm afraid you'll have to wait a few more weeks."

Hermann pressed on. "I seriously hope it will be arranged quickly. And by the way, I believe I've done a good job and there's no room for any doubt whatever about the identity of the man—he is definitely Adolf Eichmann."

"What you say is pretty convincing," Hofstaetter said, "but it isn't a conclusive identification. Vera Eichmann may have married again—we've heard many such rumors—and her children may have continued using their father's name."

"I think Eichmann had plastic surgery, which is why it is difficult to identify him from old photographs. And as for Vera Eichmann, she may have married again, but if she did, it was her first husband she remarried and not another man."

Hofstaetter tried to explain the delicacy of his position. "You may be right, but then again you may be wrong. You must understand that we have to have decisive proofs which leave no room for doubt before we can take practical steps."

"I'm certain I'll be able to get you your proofs," Hermann said. "I know the neighborhood and its residents, and I can work more efficiently and more safely than anybody brought from outside. So I'd like to suggest to you that you work only through me. I don't have to remind you that any attempt to identify Eichmann by direct action is liable to arouse his suspicions and chase him away. Maximum caution is required here."

Hofstaetter nodded agreement.

The blind man went on. "I must also warn you against the personnel of the German Embassy in Buenos Aires. If they find out that Eichmann has been traced, I have no doubt whatsoever that somebody from there will rush to warn him about the danger confronting him. I'm prepared to go still further and say that the same applies to any and every German Foreign Service person as far as anything to do with Nazi war criminals is concerned."

In his role as Huppert, Hofstaetter considered it his duty to defend "his" country's authorities: "You're exaggerating, Mr. Hermann, you're overdoing it."

"There's even more than that," Hermann went on. "I tell you that Eichmann has considerable means at his disposal. He's also got a Jeep."

At this stage Hofstaetter realized that Hermann had no further information, and he decided to divert the conversation into practical channels. "Mr. Hermann," he said, "I want to explain what we need for a definite identification of the man: his present name, his place of work, details about his car, a photograph like the one on his identity card, and any other official document we can lay our hands on. And most of all, I'd like to get his fingerprints, which are an infallible means of identification."

"I've got many friends in Olivos, as well as connections with the local authorities. It won't be difficult for me to get the things you enumerated," replied Hermann, "but it's obvious I'll have to travel to Buenos Aires again, my daughter too, and we'll have to stay there for a week. This will involve further expense, and I can't afford it."

Hofstaetter said, "I promised you I'd see to it that you get back the money you've already spent, and I'll also have your future expenses covered. What's more, I suggest that you don't do anything until you have the first payment in hand. However, when it comes, it's understood that I can expect you to go to Buenos Aires without delay and make every effort to obtain all the data we spoke about."

"Just as you say," Hermann replied.

"I'd also like to suggest that you stop all direct correspondence with Germany and that you send all future letters to an address I'll provide for you," Hofstaetter said. "By the way, do you have visiting cards?"

"Yes, of course."

"Perhaps you'll give me some cards with your signature on them. I'll attach one of the cards to each letter I send you, to show that it does in fact come from me, no matter who signs it."

"Excellent idea!" exclaimed Hermann admiringly.

Hofstaetter took an Argentine banknote out of his pocket, folded it, and cut it in two with his nail file. "I'll leave you one half of this note. If anybody comes to you and shows you the other half, you may be sure he comes in my name and you can trust him completely." Hofstaetter looked at his watch: he had been there nearly two hours.

Hermann's daughter brought the visiting cards and helped her father sign them. Hofstaetter took them, then stood up, saying, "Thank you very much indeed, Mr. Hermann, for all you've done up to now and for your kind hospitality. I'll have to be going, but we'll keep in touch as arranged."

"Thank you for coming, Mr. Huppert. I hope to hear from you very soon."

Hofstaetter said good-by to Hermann and his wife and daughter and went out. He strode off in the direction of the railway station. He hadn't gone a hundred yards when a taxi drew up beside him.

"Can I give you a lift, sir?" asked Talmi in English.

--------

A few minutes later they were at the tumble-down little railway station, and by late evening they were back in Buenos Aires. On the train Hofstaetter had told Talmi about his conversation with Hermann and his family. He made no secret of his impression that Hermann was impetuous and overconfident and that if the story had not been confirmed by the wife and daughter he would have been less likely to believe Hermann. All the same, he decided to recommend that contact with the man be maintained, on the assumption that there was no particular danger in the blind man's interest in Eichmann's identity.

Hofstaetter described the meeting with Hermann in great detail in the report he sent to Israel. He added that he had also drafted a letter to Hermann stating that he, Huppert, was anxious to get things moving and was sending 5000 pesos (about 130 dollars) out of his own pocket to cover expenses; a mailing address would follow soon. Hofstaetter left the letter and money with Talmi to forward to Hermann as soon as Israel confirmed the action; he also suggested that a few days after the dispatch of the letter with the money a second letter be sent to Hermann with the new address, and that a post-office box in another country be rented for the purpose. Talmi kept some of the visiting cards and Hofstaetter's half of the banknote.

Hofstaetter suggested in his report that we act quickly: Hermann's daughter, whose help he considered extremely important, was going abroad in two months, and once she was gone her mother might prevail on Hermann to wash his hands of the whole affair.

# 4

Hofstaetter returned to Tel Aviv in the middle of March 1958 and put the finishing touches on his Buenos Aires report. I met him to hear further details. He repeated his reservations about Hermann, but his opinion of the wife and daughter was favorable.

I could see that a distinction had to be made between the facts themselves (most of which came not from Hermann but from his wife and daughter) and the evaluation of those facts (which came from Hermann alone), which was open to doubt—the reference to Eichmann's plastic surgery, for example, was totally unsubstantiated. However, the starting point remained the same and was not to be regarded lightly.

There was no reason to presume that Hermann had collaborated with his wife and daughter in concocting an imaginary tale. Why should they do such a thing? What motive could a whole family have in becoming involved in a senseless adventure, and a dangerous one at that? Their story was fairly rational: a young man, even Eichmann's son, would speak freely to his friends on any subject—including the Jews—according to the way he'd been brought up. At the same time, some things could be taboo and he might not be free to bring people home or to reveal his address to strangers. But what's wrong with telling a girl friend that his father was an officer in the German army and "did his duty for the fatherland"? It would also make sense for Nicolas Eichmann to have her write to him at someone else's

address: he might not want his inquisitive family to
read his letters. Mrs. Hermann's remarks also struck me
as being reasonable. What could be more natural than
a mother's desire to know something about the young
man her daughter was going out with? The young
man's reply to her question about his accent, and his
explanation that his father's duties had kept the family
on the move, would not be suspect to a German woman
who had been living in Argentina for ten years or more
and who, as far as he knew, would not think ill of them
in the first place. And hadn't there been a great many
German officers who kept moving from place to place
in the German areas of conquest during World War II?

As for Hermann himself, he could well be rash and
overconfident, as Hofstaetter said, but there was no
ignoring the fact that he had demonstrated a quick per-
ception and an acute intelligence in correlating all the
data about the young man and his family. Therefore, if
his primary evaluation was correct, he could indeed be
useful in identifying Eichmann. If, however, it should
prove that the whole story was a fabrication, the undertaking itself wouldn't suffer if we let him and his
family carry on embroidering their fanciful tale.

These considerations led me to authorize Hofstaetter's recommendations on general lines. A cable was
sent to Talmi informing him that he could now send
Hermann the letter with the money. I also made arrangements for Hermann's correspondence.

Hofstaetter returned to his regular duties in the police force and had no further hand in Operation Eichmann.

––––––––

Hermann's first letter to the new address was dated
May 19, 1958. He confirmed the receipt of Huppert's
letter with the money and reported on his activities in
Buenos Aires and environs between April 8 and 15. He
wrote that he examined the property register in the
town of La Plata, Buenos Aires Province, and found
that on August 14, 1947, a Francisco Schmidt, an
Austrian citizen, had purchased a plot of land at 4261
Chacabuco Street, Olivos. Toward the end of 1947 and

the beginning of 1948 a house was built on the plot, with two separate units, one facing Chacabuco Street and the other facing the yard. The Olivos electric company, Hermann found out, had installed two meters, one in the front apartment in the name of Dagoto, the other in the rear in the name of Clement or Clements (he did not find out any first names). In 1955 Francisco Schmidt sold a portion of the plot that had not been built on, but the house at 4261 Chacabuco Street was still registered in his name.

On the strength of these findings, Hermann unhesitatingly stated:

Francisco Schmidt is the man we want, and the personal description of Adolf Eichmann we got from Frankfurt fits him. From what I can make out, he chose two people at random and registered the meters in their names. Francisco Schmidt and his family live in the front of the house and he has rented the rear apartment to a family whose identity I haven't yet been able to discover but who apparently know who he really is. From what I was able to find out from people who saw Francisco Schmidt when he bought the land, his appearance matches the description of Adolf Eichmann exactly. Rumor has it that Schmidt was landed from a German submarine on the shore of Argentina in 1945. The same sources report that he claims his face was injured in an accident. These facts and data provide grounds for presuming with certainty that Francisco Schmidt (who is Adolf Eichmann) had his face changed completely by plastic surgery.

After this section of the report, which seemed clear and plausible, the second part came as an unpleasant surprise. Not only was the wording obscure, but it also contained material which gave rise to doubts about the first portion. This is what Hermann wrote in continuation:

After further inquiries into the Eichmann matter,
which I carried out in Buenos Aires from May
13 to 18, I can now determine that when Eichmann came to Argentina in 1945 he made his
way to the interior of the country. It will therefore be necessary to follow his trail there in order
to find out where he lived at that stage. I must
point out that the investigation in question will
have to cover a wide field and I will have to take
numerous journeys to northern Argentina, a distance of thousands of miles—a complicated matter
for me, and also very expensive.

Hermann went on to detail his financial requirements
and the arrangements for transferring the money to
him, and he concluded:

If you, or the authorities, want the material necessary for advancing the matter, you will have to
let me hold all the strings. . . . There's no need
to tell you that the expenses will be enormous or
that I won't be able to defray them from my own
pocket. As soon as you reply and carry out my
request, you will hear from me again.

It all sounded most peculiar to me: if he's so sure of
his story about Nicolas and what his daughter told him
after going to the Eichmann home, and if he states
categorically in the first part of his report that Francisco Schmidt is Adolf Eichmann, why on earth does
he want to check on Eichmann's movements after his
arrival in Argentina in 1945? It's like a hunter who
finds the fresh spoor of an animal and instead of following it doubles back to see where it came from. If
Hermann did in fact establish that Adolf Eichmann
is Francisco Schmidt who lives at a known address in
the suburbs of Olivos, he should now go all out to obtain the details required for the final identification of
the criminal, and that's that. What's the point of searching all over Argentina for places Eichmann stayed at

in the past? And why is Hermann demanding that he must "hold all the strings"?

I could see two possibilities: either Hermann's story was a figment of his imagination from start to finish and he made it up for a purpose I couldn't fathom, or his first story did have a sound basis but he got muddled up as he carried on with his search.

I gave instructions to approach him for an explanation of the contradictions in his report. All the money he had been promised was transferred to him, and at the same time Menashe Talmi was asked to find out, but not through Hermann, if there was any foundation for the supposition that Francisco Schmidt was Adolf Eichmann.

———

A wearisome round of inquiries proved to Talmi that Francisco Schmidt could not possibly be Eichmann; neither his appearance nor the data about his family fitted in with what we knew about the criminal. And furthermore, while Schmidt was in fact the owner of the house at 4261 Chacabuco Street, he didn't live there.

These findings damaged Hermann's trustworthiness irretrievably. The man continued to maintain obstinately that Schmidt was Eichmann. He didn't use the term "supposition" and never even mentioned the possibility that it was one of the tenants of the house—either Dagoto or Klement—who could be Eichmann. Once all our checking showed us that he'd made a mistake, we began to doubt his claim that Eichmann lived at 4261 Chacabuco Street.

In August 1958 instructions were given to allow our contact with Hermann to lapse gradually. However, Lothar Hermann didn't give up easily. At the end of that year he sent Huppert further news of his efforts to find Francisco Schmidt or "a man living in Argentina using the name Eichmann." He had apparently found out that nobody by the name of Schmidt or Eichmann lived at 4261 Chacabuco Street. Posing as a research worker for an alleged economic survey, he went to the registry office for temporary residents in

Argentina and asked for information about Adolf or
Adolfo Eichmann, born in Germany, and Francisco
Schmidt, a native of Austria. He said in his application
that they both used to live at 4261 Chacabuco Street
on the outskirts of Buenos Aires. Hermann explained
that he had been asked for the information by a client
in Germany in connection with a real-estate transaction.

Some more money Hermann requested was sent to
him at the beginning of 1959, and after that the correspondence petered out. Nothing remained of the high
hopes we had pinned on him at the beginning.

Somehow I couldn't reconcile myself to the thought
that Hermann's information was totally unfounded.
From time to time I went through the file we'd prepared
on Eichmann, and I believed that in spite of everything
there must be a grain of truth in Hermann's words. It
was the daughter's story particularly that I wanted to
check—it sounded very convincing. The whole Hermann family agreed on one detail: they knew a young
man named Nick Eichmann whose age and description
conformed to what we knew about Eichmann's eldest
son, Klaus. "Klaus" and "Nick" are both diminutives
of Nicolas. And Nick Eichmann's unwillingness to give
his girl friend his address was enough to point to some
sort of family skeleton.

Apart from Hermann's evidence, we had quite a bit
of information—unchecked, it's true—about Eichmann's presence in South America. Some of the items
even mentioned Argentina specifically. Bauer too, in
spite of his disappointment in Hermann, continued to
believe that Eichmann was in Argentina.

The disappearance of Vera Eichmann and her children from Austria and Germany was also not without
significance. If there were any grounds for the theory
that she had married again, why did she have to conceal where she was living? Why were the relatives,
both hers and Eichmann's, so careful not to give any
information about her or her children?

I came to the conclusion that we must renew our
attempts to ascertain whatever we could from both

sides of the family. I worked on the assumption that Vera Eichmann most likely kept up some sort of correspondence with her mother and her sisters and brothers. I thought that Eichmann might even be maintaining some sort of link with his father in Linz, or with one or more of his brothers in Austria and Germany. And if there was in fact an exchange of letters between him and his relatives, then there was hope of uncovering a lead, any sort of lead, to the family we were looking for.

With a view to advancing the investigation, I decided to appoint a special unit to deal solely with the most important war criminals—first and foremost, Eichmann. Hillel Ankor, a veteran agent, was placed at the head of the unit. All the material in the hands of the various institutions was passed on to this group, which in turn assigned agents in Israel and abroad to uncover new material on Eichmann and locate persons who might be able to identify him.

Our efforts did not bring the desired results.

Information we received in September 1959, claiming that Adolf Eichmann was seen in Bad Aussee or Alt Aussee in 1955, 1956, and 1959, was checked and found to be baseless. I had made up my mind, however, not to abandon the search. I considered it desirable to strengthen our ties with Dr. Bauer and to urge him not to spare any effort likely to lead us on a fresh trail.

And indeed, in the middle of 1959 Bauer reported that he had a new clue, leading again to Argentina. The information and its source, he stated, could be regarded as extremely reliable, but he considered it necessary to inquire further before he could pass it along. These inquiries would take some time, but he was hoping that by the time he planned to visit Israel, early in December 1959, he would be able to bring the results with him.

We had managed to conduct all our activities in secret until then, and there was nothing about them that could be construed by Eichmann as a warning or alert him to the fact that attempts to discover his hiding place were in progress. But on October 11, 1959, a sensational piece of news was published in the Israeli press: Eichmann was in Kuwait, working for an oil company. The item was attributed to Dr. Erwin Schüle, one of the heads of the Bureau for the Investigation of Nazi Crimes, in Ludwigburg.

The newspapers got their teeth into the subject and didn't let go for weeks. There were reports about teams of investigators in various countries working to find Eichmann. In the wake of the shattering news came criticism for lack of action in the past and a demand for efforts to capture Eichmann. This in spite of the fact that Dr. Erwin Schüle soon dissociated himself from the statement attributed to him and said that he had received unsubstantiated news that Eichmann had apparently been in Kuwait a few years ago. There was never any question of his being there now.

But that didn't stop the flood of publicity and demands for action. I was in no position to put a stop to all this without stirring up undesired attention. The newspaper publicity could very well put Eichmann on the alert. I decided that the best thing to do in the circumstances was to encourage the rumors about his being in Kuwait and even to make up a lot of extra details, so as to give him—and his friends—the impression that this was no serious investigation. Nothing could be done about the harsh criticisms leveled against the government. Silence was the only expedient in this respect.

Silence was not always possible. On December 25, 1959, Knesset Member Peretz Bernstein put a question in the House, asking whether the Prime Minister was prepared to take suitable steps in order to assist in the capture and legal punishment of Eichmann. I was asked how the question should be answered. I said I was confident that a man like Peretz Bernstein would not insist on a reply if the efforts being made were explained to him.

My advice was accepted. Knesset Member Bernstein willingly withdrew his question.

The reverberations of the rumor that Eichmann was in Kuwait had not yet died down when a turbid wave of anti-Semitic filth swelled in Germany and overflowed into dozens of countries all over the world. At daybreak on December 26, 1959, swastikas and anti-Jewish slogans were daubed on the walls of the new synagogue in Cologne. This did not remain an isolated incident. Within a few days swastikas and anti-Jewish, pro-Nazi slogans appeared in other cities in Germany and all over Western Europe. Similar incidents, including smearing of Jewish institutions and threatening of Jewish leaders, occurred in places as far away as Melbourne, New York, and Buenos Aires.

The worldwide scope of these paintings of swastikas and vilifications aroused grave anxiety in Israel. Admittedly, various governments had publicized their revulsion at the acts and increased the number of police guards at Jewish institutions; however, the general feeling was that these measures were not vigorous enough to stem the murky torrent. Newspapers in Israel expressed the fear that an international anti-Semitic organizaion was planning and directing the hostile demonstrations in every country.

As the epidemic showed no signs of abating, the name of Eichmann eventually floated to the surface in the newspapers. He was said to be one of those Nazi leaders who had smuggled abroad considerable funds from the treasury of the Third Reich and were now in constant touch with an anti-Semitic center in Europe and were financing its activities.

On January 20, speaking in the Knesset about the wave of anti-Semitism engulfing the world, the Prime Minister said that "one of our services, which has the facilities for it" had been entrusted to make inquiries in various countries about the possible existence of an international organization that had a hand in these outbreaks.

The inquiry entrusted to us was not inconsistent with our efforts to catch Eichmann. On the contrary, the new wave of Nazism made our operation a matter of paramount importance. It was clear to me that Eichmann's capture and his judgment in Israel would constitute a crushing counteraction to the Nazi monster's attempt to rear its head once more.

# 5

The new information Dr. Bauer brought to Israel in December 1959 was of tremendous importance. According to Bauer's new source, Eichmann went into hiding after the war in a German monastery, under the aegis of Catholic monks from Croatia. He apparently visited his wife in Austria in 1950, by which time he was already equipped with papers in his new name, Ricardo Klement. He then went by boat to Argentina with an International Red Cross passport—in the name of Ricardo Klement. In Buenos Aires he obtained an identity card in his new name, and a Ricardo Klement was listed in the Buenos Aires telephone directory for 1952. For a while Klement ran a laundry in the Olivos quarter, but he went bankrupt.

Some time in 1952 or 1953, Klement had business connections with a banking firm called Fuldner y Compañía, whose address in Buenos Aires was 374 Avenida Córdoba, telephone 328785. This company, headed by a German emigrant settled in Argentina, was interested in the exploitation of water sources for electricity and set up a subsidiary called C.A.P.R.I. for the purpose; Ricardo Klement was on the staff. In the early fifties, 1952 it seems, he worked for the company in the vicinity of the city of Tucumán. In 1958, according to the same source, somebody asked about Ricardo Klement at the Fuldner company, and the reply was: "He is still with us."

Once, during an attempted Bolivian uprising, one of

Klement's friends who knew his real identity was said to have suggested that he work for the state security services there. Klement responded: "When I hear those words, 'state security services,' my appetite for killing is whetted all over again."

———

It was absolutely impossible to make Bauer reveal any details whatsoever about the new source. But I realized immediately that this was the turning point and we were now steering toward the open road. Only one question bothered me, and I asked for clarification: How can I be sure that there is no connection, either direct or indirect, between the new source and Hermann? Bauer's reply was unequivocal: There is not, and there never could be, any connection between the two.

My mind was now at rest. First and foremost, the Hermann paradox was solved; what's more, at last we had additional confirmation of our premise that Eichmann was in Argentina. I had no means of assessing the reliability of the new source, but one item leapt to the eye and seemed to provide the key to the whole mystery: the name Ricardo Klement.

The name Klement (or Klements) had been mentioned in one of Hermann's reports, but he had regarded it as having been made up solely for the purpose of registering one of the two electricity meters in Francisco Schmidt's house. It never entered his mind that the names on both meters—Dagoto and Klement—could be those of actual tenants, although he became aware that Schmidt did not live in the house in Chacabuco Street. Rather than admit his mistake, Hermann started searching for the suspect elsewhere, under the name of either Francisco Schmidt or Adolf Eichmann. I remembered that in our first contact with Bauer at the end of 1957 he told us that his source (Lothar Hermann) refused to reveal the pseudonym of the man suspected of being Eichmann, and when "Huppert" visited him he didn't say by what name Nicolas Eichmann's father was known.

Now I understood why, and it was obvious what had

happened with Hermann: his story about Nick Eichmann was logical and reasonable from every point of view. It was based on the daughter's evidence and supported by the mother, both of whom had from the very beginning impressed us as being reliable. Even Hermann's explanation of how he came to connect Nick's father with the criminal Eichmann—whose name was mentioned at the trial of another war criminal in Germany—was perfectly logical. Had Hermann stopped there, his important discovery might have brought results before long. However, for reasons known only to himself, he wanted to carry on alone and to "hold all the strings." He seemed to think that if he were given the necessary finances he would soon succeed in finding out everything about Nick Eichmann's family, including the assumed name and exact address of the father. But Hermann may have reasoned that since Nick was using his real name the father would also not conceal his, and if this was so he could easily confirm it through his ramified connections and his many friends in Olivos.

His hopes were not fulfilled. Finding that there were no tenants in the house at 4261 Chacabuco Street by the name of Eichmann but that the occupant was an Austrian, he did not bother to look for proof but "stated" rashly that this Austrian was Eichmann. Had he told us he was guessing that Schmidt was Eichmann, we would have checked; and when it turned out that Schmidt didn't live in the house and couldn't be Eichmann, we would almost certainly have checked on the other tenants. But Hermann didn't refer to the Schmidt-Eichmann identification as a possibility or a conjecture, he laid it down as a fact and supported it with the rumor that the man had landed in Argentina from a German submarine after the war. His theory that Schmidt-Eichmann had his face changed by plastic surgery was also offered to us as a proven fact. He presented his surmises as facts, and when his errors were pointed out he asked only for a chance to trace Eichmann's movements from the day he arrived in

Argentina. In his haste to draw conclusions, Hermann
had destroyed his own theory.

---

I couldn't write it off as coincidence that the name
Klement cropped up in both our sources. A comparison of the two led me to believe that Eichmann
did in fact live in the house in Chacabuco Street and
that the name Klement on the meter was the name he
had assumed from the time he arrived in Argentina.
The more I delved into Hermann's file and all the reports on his findings, the more convinced I became
that Ricardo Klement of Chacabuco Street was Adolf
Eichmann. It struck me as farfetched that Vera Eichmann could have married another German who was
also forced to conceal his true identity and was using
the name Klement.

What worried me, however, was that Hermann's discovery of Nick Eichmann's family had been made in
1957. It was now the end of 1959, more than two
years later, and we had heard nothing further. There
was no certainty that the family still lived at the same
address.

Our next move was obvious: we must locate the
Klement family in Argentina and determine whether
Ricardo Klement was Adolf Eichmann; also, in view
of the remote possibility that Klement might be a different war criminal whom Vera Eichmann had married after her husband's disappearance, we must again
put out feelers in Europe to test just how touchy the
two families, Eichmann and Liebl (Vera's maiden
name), were on the subject of the whereabouts of the
woman and her children. If it was true that she was
remarried to a man called Klement who wasn't Eichmann, there would be no reason for the family to hide
the fact that she and the children were in Argentina—
all the more since the children continued to call themselves Eichmann. However, if Klement was Eichmann,
the family would be careful not to tell anyone the
country where Vera and her children were living. It
was reasonably worth our while, if we could, to "join

in" the correspondence between the Eichmann family in Argentina and the relatives in Europe, if such a correspondence did exist.

---

I then began to consider the choice of a self-reliant senior operator to whom to entrust the investigation of the theory that Klement was Adolf Eichmann. The assignment called for a man who could be counted on to keep his inquiries secret and his conclusions logical. I settled on Yosef Kenet, one of the best investigators in the country. A former member of a kibbutz, Kenet was born in Germany and became a specialist in the interrogation of German war prisoners while serving in the British army during World War II. I knew him as a dedicated man who never let go once he got his teeth into an assignment, and I was sure that when he'd finished his mission we would know where we stood.

I approached his commanding officer, Haggai. I knew that in any matter touching on Eichman I would find Haggai helpful and understanding—he was one of the few survivors of Auschwitz, the primary Nazi concentration camp, and was all too familiar with Eichmann's satanic deeds in Hungary, Haggai's native country.

Long before the first news of Eichmann in Argentina was brought to me, Haggai had felt that the two war criminals most responsible for the slaughter of millions of Jews should be tracked down: the bestial doctor of Auschwitz, Josef Mengele, and the fiend who engineered the "Final Solution," Adolf Eichmann.

Nonetheless, it was no easy matter to secure a release for Kenet to join our operation; he was busy with various important security investigations and couldn't be replaced. Haggai was prepared to do anything in his power to advance Kenet's release, but nothing could be done before the end of February 1960.

I was seething with impatience. At a time like this, when I knew we had reliable information, to have to wait two months was galling. But it couldn't be helped —Kenet was the ideal agent for this job and he was pleased to have been selected. And he did have the opportunity to make a thorough study of the subject in

the weeks before his departure. I explained my view
that there were solid grounds for hoping that Ricardo
Klement was Adolf Eichmann. I also managed to arrange for Kenet to meet with Dr. Bauer to hear everything Bauer knew about Eichmann and to get details
of Bauer's sources and his evaluation of the supposition that Klement was Eichmann. Present at this
meeting were Hillel Ankor and Menashe Talmi, who
had completed his research and returned home at the
end of 1958. Talmi's participation was particularly important, because of his expert knowledge of conditions
in Argentina and because he had acquired experience
in conducting inquiries, first with Goren and Hofstaetter and later on his own.

Kenet emerged from this meeting somewhat disappointed, as he had not succeeded in persuading Bauer
to reveal the identity of his source; he felt that if he
could meet the man and question him his work would
be infinitely easier. At the same time, he was impressed with Bauer's honesty and his total belief that
Klement was Eichmann. And Bauer had promised that
when he returned to Frankfurt he would put at our
disposal copies of all the documents in his possession
which could in any way assist in identifying Eichmann.

---

At this point I started delving into the possibility of
bringing Eichmann to trial in Israel—that is, provided
it did in fact turn out that Klement was Eichmann and
we could lay our hands on him. The trial of Eichmann
would clearly be the crowning point of the operation,
and I firmly believed that to present Eichmann before
a panel of Israeli judges would be an achievement of
tremendous moral and historical consequence.

For enlightenment on the judicial possibilities I turned
to a friend who was considered one of our greatest
jurists. At my request, we met at his house rather than
the office to avoid arousing unwelcome curiosity. Sitting in his study crammed with books, I told him about
our prospects for locating Eichmann and our intention
to capture him and then bring him to trial in Israel. The
question, I told him, was whether it would be possible

to try a man who had been brought into the country
under such circumstances.

My friend was very moved—though he did seem to
be a little taken aback at the very audacity of the idea.
He sat for some time deep in thought; then he rose
abruptly and took several thick volumes off his book-
shelves; he studied his law books for a while.

Then he turned to me and said, "It can be done."

He was basing his opinion on precedents, but before
giving his final answer he wanted some time to consult
with a friend who was also an eminent jurist.

A few days later he brought me their joint reply:
"Yes."

———

Toward the end of December 1959 I decided to set
up an operational team to carry out a thorough check
on the Eichmann and Liebl families. The task of
organizing the action was assigned to Ezra Eshet, who
was stationed in Europe on operational duty. Ezra
had come to Israel in 1949, after tasting the bitterness
of the Fascist regime in Rumania during the war. His
chief mission was to discover when, how, and where
Vera Liebl Eichmann and her children had vanished
in the aftermath of the war. The team was instructed
to shadow her family in Europe in case any of them
was in correspondence with Vera, which might give us
a lead to the woman's present address. Eshet was told
to conduct similar inquiries about Eichmann's father—
who, in spite of his eighty-two years, was still running
an electrical-equipment business in Linz—and his four
brothers.

The assignment was by no means easy. And I added
to its objective difficulties by imposing severe restrictions on the team: for one incautious step might apprise
the family of our intentions and cause them to warn
our quarry.

———

I was so sure that my theories about Eichmann were
about to be verified that I began to work out the operational plan for the capture.

To me Argentina was an unknown country, and it was nine and a half thousand miles from Israel. I figured that a task force would have to be set up in Israel and then dispatched abroad for action—a difficult and complicated procedure. But my biggest problem was how to get Eichmann from Argentina to Israel.

No Israeli planes flew to that part of the world, though a regular flight to South America had once been considered. At first I thought of hiring a special plane for the operation. But an Atlantic crossing would require a large aircraft, and I knew we couldn't charter a large passenger plane without attracting general attention.

I decided to share my problems with Asher Kedem, an airline manager. We'd known each other for years, so there was no need to waste time on explanations and preambles. "Is there any possibility of sending a plane to Buenos Aires?" I asked.

Kedem probably knew that my interest had less to do with extending the company's network than with an impending operation, yet he asked no questions. "Technically," he said, "such a flight could be undertaken, but I can't give you a final answer without the approval of the directors. The managing director isn't in the country at the moment, but I can speak to Moshe Tadmor, one of his deputies."

We decided he should discuss it confidentially with Tadmor, and the following week he brought the reply: "Tadmor says that any request coming from you calls for immediate action. I can confirm definitely that from the technical point of view there's nothing to stand in the way. A plane of the Britannia type could fly to Buenos Aires and back with two crews and two intermediate stops—Dakar and Recife."

"But what sort of plausible explanation do you think we can make for a special flight like that?" I asked.

"The company has been considering a plan to inaugurate flights to South America, as you know. We could say that this is an experimental flight."

I was satisfied. "That's enough for the time being,"
I said. "But I must stress that even the fact that I made
this tentative inquiry mustn't be allowed to leak out."

Kedem asked, "Can you say anything now about the
estimated date of the flight?"

"At this stage, no. When the time comes I'll call on
you."

That was in December 1959.

---

The painstaking work continued. Grain was added
to grain, document to document, testimony to testimony.

In Europe, an agent whose mission was just ending
agreed to postpone his return to Israel for a few months
so that he could work with Ezra Eshet on the Eichmann
assignment. During the last weeks of 1959 and the
first weeks of 1960, Gad Armon alternated between
Germany and Austria, checking on the Eichmann and
Liebl families. Wherever he went the relatives and
their close friends and neighbors raised an impenetrable
wall of silence. The conclusion was self-evident.

Eshet put extra men to work while he himself went
into action in Germany and Austria. All attempts to
make Eichmann's brothers talk were of no avail. The
men sent to interview them worked under excellent
cover and could not possibly have aroused any suspicion whatsoever. One of Eshet's representatives, perfectly disguised as a German commercial agent, succeeded in making direct contact with Vera's mother.
He stayed in Mrs. Liebl's little village for ten days,
but there, as elsewhere, everyone was steadfastly mum.
Her correspondence was examined, the results again
were negative. There was no mistaking it: everything
relating to Eichmann and his wife and children was
taboo to all branches of the Eichmann and Liebl
families.

Still, our operational file continued to fatten. In addition to the material in our possession, including the
documents and annotations we had obtained through
Bauer, there were the items we had unearthed while
searching through the archives of various bureaus.

Anything that might help in the identification of Eichmann and his family was meticulously recorded. It was all done in secret and with great caution to avoid public knowledge that we were interested in the criminal and his family.

According to information from a reliable source, Vera Eichmann and her children had been living in an out-of-the-way village in Europe at the beginning of the 1950s but had suddenly disappeared from there without a trace. It also became obvious that none of the German consulates in Europe were prepared, in any circumstances whatsoever, to divulge the name in which Vera Eichmann's passport had been issued.

When I went to meet Eshet in Europe to learn from him the results of his inquiries and activities, my convictions were strengthened: Adolf Eichmann was undoubtedly alive, well hidden, and apparently living with his family—otherwise his wife and children wouldn't have vanished so completely and mysteriously, nor would his family in Europe have kept their lips so tightly sealed.

At the end of February, Yosef Kenet was ready to leave for Argentina. Before his departure, I outlined the plan of action with him and set up arrangements for liaison and reporting. We went over the cover story he would be using to conceal the object of his journey, both at home and abroad. Even his family and closest friends, I told him, mustn't know where he was going or for what purpose.

# 6

On his way to Argentina, Kenet stopped in two other South American countries to see some people who had volunteered to help him in his assignment. There were four of them, all South American residents, fluent in Spanish, and thoroughly familiar with Argentina in general and Buenos Aires in particular, through frequent business or personal visits. Two were a couple by the name of Kornfeld, David, a successful young architect, and Hedda, a graduate in psychology and languages; one was Lubinsky, a middle-aged lawyer with extensive contacts all over the continent; and the fourth was Primo, a second-year engineering student. Kenet made their travel arrangements, outlined future meeting places, and furnished them with new papers under borrowed names.

He himself reached Buenos Aires on the evening of March 1, 1960, and went straight from the airport to his hotel. He immediately started looking through the telephone directories for Buenos Aires city and district. The city directory listed both a Ricardo Klement and a Carlos Ricardo Klement, but in the district directory, which included the Olivos area, the name Klement or Klements—with either "K" or "C"—did not appear.

The next morning he learned his way around by wandering through the streets with a map. Later on he rented a car, so he could drive the following day, March 3, to the café prearranged for his first meeting with Lubinsky, who was now installed at another hotel.

Kenet asked Lubinsky if he could—without arousing
undue attention or curiosity—go to a private investigation bureau to seek  information about certain people
and their places of residence. Lubinsky said it would
seem perfectly feasible if he, as a lawyer, were to explain at the bureau that he needed to find these people
in connection with a legacy. Any detective agency, he
said, would preserve strict secrecy if asked. He had
often initiated such inquiries in his own country and
had also on various occasions requested friends of his
in Buenos Aires to deal with private investigators on
his behalf. So they decided that Lubinsky would establish contact with a suitable agency to investigate details
about the identity of the tenants at 4261 Chacabuco
Street, Olivos, and to find out whether in 1952 or
1953 a woman by the name of Vera Liebl had arrived in Argentina with three children. And he would
also try to obtain the 1952 telephone directories for
Buenos Aires city and district.

Lubinsky's task turned out to be completely routine.
When he explained to the people at the bureau selected
that he had been requested to undertake an extremely
complicated inheritance suit involving the search for
heirs in several continents and their subsequent investigation, not a soul doubted his veracity. His request
that the work be carried out quickly and in complete
silence and secrecy was received with full understanding, all the more so when it was accompanied by an
open hint that his clients would be generous with
their remuneration if the results came up to expectations.

At his next meeting with Kenet, Lubinsky was able
to reassure him that the detective agency saw nothing
strange or unusual in his request. This report encouraged Kenet to entrust Lubinsky with further inquiries, this time through a different investigation
bureau in another part of the city. The subjects in this
case would be the Fuldner and C.A.P.R.I. companies
mentioned in our background material as Klement's
past or present employers, and Lubinsky would explain
his interest in the companies by telling the agency that

his clients might wish to communicate with them about carrying out certain development work.

———

Kenet's next meeting was with the student, Primo. As Primo had a large circle of acquaintances in the Argentine capital and there was always the chance that he might run across them, he chose as their meeting place a restaurant where the cuisine appealed to his personal gastronomic tastes but not to those of any of his friends.

After a short talk over a snack, Kenet and Primo set out in the rented car on a tour of Olivos. They drove along Chacabuco Street, and from the detailed descriptions he had been given Kenet had no difficulty finding and identifying number 4261. He had heard so much about its seedy and neglected appearance that he was surprised to find it larger and nicer than he had imagined and to notice that the unpaved street was flanked by a curious combination of humble cottages and luxurious villas. They asked directions here and there and gathered from the accents of the people that the district was indeed inhabited mainly by Germans—and there were several swastikas daubed on the walls.

They parked a few hundred yards from the house. Kenet took a postcard out of his pocket and asked Primo to write on it in Spanish: "Regards from George." In the space reserved for the sender he wrote "Dagosto" and below it "4263 Chacabuco Street," a number that didn't exist. Kenet chose "Dagosto" because it was similar to Dagoto, the name in which a meter had been installed at 4261.

Kenet told Primo to go up to the house, postcard in hand, on the pretext of looking for its sender. Several minutes later he returned and told Kenet he had spoken to a girl who said there was nobody by the name of Dagosto in the neighborhood. He went into the yard of number 4261, looked through the windows of the house, and was able to see that one of the apartments was empty and painters were at work in the other.

Kenet inferred that the tenants had moved and that, even if Eichmann had ever been one of them, he was no longer to be found there. That being the case, he reasoned, there would be no risk of complicating matters if straightforward inquiries were made at the house itself; the likelihood of meeting Eichmann or any member of his family had been eliminated.

He thought the inquiry would seem more innocent if they pretended they wanted to do someone a good turn. Kenet remembered that March 3 was Klaus Eichmann's birthday and felt it would not arouse suspicion if they were looking for Klaus to give him a birthday present.

———

The next day, March 4, Kenet bought an expensive cigarette lighter and dropped it into his pocket. He then went to meet the Kornfelds, who had arrived the day before. He asked Hedda to wrap the lighter as a gift and to attach to the small parcel an unsigned greeting card: "To my friend Nicky, affectionately, on your birthday." He told her to address the envelope to Nicolas Klement, 4261 Chacabuco Street, Olivos.

Kenet explained that he wanted Hedda to register at a luxury hotel for one day, find an intelligent page from the hotel, and have him deliver the gift and card —according to very specific instructions, which he outlined at some length.

A little later, Hedda was sitting in the spacious lobby of one of the best hotels in the city. She was an attractive woman and had taken special pains with her outfit that day; she looked perfectly at home in the posh surroundings, and no one would have dreamt that this elegant young woman was a fraud or that she could be taking part in a manhunt destined to take the world by storm.

There were not many people in the lobby, and Hedda's sharp eyes scrutinized its few occupants. Now and then she glanced toward a young page who appeared to be more alert and well-mannered than the others; she had in fact noticed him the moment she came in. The boy must have sensed her interest, for he blushed to the roots of his hair. She beckoned him with a nod.

"What can I do for you, ma'am?"

She looked him over and smiled. "What's your name?"

"Pedro, ma'am."

"I'm sure you know the city well. . . ." The boy answered in the affirmative, so she went on. "Well, then, I want to send you on a little errand."

"Anything you like, ma'am."

"It's a delicate matter," she said, "and I have to rely on you to be discreet. I think a boy of your age knows by now that there are certin things which have to be handled quietly, and when you come back you'll have to report on every little thing without leaving out a single detail. Keep in mind all the time that it's top secret and must be kept strictly between you and me. I'm sure I can trust you."

The boy straightened up proudly. "Word of honor, ma'am," he said.

"Are you free now? Can you go at once?" she asked.

"Yes."

"Very well. Here's an envelope with a small parcel for you to give to a man by the name of Nicolas Klement. The name and address are written on the envelope. There's a present in the parcel and you have to deliver it personally—I mean, into the hands of Nicolas Klement himself. If you can't hand it to him personally, either because the address is wrong or because he's moved away, try to find out the correct or new address so that I can send the present there. If you find that he has moved, don't go to the new place—I'll see to the delivery of the parcel myself. But please remember, don't tell anybody that it was a woman who sent you; if you're asked who sent you, say that a friend of yours who works at another hotel gave you the parcel yesterday and asked you to take it for him, and that's all you know about it."

A spark of excitement flashed in the youngster's eyes. It was obvious that he was conjuring up in his imagination some mysterious and romantic affair in which he was being allowed to play a decisive role—and who knows, maybe this elegant young woman's happiness depended on his resourcefulness.

"I won't let you down," he replied. "I'll do just as you said. I'm on my way."

"Excellent. Here's some bus money." The amount she handed him put an extra sparkle in his bright eyes. Off he went at a run.

Pedro had no trouble finding Chacabuco Street and the house numbered 4261. He looked for a bell at the gate, but there was none, so, after calling out and getting no response, he crossed the yard and walked straight into the house. The door and windows were open, and he could see that painters were working inside. Pedro passed through the living room and crossed the patio into a bedroom, where he saw an unmade bed, shoes, and other personal effects. To the right of this room was a kitchen with a table set with food. The kitchen, bathroom, and another bedroom faced the yard. Through the open door he could see part of a small room with an old man sitting at the door.

He went back out to the yard and walked along a side path to an unplastered shack. A young man of about thirty and a woman were busily cleaning it out. Pedro went up to them, the envelope and gift box in his hand, and asked, "Does Klement live here?"

"Klement . . . Klement . . . mmm . . . oh yes, Klement . . ." the man replied after a moment of hesitation.

"Yes, Klement," the woman confirmed.

"Klement. . . .

"Isn't that the German?" asked the man.

"I don't know," said Pedro.

"He's got two grown sons and one youngster, isn't that so?" the man asked.

"I don't know a thing about him," said Pedro. "I've got something to give him. Where can I find him?"

"He used to live here but doesn't any more. He left, I don't know exactly when . . . about twenty days ago," the man explained.

"Where did he go?"

"I haven't a clue. But he will know." He indicated the small room where Pedro had noticed the elderly painter and then led Pedro back through the house.

"I've got a message for the man whose name's written here," Pedro began, pointing to the envelope.

"He wants the new address of the one who moved out of here," the young man chimed in.

"Ah ... the German," said the painter.

"Yes. Can you tell me where to find him? I've got something for him."

"All I know is he moved to San Fernando, but I don't know how you'll find it—I don't know the exact address. You go there by the number 60 bus ... Wait a minute: the son works near here. ... ." He turned to the other man and said, "Maybe you could go with him and show him where it is."

"It'll be a pleasure. Come with me."

They left the house and walked down the street to the corner. The young man started to explain how to get to the workshop where he could find the German's son, but he saw that Pedro was having trouble following his directions and offered to take him there. They crossed the street, and the man pointed out a scooter parked next to the curb.

"You see that *motoneta?* It's the young German's. You'll know him by his very fair hair."

They crossed the road about thirty yards from Paraná Street, at the continuation of Chacabuco and went into a one-story building. A number of technicians were busy at various jobs, and in the corridor a typically Teutonic-looking lad, about eighteen or twenty years old, was at work. Pedro's escort called him over and they shook hands.

"This young gentleman wants to talk to your father."

"I've got a letter for the man whose name's written here," said Pedro, showing him the envelope. "They tell me he doesn't live here any more. Maybe you can tell me where to take the letter."

"We've moved," the blond fellow said.

"Where to?"

"Don Torcuato."

"Well, they told me I must deliver this letter and parcel personally into his hands," Pedro said.

The German examined the envelope again. "Who sent it?"

"I don't know exactly. One of my friends gave it to me. He got it from a guest in the hotel where he works, but he was too busy so he asked me to do it for him. I've had it since yesterday really, but yesterday I didn't have time."

"I'd still like to know who it came from," the blond man insisted.

"What do you want from him?" the young man interrupted. "They gave him these things and all he's got to do is hand them over. He came to look for you where you lived before and I told him you've moved and you work here. I think you should take it."

"Yes, but I'd still like to know who sent it."

Pedro pointed mutely to the envelope in his hand.

"Mmm . . . I see what you mean. The sender's name may be inside the envelope," said the fair-haired lad.

"I still think I've got to put the letter and parcel in the hands of this person," said Pedro, pointing again to the name on the envelope. "Maybe you could give me the address?"

"No . . . the houses aren't numbered where we live. And besides . . ."

"Oh, really?" said Pedro. "Then I guess I'd better give them to you—unless you can tell me how to get there."

"There aren't any street names in Don Torcuato," Pedro's escort remarked.

Pedro sighed. "O.K. Here's the envelope and here's the parcel."

"If you have any trouble about this you can always find me here," the blond fellow replied.

"All right. Good-by and thanks."

As they left the building, Pedro made a note of the street number: 2865. The scooter was a Siambretta 150–Sport, and it was in filthy condition.

Pedro thanked the man who had acted as his guide and hurried back to report to the lady on how he had carried out his mission. He wasn't sure if he'd done right handing over the letter and parcel to the blond young man, on the strength of the neighbor's word that he was Klement's son.

But the young woman wasn't angry with him. When he told her the whole story, she said he had acted correctly. For some reason, she attached great importance to every single detail of his story and even made some notes. She asked him if he had caught the name of the young man he'd given the letter to, and Pedro thought about it and recalled that he'd heard the men at the workshop call him something that sounded like "Dito" or "Tito" or even "Tieter."

She paid him generously, shook hands and thanked him, and went away.

Hedda Kornfeld reported to Kenet every word the youngster had told her. The next day she moved back to her former hotel.

# 7

The new information in Hedda's report led Kenet to conclude:

Until a few weeks ago a German family with three sons lived at 4261 Chacabuco Street. It was almost a certainty that the name of this family was Klement. It was also extremely likely that, if Pedro had indeed met one of Eichmann's sons, it was the third, Dieter. He was born on March 29, 1942, which would make him about the age of the blond young German at the workshop, and the name might easily come out sounding like "Tito" or "Dito." The fact that the family moved out without leaving any forwarding address strengthened the assumption that they were the Eichmanns.

Kenet attached particular importance to what the painter had told Pedro about the family moving to San Fernando, and the blond young man's statement about their living in Don Torcuato. Since the map showed these two areas to be about six miles apart, it was possible that Dieter Eichmann was deliberately trying to mislead Pedro (we found out later that it was Kenet who was wrong on this point and that, in a way, both the painter and Dieter were telling the truth).

The next step was to find out the family's exact address. Kenet decided to try checking on the young German as he was leaving the workshop; the same day, March 4, he drove with Primo and Lubinsky to an intersection "Tito" would have to pass on his way from the workshop on Monteagudo Street to San Fernando,

55

or Don Torcuato, and there they waited. He hoped to be able to identify the young man from Pedro's description.

They waited from three-thirty until six o'clock, but no blond young man of Teutonic appearance passed the spot.

Kenet thought it would be worth having another try at finding out the Klement family's new address from the tenants at 4261 Chacabuco Street. After making sure that Dieter had finished work and there was no danger of bumping into him, he told Lubinsky to go to the house, posing as an insurance agent making inquiries about Ricardo Klement. Lubinsky found two painters inside. One of them, who spoke Spanish with a German accent, replied to his question about Klement. "No, he's not here. Ricardo Klement and his family moved out three weeks ago."

"Could you perhaps give me his new address?" asked Lubinsky.

"I don't know it. All I know is that they moved to San Fernando."

"Have they rented a bigger house?" Lubinsky asked. "Has the family grown?"

The painter shrugged. "They've got four children, three grown up and one small, and as far as I know they haven't had a fifth. The eldest is married, one's in the navy, and one works in a shop about half a block from here. The little one's about eight."

"Couldn't you perhaps still help me with the new address?" Lubinsky urged. "You'd save me an unnecessary journey and a lot of searching."

At that moment two men walked in and stood listening to the conversation. Lubinsky thought he'd better cut it short, but the painter kept on talking. "You can ask the son who works near here," he said. "But he's not there now because he finishes work at five."

"What's his name?"

"I don't know. If you ask for 'the German' everybody will know who you mean."

Lubinsky went back to the car and repeated the conversation to Kenet. So a surmise had become a certainty: the German living in that house until a few weeks ago was definitely Ricardo Klement. What Lubinsky had heard about the family setup generally fitted what was known about the Eichmann family—except that if Vera Eichmann joined her husband in 1953, they could not have an eight-year-old; the child born to them in Argentina could be no more than six.

This was a Friday, so they had no choice but to postpone checking up on "Tito" until after the weekend. Kenet took advantage of the opportunity to have a rest and to send his first report to Israel.

And we received it as good news that Klement had been living until recently in the house at 4261 Chacabuco Street and that Kenet believed he had found Eichmann's third son.

————

This first report was hailed as encouraging news by everybody who was in on the secret. I had really been convinced all along that the Hermann family's story about Nicolas Eichmann was true in its entirety, but a long time had passed since Hermann's daughter had been friendly with Eichmann's son, and it was impossible to be sure that the Eichmann family hadn't vanished again without trace since then. And now came the good tidings that Eichmann was still living in the vicinity of Buenos Aires, and what's more his son's whereabouts were known with near certainty. Without further delay, I intensified the planning of the operational steps we'd have to take immediately upon verification of our assumption that Ricardo Klement was Adolf Eichmann.

I summoned Leora Dotan, an expert in matters pertaining to administration, finance, and manpower. I didn't tell her what it was about and she asked no questions, but I knew that generally she intuited far more than she had been told. You can't work with people who are quick-witted and resourceful and expect them not to exercise their talents to figure out all kinds of things. I couldn't really hide anything from most of my principal assistants, but I could rely on them to keep quiet and not ask superfluous questions.

I assigned Leora to prepare certain details we might

need when the time for action came, and I knew that whenever we required them they would be ready. Leora was endowed with a rare talent for organization, and the concept "impossible" didn't exist for her; she was outstanding for her energy, her resourcefulness, her quick grasp, and her qualities of leadership.

That following Monday, March 7, Kenet and Primo waited again at the same crossing, the one all their data told them the young German would have to pass on his way home. Again he didn't turn up.

The same evening Lubinsky brought the first results of the inquiries conducted by the private investigation bureau he'd visited a few days earlier. The Argentine investigators told them that Eichmann and the Klements whose names were in the telephone directory had nothing to do with each other. As for the house at 4261 Chacabuco Street, the agency reported that à large garage had been added to it, which—judging by its width and height—could also serve as a storeroom. About ten days earlier a German family by the name of Schneider had cleared out the part of the storeroom which they had been renting and had moved to an unknown address. Now there remained one tenant only, a foreigner—apparently Hungarian or Polish—named Francisco Schmidt. He was the owner of the whole house and was now busy having it painted and renovated with a view to selling it. Nobody knew where he would go.

Kenet asked Lubinsky to request further particulars about the people named in their report, since there was the possibility that one of them, Schneider or Schmidt, might be the "Klement" he was looking for. Kenet also wanted him to find out the name of the firm that had handled the removal of Schneider's furniture. Following his instructions, Lubinsky explained at the bureau that complete secrecy was essential as Klement was liable to disappear if he found out that they were looking for him, then "great financial loss would be incurred."

On March 8, from seven-thirty in the morning until ten, Kenet maintained a surveillance of the Fuldner

Company's offices on Avenida Córdoba. He was lucky —it was raining heavily and he was able to stand for a long time in the doorway of a house without arousing suspicion. During all that time he saw nobody who could be Eichmann.

In the afternoon Kenet and Primo went once more to the same intersection to watch for the young German on his way from the workshop. At five-fifteen they saw a scooter that looked like the one the youngster Pedro had described coming from the direction of the shop. The scooter shot out into the main road and, a little farther on, turned left, in the direction of San Fernando. The driver was a swarthy man between forty and forty-five wearing dark-rimmed glasses, and riding in the seat behind him was a fair-haired lad dressed in mechanic's clothes who fitted Pedro's description of "Tito." The scooter's number plate was so dirty that it was illegible —however, its very filth conformed to Pedro's identification.

They followed the scooter, keeping a good distance behind. They had traveled just over half a mile along the main road, Avenida Santa Fe, when they saw the scooter turn left near the Beccar railway station. Kenet drew closer at that point and saw it stop in front of a house near the corner of Juan B. Justo. The driver waited while the young man went into the house for a minute or two; it was twenty-five minutes past five. The young man came out and they returned to the main road and continued on toward San Fernando, where they turned left into Sarmiento Street.

Here Kenet and Primo lost them when a funeral cortege making its way through the center of San Fernando came between them, alongside the square, at the corner of Tres de Febrero and Sarmiento. They drove all around the neighborhood looking for the scooter but didn't find it. From a distance they could make out a young man in mechanic's overalls going into a house on Tres de Febrero, number 461, but they had no way of knowing whether this was the youth they had tailed from Olivos. Luck continued to frown on them—on the return journey the car's electrical system acted up and it was only with a great deal of difficulty that they managed to limp back to Buenos Aires.

Having failed to shadow their quarry to his destination, they began to question whether they had trailed the right man. True, the scooter riders did go to San Fernando, the area mentioned by the man in Chacabuco Street as the home of the Klement family, but how could they know if it was the young man from the workshop they'd been following? After all, Pedro had said that the scooter belonged to the young man himself, but this scooter had been driven by an older man, with the young one on the rear seat. Neither Kenet nor Primo had ever seen young Klement, so how could they be sure they had shadowed the right person?

It was raining the morning of March 9 when Kenet sent Primo to the workshop in Monteagudo Street to look for the scooter and get its number. The weather was likely to make their trailing activity harder, and they also had to take into account the possibility that because of the rain young Klement would travel to work by train or bus.

In the afternoon Primo came back with the information that the scooter was there, after all, and its number was 84099.

This time Kenet organized three shadowing parties. He waited with Lubinsky at the intersection where the scooter had first been seen the day before. Primo waited at the square in San Fernando, at the spot where they had lost sight of the scooter because of the funeral. David and Hedda Kornfeld wandered around near the workshop, prepared to follow the young man if he got on a bus.

Kenet and Lubinsky waited until six o'clock, but the scooter didn't appear. They drove past the workshop but didn't see the Kornfelds. Parked on the pavement next to the workshop was a black scooter, its number: 160934. They drove to San Fernando to pick up Primo, who had not seen the young man.

Kenet didn't hear from the Kornfelds until the next day. They said they had waited opposite the workshop until five-twenty, when a fair-haired young man who

seemed to fit Pedro's description came out and walked
to the corner of Monteagudo Street, where he boarded
a bus. They got on after him and followed him off at
the Martinez railway station. From there the young
man could have taken a train to San Fernando or to
Don Torcuato. But he didn't even go into the station;
he walked away and turned into a side lane. In accordance with their instructions, they broke off their
shadowing at this stage.

The afternoon of March 10 Kenet again divided
his people into three parties: Primo waited at the center of San Fernando as before; Kenet sat in the car on
Monteagudo Street about a hundred yards from the
workshop; and the Kornfelds waited on Paraná Street
not far from the corner of Monteagudo Street, leaving
their car nearby.

They waited from four-thirty until almost ten minutes to six, when a scooter similar to the one belonging
to the young man they were after was seen driving out
of the workshop yard. Again two men were riding on it,
the older man and the fair-haired youth. Kenet drove
quickly to the Kornfelds' observation point, picked
them up, and dashed after the scooter. Fortunately for
them, the scooter was pulling a small tender, a kind of
cart, which slowed it down considerably and made it
easy for them to catch up. The scooter took the same
route as two days before, and this time too the riders
stopped for a few minutes at the house near the Beccar
railway station and then continued on to San Fernando.
In the central square of San Fernando, next to Sarmiento
Street, Kenet saw Primo sitting on a bench and picked
him up.

The scooter parked for a minute or two in San
Fernando—from a distance it looked as if they were
buying something at an outdoor candy stand—and then
nearly disappeared in a maze of alleys, emerging onto Route 202 and driving in the direction of Bancalari–Don Torcuato. After about a mile and a half
the built-up area of San Fernando was behind them,
and in the open country stretching ahead Kenet was
obliged to increase the distance between his car and

the quarry to about half a mile because of the lack of traffic on route 202. Kenet looked at his watch. It was close to six o'clock.

The scooter stopped about a hundred and fifty yards before the railway bridge over Route 202, five hundred yards before Bancalari station. The shadowing party turned into a side street some five hundred yards before the bridge and Kenet parked the car behind a deserted house at the crossroads. In the distance they saw one of the scooter riders—it was impossible to make out which one—get off at a kiosk on the left side of the road, while the other drove on for fifty yards. There he parked next to a cottage and went inside. Meanwhile they had lost sight of the first man. Kenet drove away but returned half an hour later, when it was dark. This time they left the car a considerable distance from the kiosk and approached it on foot. They went past the cottage and asked some workmen walking by if they knew a family by the name of Rodriguez in the neighborhood. One of the men pointed toward a distant compound that looked like a refugee camp and said he thought a family by that name lived over there. When asked who lived in the cottage, the workman said a young man and his mother lived there and, yes, the young man had a scooter. Kenet decided to call it a day and leave the rest of the inquiry for another time.

A hundred yards or so from the cottage, and about the same distance from the kiosk, stood a brick house that looked unfinished. No one in the party gave it a second thought.

# 8

The next morning Kenet reckoned it was time to change his rented car; it may have been seen too often wandering in the neighborhood of Chacabuco and Monteagudo Streets.

Then he met Lubinsky, who told him that the investigation bureau had found nothing in the official records to indicate that in 1953 a woman by the name of Vera Liebl had arrived in Argentina with her three children. Kenet asked Lubinsky to put pressure on the second bureau to hurry its investigation of the Fuldner and C.A.P.R.I. companies.

In the afternoon, surveillance of the workshop was renewed. Sitting in the new car, Kenet and Primo saw a fair-haired young man drive past on a black motorcycle, number 118111. They followed it in the direction of the Martinez railway station. The young man stopped in front of a house at 186 Ladislav Martinez Street, secured the motorcycle to a tree, and went inside. Kenet parked across the street and walked to the house. It was a dentist's office.

Nearly twenty minutes later the young man came out, and they realized they'd made a mistake: beyond the blond hair, he bore no resemblance to the "Dito" or "Tito" Pedro had described.

Kenet concluded that he didn't have enough facts or enough aides to continue the shadowing. And they still didn't even know if this "Dito" or "Tito" was really Eichmann's son. So Kenet decided that, rather than risk being caught lurking around, he'd better first clarify this key point.

———

Kenet felt that it would be safe to send Pedro back to 4261 Chacabuco Street, in another attempt to learn the Klements' new address and also to get further particulars about the young German in the workshop.

So the next day Hedda Kornfeld did her act again. She sat down in the hotel lobby and ordered coffee. Pedro noticed her immediately and was very pleased to see her. He started to walk slowly toward her table, but at the first sign from her he came hurrying up. She looked worried, and he thought she must be in trouble. She asked him if he'd go back to the house in Chacabuco Street and have another shot at getting Nicolas Klement's address. He was to say, she expained, that the sender of the letter and parcel had complained to his friend that the things hadn't been delivered, so the friend was demanding five hundred pesos compensation from him because that's what the parcel was worth. She also told him to go see the young man at the workshop again and to fix an exact description of the fellow indelibly in his memory, as well as every single word that came out of his mouth. Pedro set off without delay.

When he got to the house, he related later, he first looked for the man who had told him the German's son worked nearby; he found him in one of the rooms and greeted him like an old friend. The man recognized him, remembered that he had asked for the German tenant's address, and this time had precise directions. First, he said, you've got to get to the San Fernando station, and from there you go by the San Fernando *colectivo* (a small bus) number 203, and ask the driver to put you off at Avellaneda. The fare is four and a half pesos. When you get off the *colectivo* and cross the street you'll see a kiosk, and there you can ask for the German's house. And if Pedro didn't want to ask at the kiosk, he just had to turn his head to the right and he'd see an unplastered brick house with a flat roof. That's the German's house.

The man had evidently traveled there himself, but to make sure Pedro asked him if he was quite certain about the way. The man said he'd done some work on the German's house and the German still owed him money.

Pedro then asked about the son who worked nearby. The man said "Tito" wasn't exactly the German's son, the German lived with the fellow's mother and had a son of about four by her.

Pedro noticed that he wasn't very keen on talking about the German's family affairs, but he did say that "Tito" had two brothers, one married and one in the navy. And he added that the young man didn't have a scooter but traveled every day with a next-door-neighbor.

At the end of the conversation Pedro asked the man's name in case he should need him again.

The man answered, "What do you need to know my name for? When you need me come here and ask, 'Where's the carpenter?' I live here, in this room."

The carpenter, Pedro made a mental note, was a man of about fifty and spoke with a marked European accent. They were still talking when a fat man who looked about the same age came in. Pedro wondered if he was the owner of the house.

When the fat man heard Pedro's questions he said, "That must be the son who works at the workshop half a block from here. Why don't you go there?"

Pedro thanked the man and walked over to the workshop. A scooter, a "Siam" model 099 with a side-car, was parked at the door.

In the office he saw the young German, who asked him jocularly, "And what do you want this time? Have you come about the letter? I'll tell you the truth. When you gave me the envelope I opened it and read the letter inside. It said 'happy birthday,' and since it was my brother's birthday, not my father's, I gave my brother the present."

"Yes, but the name . . ."

" 'Nicolas Klement' could be either my father or my brother."

"But I'm in trouble now," Pedro said. "The letter and the parcel were given to me by a friend who works at another hotel. A lady guest at his hotel had asked him to make the delivery. Now he claims that the things weren't delivered and he's demanding that I pay him five hundred pesos."

"The lady should have been more exact when she wrote the name on the envelope, and then we'd have no problems. Why did she write 'Nicolas Klement' and not 'Nicolas Eichmann'?"

Pedro shrugged. "How should I know?" he said. "Why don't you give me your brother's address."

"Tito" handed him a piece of paper and said, "Write '3030 Avenida General Paz.' "

"Thanks," said Pedro. "And could you tell me where to find Mr. Klement? The lady may want to know his address."

"He's in Tucumán now, on business, and we don't know when he'll be back."

A man of about thirty who had apparently heard part of the conversation came over and asked "Tito," "Where did you say your father is?"

"In Tucumán," "Tito" repeated. "He went on business and we have no idea when he'll be back."

Pedro went back to the hotel and Hedda questioned him over and over again, writing down every fact he could remember. He told her how sorry he was that he hadn't succeeded in his errand—he hadn't managed to find the Klement family because the young German said that his name and his brother's name wasn't "Klement" but "Eichmann." And to his surprise, she paid him generously once more.

———

Late that night, Hedda gave Kenet her report on Pedro's errand, referring to the notes she had made. Even she had no notion of the decisive importance of what she was telling him. Kenet was the only one who immediately realized the significance of what the youngster had found out. He had learned that Eichmann's eldest son, Nicolas, was living in Buenos Aires and calling himself by his real name. Furthermore, it was

positively established that the Eichmann family was in
Argentina and living at a new address, someplace between San Fernando and Don Torcuato. And above
all, it now seemed possible to state categorically that
Ricardo Klement was Adolf Eichmann, husband of
Vera Eichmann and father of her four children, the
three older ones born in Europe, and the little one born
in Argentina. True, it still might be that Klement was
not Eichmann but another man who had married Vera
Eichmann after the war and was now accepted as the
father of her sons, but there were sufficient arguments
to quash this theory.

At this juncture, Kenet was confident that a crucial
stage in his investigations had come to an end.

He reported to Israel that the young German at the
workshop had been identified as Dieter, Eichmann's
third son, that he was calling himself by his real name,
and that he lived with his mother. Kenet said he would
soon know the family's exact address and that he already had the address of the eldest son, Nicolas, who
was also using his real name. The family was apparently circulating the rumor, Kenet reported, that Vera
Eichmann was remarried, to a man by the name of
Ricardo Klement; at the moment, this man was said to
be away on business, in Tucumán, a city nearly a thousand miles from Buenos Aires. And, on the strength
of the information gleaned by Lubinsky through one of
his investigating agencies, Kenet was able to add to his
report that it was established once and for all that
Francisco Schmidt was not Eichmann.

In light of Kenet's report, I decided to call off the
investigations into the Eichmann and Liebl families in
Europe. Vera Eichmann and her children had been
located, and any superfluous inquiries among her relatives in Europe were liable to arouse suspicions and
lead them to warn her.

It was my opinion that before long the whereabouts
of Klement himself would be uncovered, and then we
would be able to determine definitively whether or not
he was Eichmann. If our theory should turn out to be

correct, we would have to be doubly careful in every step we took. But if it should be proved that Klement wasn't Eichmann, then we would have good grounds for supposing that Adolf Eichmann was no longer alive —unless he was deliberately steering clear of his wife, in which case she and her sons could prove a sure source for finding him.

Relying on Pedro's information, later that afternoon Kenet went to San Fernando, where he soon found the house in which the Klement family was said to live. It was an isolated one-story house without a fence; the door was fiberboard, the walls unplastered, and, as far as Kenet could make out, it was not connected to the local power lines. Indeed, the whole neighborhood looked neglected: nearby were a cottage and a kiosk, and apart from those no houses were to be seen within a radius of several hundred yards.

Driving along the highway some thirty yards from the front of the house, Kenet saw a stout woman of about fifty sitting on the porch, a boy of five or six playing beside her. He presumed they were Vera Eichmann and her youngest son.

He went back later that evening, and this time he walked along the path behind the house. He heard a dog barking in the distance, but saw no sign of a dog at the house itself. Next to the house was a small brick structure that looked like an outhouse or a storeroom. Inside both the house and the little brick structure dim lights were burning. As Kenet was nearing the house, a young man—Kenet assumed it was Dieter—came out of the little outhouse. Kenet hurried away as fast as he could.

On March 12 he returned to San Fernando with Primo. Primo drove and Kenet sat beside him with a Leica camera with a telephoto lens and also a "brief-case" camera—a concealed camera easily operated by a button at the top of the case. As they drove past the house, he photographed it. On the way back they parked the car some thirty-five to fifty yards from the house. Primo got out, opened the hood, and bent over the

engine as if examining it, while Kenet used his Leica
to get a shot of the house with Dieter working in the
garden.

The next day he went to the main post office on
Avenida Santa Fe to look at the Tucumán telephone
directory. In the 1959 edition he found a listing for
"C.A.P.R.I.—Industrial Planning and Development
Company."

Kenet had strong grounds for believing he had located
the Eichmann family, but he wasn't satisfied with a
belief. What he wanted was a certainty. He hoped to
get final positive proof by examining the official records
or by consulting the property register to find out in
whose name the plot and house were registered. As
for Klement himself, Kenet considered that the time
was not yet ripe for a trip to Tucumán to look for him.
He preferred to wait for additional information about
the Fuldner company and its subsidiary C.A.P.R.I., but
he could allow himself to believe that if Klement was
Eichmann, and if he really was in Tucumán, it was
virtually certain that he would come home for his silver
wedding anniversary which—according to the Eichmann
file—fell on March 21, just days away. In the meantime, he would carry on with his inspections in the
neighborhood of the house.

On March 16, at six A.M, Lubinsky called for Kenet
in his rented car, and an hour later they were at the offices of the San Fernando Local Council. After examining various maps to find the area number of the plot
the Klement house stood on, they sent in a written
request under a fictitious name for particulars about the
owners of all the plots in that block. Kenet told the
clerk who took their application that he represented a
large company in North America interested in buying
land in that area. The clerk promised to give them the
required information the next morning.

At about ten o'clock they drove to the house and
parked next to the cottage which stood twenty yards
from the Klement's house. A middle-aged woman came
out of the cottage, and they asked her the name of the
side street. They told her that they represented a North

American company which wanted to put up a factory in the neighborhood and was interested in acquiring land. She said her cottage was for sale. Then they asked about the occupants of the house next door. She said they were Germans who had only recently arrived there and she didn't know their name, but she'd willingly call the woman from the house. Meanwhile, Kenet was able to get a close-up of the house with his briefcase camera.

A few minutes later an attractive young woman with black hair came out of Klement's house. They explained what they wanted and she said that the house wasn't hers, it was her mother-in-law's, but she knew it wasn't for sale. Kenet took a close-up shot of her too.

Through the window they saw a fair-haired boy about six years old. They asked the young woman what the side street was called, explaining that they had land in the neighborhood but didn't exactly know where. She said she didn't know the name of the street, and when they asked her if they could ask her mother-in-law—in the hope that she'd come out and they'd be able to photograph her—she replied that her mother-in-law hardly spoke Spanish.

The young woman then started questioning them about what company they represented and what sort of factory they intended to put up in the area. When she heard them speak English, she also switched to English; Kenet was afraid that her knowledge of the language might be enough for her to realize that he wasn't a North American. She explained that there was no electricity or water there, and in winter there were frequent floods in the district. But still, she said, they weren't thinking of selling the house.

They said good-by to her and left.

At about six o'clock in the afternoon Kenet went past the house twice. The shutters were up, but there was nobody outside.

In the evening Kenet gave Lubinsky another assignment: to obtain, through one of the investigation bureaus he was in contact with, everything they could

get on Nicolas Eichmann from the address in Olivos
that his brother Dieter had given.

The surveillances continued. On March 17 Kenet
and Lubinsky approached the house at six-fifteen A.M.
They hid in a clump of trees about a hundred and sixty
yards away. At about seven-fifteen they saw the young
man come out of the house and go toward the bus
stop. They saw no further movement about the house,
and at eight-twenty-five, when a stranger wandered
by, they had to leave their post.

They went back to the Local Council, but the reply
awaiting them was disappointing—there were no official
records on any of the houses in the area they were
interested in. It was explained to them that practically
every winter the entire neighborhood was flooded, and
the area was in fact regarded as ownerless property.
People built there without licenses and paid no taxes to
the local authority. An inquiry at the Council's legal
department elicited the same answer.

They went into consultation about their next step.
Lubinsky's opinion was that their only prospect of getting any sort of record of the owners was from the
company that was developing the land and selling it to
the builders. They decided that Lubinsky would try
working along these lines, through a commercial inquiry
agent, on the pretext that he represented a company interested in acquiring large stretches of land for building
and for industrial development, so he had to know who
had bought plots and houses in the neighborhood in
case the company should need to buy the ground from
them.

Lubinsky also undertook to find out if the cottage
near the Klement house could be purchased at once. He
estimated that they would need about a thousand dollars to buy the place and thought they could quite
easily buy it under a false name. It was Kenet's intention to acquire the house for use as an observation post,
and also in order to get rid of the tenants who might be
a problem if and when they decided to capture Klement.

On March 18 Kenet bought night binoculars for surveillance in the dark. In the morning he went by car on another reconnaissance trip around the house. He saw the boy close up and judged that he was four or five years old; every time Kenet had seen the child he was dressed only in underwear. This time he also got a close look at the lady of the house, though only from the back; she was about fifty, full-bodied, black-haired, medium height, wearing a cheap summer dress.

In the afternoon he had a rendezvous with Lubinsky at a café. Even before they started talking, Kenet gathered there was good news—Lubinsky was smiling. He explained that he had obtained access to the records of the company that sold the plots, and he gave Kenet written particulars about plot number 14: it was registered in the name of Veronica Catarina Liebl de Fichmann of 4261 Chacabuco Street, Olivos. The "Fichmann" didn't worry Kenet unduly: the clerk might have made a mistake in copying (because of the similarity between the letters "E" and "F") or it could be an intentional "mistake" on the part of the family. In any event, it was obvious to him that this was the most important item of information they had obtained to date.

Vera's maiden name was Liebl, but the fact that she was now going under the name of Liebl de Eichmann (or Fichmann, it didn't matter which) certified that she wasn't married to a different man; while the fact that the house was registered in her name and not her husband's seemed to indicate that he had no desire to appear in any official records.

In the evening Kenet got further confirmation of this last assumption. With David Kornfeld's assistance, he examined the voters' roll for Olivos. The register was open to the public because elections were about to take place. To make doubly sure, they examined the register displayed at the municipality as well as the one at the offices of the largest party. No Klement, Eichmann, or Liebl appeared on any of the lists. The same day Kenet transmitted the following message to Israel:

The woman Eichmann has been positively identified. I have photographs of the house where the
Klement family lives. About twenty yards from
the Klement-Eichmann house is a small cottage.
It may be for sale. Its estimated cost is one thousand dollars. If you authorize the purchase, I'll
carry it out without leaving any trail.

————

Their frequent trips to San Fernando were becoming
dangerous. They had to change cars often so that no
one vehicle would become familiar to the local residents. On March 19 Kenet asked the Kornfelds to rent
an American-model passenger car. After no little effort, David managed to find one and leased it for a
few days.

This time Kenet took Hedda with him, and together
they reconnoitered the vicinity of Klement's house. As
they were passing the house a second time, at about
two o'clock, they saw a man—medium height, a high
forehead, balding—taking wash off the line in the yard.
Kenet tried to snap him with his briefcase camera but
wasn't successful. The man went back inside, and they
returned to Buenos Aires.

Kenet believed that the man in the yard was Eichmann. He saw a resemblance between the photos of
Eichmann in the thirties and the man in the yard, and
the particulars of his height and build, as recorded
in his file, described the man he saw. Since he was taking down the wash, it could be assumed that he lived
in the house and wasn't just a chance visitor. Kenet
supposed that Eichmann had returned from Tucumán
for his wedding anniversary in two days.

That evening he sent another message to Israel:

In the Eichmann woman's house a man was seen
today who fits the description of Adolf Eichmann.
  It was my hypothesis all along that if Ricardo
Klement is Adolf Eichmann he would try to come
back from Tucumán before his silver wedding anniversary, which is the day after tomorrow.

Since Klement did in fact turn up at the estimated time, there is no further doubt that he is
Eichmann.

I assume that Klement will return to his work
in the Tucumán area this coming Tuesday. I will
follow him even though I presume that locating
him there will involve difficulties.

I suggest that I be permitted to return to Israel
soon for the purpose of reporting in full and considering further action.

———

This message removed any remaining doubts in my
mind that it was essential to act quickly and decisive-
ly. With the few people Kenet had at his disposal he
couldn't carry on his investigations much longer without being found out, and the slightest hitch was liable
to alert Klement to the danger threatening him. It was
my opinion that, even if we were not completely certain that Klement was Eichmann, we must undertake
the necessary preparations for the operation at once; it
was always possible that the final identification of the
man would be made only while the operation was being
carried out. This was a calculated risk. But in view of
the importance of the assignment, I considered it rational and essential.

I immediately summoned Asher Kedem and explained that the airplane matter I had touched upon
during our conversation in December 1959 might soon
become an actuality. Kedem was due to go overseas on
behalf of his company in a day or so, to look into the
purchase of new planes. The trip was important to him,
but he was ready to forgo it if necessary. I told him I
didn't want to upset his plans and if I needed him I
could find him through Dan Avner, a senior employee
of the company who, like his friend Kedem, was always
prepared to volunteer help when needed.

# 9

Sunday, March 20, Kenet met with Lubinsky to hear the investigation bureau's report on the tenants of 3030 Avenida General Paz, Nicolas Eichmann's alleged address. The same morning Kenet went to San Fernando in a small broken-down old truck, the back covered with a tarpaulin; Primo was driving. They drove past the house twice, and Kenet, sitting in the back, photographed it from every possible angle. Then they parked the truck about a hundred and sixty yards from the house and fifty-five yards from the kiosk. Primo walked to the kiosk to have something to eat while Kenet used his binoculars to observe the house through a small opening in the tarpaulin. The boy was playing outside alone.

At about eleven-forty-five the man Kenet had seen the day before came walking toward the house from the direction of the main road—the peephole in the tarpaulin was too small for Kenet to see exactly where the man had come from. He was fairly well-groomed, wearing light-brown trousers, gray overcoat, a plain green tie, and brown shoes. Kenet estimated his height at about five feet eight inches. Other details he noted were: "about three-quarters bald, fair hair on either side of his head, large nose, wide forehead, spectacles, maybe a mustache, walks slowly."

The man entered the property from the other side, not through the front, bent down to pass under the wire marking off the boundary of the plot, and walked into the yard. He stopped for a moment next to the child, said something to him, and stroked his head and straightened his clothes—this time the child was fully dressed, perhaps because it was Sunday. With a slow tread the man climbed the steps to the porch, brushed away the flies with a newspaper he was carrying, and was about to open the door when the stout woman opened it from the inside. As he walked in, they both waved the flies away from the open doorway.

A minute later the man reappeared, walked to the road next to the house, and bought two small loaves of bread from a cart standing there. He returned to the house, but in five minutes came out wearing an undershirt and pajama bottoms and took a siphon bottle out of a small wooden storeroom. At that moment the fair-haired young man appeared from the direction of the cottage, where he had been standing talking to the scooter driver. The two men stood talking for a few minutes and then went inside.

That evening Kenet wrote his summing-up report, concluding:

> In my opinion, the cottage must be purchased and a reliable watchman installed in it. From a man like that we can obtain information about the Eichmann family. In addition, we will be rid of potential witnesses to the operation. In my opinion, there is no point in running to Tucumán after him, for even if we locate him there—almost an impossibility without attracting his attention—I see no possibility of operating there. It is a twenty-four-hour train journey away, and it would be extremely difficult to transport him from there. It is necessary to have everything ready here and to sit and wait patiently until he comes.
>
> I await instructions.

Kenet didn't content himself with the achievements he had reported. That evening, at nine-fifteen, he went again to San Fernando. This time he asked David and

Hedda Kornfeld to accompany him. His object was to get as close to the house as possible under cover of darkness and to observe what was going on inside. He was afraid that if he drove alone and parked in the vicinity of the house he might arouse the curiosity of passers-by; and if he went by bus he would still attract attention because he was a stranger. However, a young couple sitting in a parked car at the side of a suburban road was by no means a rare sight. Consequently, he decided to go by Jeep and to leave the Kornfelds in it while he crept up to the house.

The house faced the side street—Garibaldi Street—about thirty yards from Route 202. The entire area was crisscrossed by a network of suburban roads, paved to a height of about three feet on account of the severe floods, but the difference in height was not very noticeable since a tangle of plants grew at the edges.

When they arrived it was completely dark. They parked the car at an intersection three corners away from Klement's house, and Kenet asked the Kornfelds to sit quietly in the car and wait for him.

Kenet was dressed in overalls, the binoculars hung at his hip. Not a glimmer of light showed from the house as he approached. He walked around looking for a window to watch or listen through. Finally he stationed himself fifteen yards from the house, but he soon realized that at this distance, though it was safe, his efforts were being wasted—he could see nothing inside the house and hear nothing from it.

He retraced his steps toward the Jeep, but was amazed to discover that it wasn't at the intersection where he had left it. Could he have lost his way? He went back and counted the streets. No, he wasn't mistaken, this was the corner where he'd left the Jeep, yet in the few minutes he'd been away it had disappeared.

Suddenly he caught sight of the Kornfelds standing at the edge of the road, and when he got closer he saw the Jeep lying on its side. David had been trying to turn it around, but in the darkness he didn't notice the dropoff at the edge of the road, and in a few seconds he and his wife found themselves trapped in the over-turned Jeep. Luckily they weren't hurt, and after a struggle they managed to extricate themselves.

Even when Kenet returned, their combined strength wasn't enough to right the Jeep on its wheels. It was obvious they'd have to call for help. Kenet was afraid to leave any of the party at the scene, lest a casual passer-by notice a stranger involved in an accident and report it. The news might reach the ears of the Klement family.

The three of them set off on foot along Route 202 in the direction of San Fernando. When they had been walking for half an hour a bus came along, so they stopped it and traveled to the town. From there they telephoned Lubinsky and Primo and asked them please to come to San Fernando immediately in a car with a tow-chain.

When the two of them turned up, after what seemed to the others an endless wait, they all went to the scene of the accident, but to their dismay they saw that someone had already been there—one of the Jeep's wheels was gone. The spare was, of course, very difficult to get at, but they finally reached it. Then they discovered that the thief had taken the nuts as well, and they had to "borrow" a nut from each of the other three wheels in order to put on the fourth one.

At long last they succeeded in setting the car right side up. In his fluent Spanish Lubinsky told curious on-lookers that a drunk had crowded the Jeep off the road. To their relief, nobody came out of Klement's house—it was still dark. (They found out later that the accident hadn't caused much comment in the neighborhood and that the Klements never did hear of it.)

It was after midnight before they could get moving. As Kenet began driving he noticed that there was bare-ly enough gas to get them to the service station in San Fernando; then he saw oil dripping inside the car, and by the time they were back in Buenos Aires he was stained with oil from head to foot.

Early the next day he took the Jeep in for a thorough cleaning—and a new spare.

This was March 21, Vera and Adolf Eichmann's silver wedding anniversary. That evening Kenet drove alone to San Fernando. Passing the house at nine-thirty, he saw a faint light flickering in one of the rooms. When he went past again about fifteen minutes later the house was already blacked out.

On March 22, at about six-forty-five, he drove past the place again. The woman and the boy were in the yard, wearing nice clothes, quite unlike their customary slipshod way of dressing. A few minutes later he saw the woman sitting on the porch.

———

Kenet decided he was overdoing his surveillances, and such activities could be resumed only if he could get trained reinforcements from Israel.

At the same time he set himself several goals before his departure for Israel: to photograph the house, its vicinity, and its surroundings from all angles; to go all out to get a good photograph of Klement; to find out where Klement worked; and to examine the population register once again to make sure that Klement wasn't legally registered.

The morning of March 23 he met with Lubinsky, who brought him the investigation bureau's detailed report on Nicolas Eichmann and his brother Horst Adolf Eichmann. He also brought the 1951 and 1952 telephone directories for Buenos Aires. They looked in vain for Klement.

Lubinsky also had the results of the inquiry about C.A.P.R.I. In the 1959 Tucumán telephone directory, "C.A.P.R.I., Proyectos y Traliz Ind." (Company for Real Estate Projects), was listed, but the bureau said that there was not now, and had never been, any such company at the address given in the directory.

At six-thirty that evening Kenet again reconnoitered in the neighborhood of Klement's house and he saw the man working in the small storeroom in the yard. A few minutes later he tried photographing him but drew a blank.

The next three days were devoted to resting, touring the city and getting to know it better, and trying to rent a passenger car. He couldn't get the sort of car he wanted, so—Hobson's choice—he took a Jeep again, but this time of a different color.

March 27 found Kenet once more roaming the San Fernando area. Driving through Tigre, he found a pathway to the Reconquista river, across an open field about half a mile from the house, and he thought this would be a good safe spot for an observation post. The next time he went past the house he saw a man and the young fellow working in the garden, and he snapped them from the moving car.

The next morning he and Primo arrived at eight o'clock in a pouring rain. Primo stationed himself at the bus stop, while Kenet sat in the Jeep about half a mile from the house. They didn't see any of the family, and after half an hour left.

Three days later Kenet drove to San Fernando and photographed the house from various angles. He then clambered up the railway embankment and photographed the entire area from there. At six-fifty in the evening he was passing the house when he saw the man in the yard. He came back after dark, left the car about five hundred yards away, and proceeded to the house on foot. He made a fairly wide circle around the place. At the west side, the side facing the railway line, he found an open shutter and a lighted window. He went close enough to the window to see the man standing in the room, which was lit by a kerosene lamp. In contrast to its neglected outside appearance, the house looked clean and well kept inside.

---

On April 3 Kenet rented a truck covered with a tarpaulin (naturally not the one he had used before) and asked Primo to meet him in the morning. He wanted to make one last effort to get a close-up photograph of their man, and it was evident that only a person who spoke fluent Spanish could get near enough to do so. He thought Sunday would be the only day they could be sure of finding Klement at home. He showed Primo how to use the briefcase camera and taped the shutter in place so that Primo had nothing to do put press the button, which he practiced a few times to make sure he had the knack.

David Kornfeld drove the truck to the target area. They stopped under the bridge at San Fernando, and Kenet lay down in the back and focused his binoculars on the house through the hole in the tarpaulin. The other two pretended to be tinkering with the motor. When Kenet saw Klement walk from the house to the storeroom in the yard he signaled to Primo, who started toward the house carring the briefcase camera.

Kenet had waited for the man to go to the storeroom because he was afraid that if Primo went to the house itself, on whatever pretext, it was almost certain the son rather than the father would come out. However, if the father were alone in the storeroom he couldn't avoid talking to Primo. Kenet also thought that if Primo went into the garden through the front entrance and then walked straight to the storeroom it would look funny, so they arranged for Primo to cross the field and go in that way.

Kenet and David watched Primo with bated breath, ready to rush to his assistance—if, for instance, the Klements realized he was taking photographs and tried to snatch the briefcase from him. Primo had reached the edge of the plot when Klement and his son Dieter came toward him from the other side. Although Kenet had little hope that such a long-distance shot would be successful, he took a picture of them through his telephoto lens from under the tarpaulin. A minute or two later the man went back to the storeroom. Primo stood and talked to the young fellow, and then went to the cottage next door, where he also stood talking for a few minutes.

In accordance with Kenet's instructions, he didn't go back to the truck but made for the road and from there traveled to San Fernando by bus.

Kenet and Kornfeld caught up with Primo at the San Fernando railway station. He told them that he had asked the men if there was a house for sale in the neighborhood—and he had photographed them. They had pointed out the little cottage near their house,

which is why Primo had gone there. He had talked to
the tenant and said he might be back in a week's
time.

On April 4 Kenet received the long-awaited message
from Israel:

> In order to obtain a full report for the purpose of
> planning the operation in detail and determining
> its various stages, you are requested to return home
> as soon as possible.

Now, if he had photographs of Klement, Kenet was
prepared to return forthwith. But he still didn't know
if they had come out well. Primo had no previous experience in photography; all he knew was what he had
learned in that one ten-minute lesson. The conditions
under which he had carried out his assignment—in the
middle of a conversation with Klement and his son
about real estate—were not conducive to success. And
Kenet didn't want to go home without a really good
photograph of the man they were convinced was Eichmann. He thought that the decision of whether or not to
go ahead with the operation might depend on the
quality of Primo's photographs.

In case the pictures were not adequate and he
might have to try again, Kenet decided to have the
film developed in Buenos Aires; yet he had to take into
account the possibility that the camera shop might
print copies and perhaps even enlarge them. There
was also the chance—a very remote one, it's true—that
the man might know Klement, and in that case he'd
be sure to tell Klement that some stranger had been
taking pictures of him.

Eventually Kenet picked a large camera store in the
hotel and tourist-shop area. He explained to the owner
that the film must be developed quickly as he was making only a very brief stop in Buenos Aires on his way
somewhere else. Knowing that it usually took six or
seven days to get developed film back, Kenet said he
was prepared to pay more if it could be done in a great

hurry. The man solemnly assured him that it would be done by the following evening.

From there Kenet went to an airline company to book passage, only to be told that all the planes were full up to the end of May or beginning of June. With a great deal of trouble he managed to get a seat on a plane due to leave for Europe on April 7. When he thought it over he wasn't really sorry it had turned out that way, because now he had time to try his luck again if the photographs were not a success.

Kenet went to the camera shop at the appointed hour, but he was greeted with profuse apologies that the prints were not ready yet.

"What prints?" Kenet asked in dismay. "I only asked for the film to be developed."

"Oh yes, it's been developed, but the enlargements aren't ready."

"I didn't order enlargements. I want the developed film, and I want it immediately."

The shop owner said, "As you wish, sir. But I must tell you we don't do the printing and enlarging here. A photographer who works for us has the film."

For a moment Kenet was speechless. Then, "Give me his address. I'll go there myself and get the film," he said peremptorily. "Didn't I tell you I've got to be on my way and I must have the film?"

"The photographer lives at the other end of town and the place is hard to find. Even a taxi driver wouldn't be able to find it."

I think he's lying—the thought flashed through Kenet's mind—he's trying to gain time for some purpose or other. What's he getting at? Aloud he said, "I demand that you telephone your photographer at once, here in my presence, and tell him to take a taxi at my expense and bring the negatives here, whether they're printed or not."

Kenet spoke in an agitated mixture of English and Spanish, and the owner of the shop could see that his customer was in a rage. He telephoned immediately, and Kenet—despite his poor knowledge of Spanish—

heard him say something about getting a taxi and coming or sending somebody instantly.

It was nearing closing time for the shops. The minutes went by and nobody came. Kenet was becoming more and more convinced that the film wouldn't arrive in time, but eventually a youngster turned up with a small parcel in his hand.

When Kenet opened the package his anger dissolved: the pictures had succeeded beyond all expectations. He knew at once that they were going to be invaluable as the operation progressed.

Kenet used the intervening days until his departure to gather certain items of information his superiors in Israel had asked for. On April 6 he said good-by to the Kornfelds, Lubinsky, and Primo. They were also going their various ways, back to their own homes.

The next day Kenet flew to Europe.

I met him on the plane from Paris to Tel Aviv. After exchanging a few words with him, I asked one question: "Are you certain he's the man we want?"

Kenet took a photograph out of his pocket and said, "There's not an iota of doubt."

# 10

As soon as I began playing with the idea of capturing Eichmann in Argentina and bringing him to Israel to stand trial I knew that I would have to supervise the operation personally, which meant that I had to be on the spot.

I regarded this action of ours as more difficult operationally and more delicate politically than any our Secret Services had hitherto undertaken, and my presence in Buenos Aires was essential for the complicated problems likely to crop up.

Our main difficulty—the one we had recognized earlier—was the very fact of having to put a task force into action at an enormous distance from home, with no speedy or efficient means of communication, and in circumstances demanding instantaneous decisions. I knew our team would have no local body, Israeli or Jewish, to depend on but would be working alone all the time, faced with three crucial tests: to perform the capture without any mishaps, to keep the prisoner in private custody for a length of time impossible to estimate in advance, and to transfer him in secret to Israel the moment conditions were favorable. At each stage, but especially at the last, the task force could be confronted with problems that only the highest echelons were capable of dealing with authoritatively.

Politically, it was evident that even if the operation was successful there was still the danger of our being charged with having violated the sovereignty of a friendly state; and if any hitch occurred and our intentions were discovered before we reached the operational stage, then decisions would have to be made on the spot at the moment of action, since we would have neither the time nor the means to ask for help or instructions from home.

I could not conceivably place the responsibility for handling potential political complications on the shoulders of the commander of the task force. Clearly, I would have to be with the task force, at the scene of action, and stay in Argentina to handle the details of the operation from beginning to end.

Before allowing the preparations to reach an advanced stage, I wanted to do everything I could to verify that the Ricardo Klement whose photograph I had was indeed Adolf Eichmann. As far as age and physique were concerned, there was no discrepancy between what we knew about Eichmann and the data about Klement brought to us by Kenet. For all that, there was still the contingency that Vera Eichmann's present husband might not be our man, and, bearing in mind the seriousness of the step we were contemplating, I wanted all doubts reduced to the absolute minimum.

There were no fingerprints available, and the other means of identification we had were limited. There were, in fact, only three possible courses of action: to have a laboratory compare the old photographs of Eichmann with Kenet's pictures; to show the photographs of Klement to people who had known Eichmann in the past; to send one of these people to Argentina to take a look at Klement in person. Even if we adopted all three methods, there was still the chance that none of them would bring conclusive results. Eichmann's old photographs were of low quality, and Klement's, taken in adverse circumstances, were not particularly clear. Furthermore, a personal identification after twenty years or more might also be doubtful.

Nevertheless, I decided to act on these lines without delay.

It wasn't easy to find people who had seen Eichmann face to face. We couldn't advertise publicly for such people to present themselves at our office, nor did we dare let it be known even in the most restricted circles that there was any official interest in the criminal. So I decided to confine the search in the first stage to a small circle of veteran Zionist workers from Germany.

One of our senior operators at the time was German-born Miriam Savyon who came to work for us in the early fifties because she was looking for something to do that would prove a personal challenge. At first her duties were nonoperational, but it wasn't very long before her skill and her knowledge brought about her transfer to the operational section. Her particular specialty was devising cover and documentation for operators on undercover missions. I summoned her and, without explaining my purpose, asked if she knew any people of German origin who had met Eichmann personally. I hit a bull's-eye. She told me straightaway that from 1936 to 1938 Benno Cohen and Dr. Hans Friedenthal had served as cochairmen of the Zionist Organization in Germany, the former in charge of internal and the latter of external affairs, and by virtue of his office Friedenthal had maintained contact with the German Foreign Ministry, with the British Consulate in Germany, and with the Gestapo. She had heard Friedenthal himself say that he had occasionally been with Eichmann in his office in Berlin, and as far as she could remember Benno Cohen also knew Eichmann at the time.

I sent Kenet to Dr. Friedenthal with the photographs of Klement. Friedenthal said he didn't recognize the man. Then Kenet asked him if he had known or met Adolf Eichmann.

"Yes," Friedenthal answered, "I saw him twice, each time for a quarter of an hour. That was in 1938, when I was a chairman of the Zionist Organization in Germany."

"Where did you meet?" asked Kenet.

"In his office in Berlin. The first time, I went to him about a certain Jew who had been arrested. Eichmann asked me if I was prepared to guarantee that the man would leave Germany immediately on his release. I agreed to this, but I requested him not to give us a time limit because I would have to set about obtaining a certificate of immigration to Israel or a permit for some other country. Two or three days later he was in fact released."

Kenet asked, "And how did Eichmann behave toward you?"

"On both occasions his behavior was correct, even though the second time I stood before him under accusation. He claimed to have been told that I had criticized the German government at a Zionist meeting. I rejected the accusation and explained that I was referring only to the new anti-Jewish legislation in the news at the time, and I had said that the Jews could draw their own conclusions. I left Germany in November 1938, after the 'Crystal Night.' "*

"And now," Kenet asked, "do I need to tell you who the man is whose picture I showed you?"

"No, I can guess who he is." Friedenthal smiled.

"We have no certain proof of his identity," Kenet explained. "Will you take another look at the photographs?"

Friedenthal pored over the pictures for a long time. Finally he shook his head. "I'm sorry. Even after what you've told me, I can't say definitely that the man in these pictures is Eichmann—though, on the other hand, I'm not prepared to state that he is not."

The laboratory identification brought more encouraging results. The head of the Criminal Identification Department of the Israeli Police, whose aid we had enlisted, gave the photographs to Eli Ilan for comparison. Eli, who came from Canada, specialized in comparison of photographs for identification purposes. He didn't know who it was he'd been asked to identify. He was

---

* *Kristallnacht*. Pogroms against the Jews occurred throughout Germany in reprisal for the assassination of Ernst von Rath, at the German Embassy in Paris, by the seventeen-year-old Polish Jew Herschel Grynszpan. Six-millon-marks worth of shop windows were smashed, hence the name.

given some photographs which had obviously been taken secretly under operational conditions and asked to compare them with another set of photographs showing an SS officer in uniform.

On both sets of photographs Ilan drew lines joining the extremities of the various limbs to form polygons, on which certain comparisons were based. Another method brought him still better results: checking and comparing one ear in each of the two sets of photographs. From the size, the point at which the ear joined the head, the angle at which it was attached to the face, and the shape of the outer ear, Ilan was able to establish that there were reasonable grounds for identifying the man in the operational photographs as the SS officer in the old pictures. In his report he stated that he found eight points in favor of identification in the two groups of photographs, and not one point against it. He wasn't prepared to go so far as to state unequivocally that it was the same man who appeared in both series of photographs . . . but the report he drew up describes the identification as a virtual certainty.

Judging from the failure of Dr. Friedenthal's attempt at identification, I didn't suppose anyone else who had seen Eichmann more than twenty years ago would be able to identify him from a photograph. On the other hand, I considered it dangerous to send somebody from Israel to Argentina for a "live" identification of Klement—Kenet and his men had already spent too much time in the neighborhood of Klement's house, and any additional activity there could jeopardize the entire operation. I was beginning to doubt whether it was worth choosing one of the people who had known Eichmann before and attaching him to the task force due to leave for Argentina. Special preparations would be involved in making surveillance comfortable and safe for a nonprofessional with no experience in such matters, all the more so since it would necessarily be a person of middle age. But I believed we'd be able to surmount this difficulty too, provided we planned the operation in such a way that the identification was part of the operation itself, and the instant Klement was identified as our man we could go ahead with the capture.

After a prolonged search—needless to say, in absolute secrecy—we found a woman who had met Eichmann. She was asked if she would be prepared to participate in a dangerous and strenuous undertaking. She said she could do it, but the state of her health was questionable, and this made us fear for her safety, for considerable physical and mental demands would be made on her.

After weighing all the circumstances, I decided it would be best to count her out. But all the same, arrangements were made for her to be standing by in case of emergency.

The wheels of the operational machine were turning fast. As soon as it became obvious to me that we had to give up all further attempts to identify Klement, and that we had to act on the assumption that the final identification could be made only when the man was already in our hands, I began giving some thought to the preparation of the actual plan of operation. It didn't take me long to conclude that the team who prepared the plan would have to be the ones to carry out the action. True, I knew that this would entail complicated arrangements and also increase the number of people we would have to send. However, I was unwilling to take a chance that, between the time the planning team finished its work and the time the operational team would go into action, conditions might change or Eichmann's suspicions be excited.

Accordingly, I decided that the task force must be assembled immediately and that it should be divided into two sections: an advance party to go to the target site to establish that Ricardo Klement was still there and that conditions for carrying out the capture were reasonably good, and the main body to be primed and ready for action but waiting for the advance party's call before setting out.

The means of transporting Eichmann to Israel had to be ready before we fixed the time for the task force to go into action, I reasoned, for there was no point in making the capture without assured transport. Furthermore, the manner and conditions of transportation could affect the time of the capture and maybe even the method of carrying it out.

The operational team of the task force could be recruited from one source alone: a group of operations men who, almost from the very beginning, were outstanding for the daring of their actions and their infinite resourcefulness. Each one had been chosen with meticulous care, to create a body of courageous men who regarded no assignment as too difficult and were both modest and ready to risk their lives in an unseen struggle and for no personal glory.

I knew the leaders of the group personally, from the days when I was their commander, and since then I had kept in contact with them and had on several occasions gone into action with them on assignments abroad.

I approached another senior intelligence officer—the one I have called Haggai—and asked if he would put at my disposal the men I required for the assignment. He responded willingly, offering me the head of the operations group himself and several men who in his opinion were likely to get on well together in an undertaking of this kind.

I promptly summoned the leader of the group, Gabi Eldad, an old acquaintance of mine and a person with outstanding operational ability. I knew him to be a fine commander, a man of good, common-sense judgment and great resourcefulness. Gabi Eldad came from a Jewish village in pre-Israel Palestine and at the age of twelve was already active in the ranks of *Hagana,* the Jewish self-defense organization, forerunner of the Israeli Defense Force. At eighteen he was recruited into *Palmach,* the striking force of the *Hagana,* where he first acquired the taste for daring operations. He participated in the attack on the camp at Atlit to free the illegal immigrants, and after that in the destroying of the British radar installation on Mount Carmel. On the eve of the War of Independence he was appointed com-

mander of a reconnaisance platoon, and the day the
state was declared—March 15, 1948—he was
wounded in the leg in the battle for Galilee. He crawled
back to his base, and before he had properly recovered,
his leg still in a cast, he rejoined his battalion, took part
in Operation "Dani," and went to the Negev, where he
became an expert at guiding troops at night to the battle
areas. Gabi finished his military service in 1950 and
joined the operations group.

Our conversation, when I told Gabi what sort of
operation he was going to lead, was practical and to the
point, like all the conversations we had had over the
years. Nothing in the world could excite this lean
smiling sabra: "It's a big action," he said. "We've never
yet had such an operation." I knew that this was the
highest pitch of enthusiasm he would display.

Gabi was known to his friends as a person who estimated everything in percentages. "What are the odds
that this man is really Eichmann?" he asked.

I told him about everything we'd done and about my
conclusion that the definitive identification could be
made only once the man was in our hands. "From one
angle," I said, "this operation is different from any we
have done up to now. This time it's not just a mission
under orders. This time we are being sent by the Jewish
conscience as well. So I want to take only those who
are in whole-hearted agreement with the idea. Participation in this operation has to be voluntary. Anyone who
shows the slightest hesitation mustn't be taken."

"None of them will hesitate," said Gabi confidently.

"I don't think they will either," I agreed, "but I insist
that every person chosen for this operation must know
that we are going into action with one goal, and only one,
in mind: to bring to judgment one of the monsters that
rose up to put a bloody end to us. If we succeed,
this will be the first time in history that a court of justice of the Jewish people will judge a man who slaugh-
tered multitudes of Jews. That is why I see in this action a humane and moral significance that cannot be
applied to anything we have ever undertaken before."

"Everyone will understand that," said Gabi in his quiet voice.

"I'd like you to begin an immediate study of the file," I said. "Kenet will tell you all about local conditions. I expect you to hand me, as soon as possible, a plan of action and a list of the men you suggest for the team."

I knew that I could now devote my attention to considering ways and means of transporting Eichmann to Israel. I went again to Leora Dotan and asked her to check the sailing dates of the Israeli shipping lines and to find out if any Israeli ship was expected to be in or near South American waters during the coming weeks. I also asked her to inquire into the possibilities of sending a freighter or refrigerator ship to Argentina on the pretext of importing frozen meat, or something like that. She was also to explore the chances of diverting a large cruise ship to Buenos Aires without arousing suspicion.

A few days later Leora reported that no Israeli vessel was likely to be in the target area in the near future. Changing the course of any ship, she said, would involve serious complications because of prior commitments and because it would look strange from the technical and economic point of view. The only possible way would be to provide a special ship to sail with some kind of cargo either from Israel to South America or vice versa. However, the preparations for a special sailing of that nature would be very drawn out, and the round-trip journey would take about sixty days, as the ship would have to stop at various ports on the way.

I decided that transportation by sea would be too slow and might delay the operation by some vital weeks, and the necessity to anchor at foreign ports on the way would increase the security risk considerably. So I applied myself to a thorough investigation of the possibilities of air transport.

The main problem was to find plausible grounds for an Israeli flight to Argentina. At one point we considered announcing it as a trial flight to examine the prospects of opening a new line to South America, but it was the height of the tourist season, and taking a large plane out of regular service to carry out a trial flight at a time like that would cause justifiable astonishment.

Luck came to our aid. News about preparations to mark the one hundred and fiftieth anniversary of Argentina's independence appeared in the press. Extensive celebrations were being organized for late May 1960. Israel had been invited to participate in the celebrations, and we found out that the Foreign Affairs Ministry attached great importance to Israel's being suitably represented at this international event and intended sending a high-ranking delegation.

I sent out feelers to test the reaction of the Foreign Office to the idea of flying the Israeli delegation to Argentina by special plane. The Department of Latin American Affairs, which was handling the arrangements for sending the delegation, received the suggestion very favorably; they considered that the arrival of a plane direct from Israel would enhance the prestige of the state still further, especially in the eyes of the Jewish community in South America.

I summoned Moshe Tadmor, the airline deputy director we had contacted before. He could foresee no insurmountable difficulties, he said, but requested that the final answer be put off for a few days, until the managing director's return, because our plan would upset the timetable of the company's regular flights and involve heavy financial loss. Tadmor knew that flight arrangements for official delegations on behalf of the State of Israel were not in my province and realized that I was interested in the flight for totally different reasons. When I told him that the composition of the plane's crew would be subject to my confirmation and asked that Asher Kedem be available to work under direct orders from me or my aides until the completion of the operation, he appeared to grasp what it was all about. As he was leaving my office, his hand already on the doorknob, he turned to me with a hesitant smile: "Does it have anything to do with Eichmann?" I nodded. Much later Tadmor admitted that he had felt very embarrassed at that point: "I couldn't forgive myself for having spoken to you a few minutes earlier as though my only concern was the company's commercial interests, talking about things like upset schedules and financial losses."

A few days later I met with the airline's managing director, who expressed his complete willingness to comply with any request from the Foreign Affairs Ministry and to tender me and my aides all the assistance the company could give. I indirectly informed the people handling the delegation's journey that the airline would most likely agree to fly the delegation to Argentina by special plane, since it was interested in running a test flight and would like to be in Buenos Aires during such an important international gathering. It was already common knowledge that several states intended flying in their delegations by special planes. On April 22 the Foreign Office made its request to the airline and a few days later received confirmation.

Shortly before that, on April 18, Asher Kedem returned from his mission abroad and came straight to me. I told him about the operation and informed him that he would have to be ready to leave for Buenos Aires very soon.

Kedem was ready for anything. Born in Holland, he had been subjected to Nazi persecution for more than a year but managed to escape in 1941, at the age of twenty-one. He reached England and enlisted in the R.A.F. On his return to Holland after the war he found that the Germans had left practically no survivors in his family. His parents, his brothers, his sister and brother-in-law had all perished in Nazi camps. For a while he took an active part in "illegal" immigration into Israel, then he also emigrated there with his wife and his brother's four-year-old son, who had been hidden during the German conquest and whom Kedem managed to retrieve. He served in the air force in the War of Independence and then went to work for the airline. It was no wonder that throughout our operation he never once said no to anything.

The celebration in Argentina was scheduled to begin on May 20, 1960, and all the visiting delegations were supposed to gather in Buenos Aires before then. I was interested in advancing our special flight as much as possible. If the plane made a prolonged stay in Buenos Aires, it was liable to cause surprise: it was permissible to consider at the very most a stay of three days. The time for the capture had to be as close as possible to the day the plane would take off, in view of the difficulties inherent in keeping a man in private custody on Argentine soil. It was therefore necessary to maintain close coordination between the time of the capture and the time of the flight. If the plane could arrive a week before May 20 and the operation arranged to correspond with this, all the better. Then if it should become necessary to postpone the capture at the last minute, it would still be possible to delay the flight until a time nearer to the opening of the celebration. However, if the flight were planned for just before May 20 and the operation had to be postponed, we would be in a difficult situation; the plane would not be able to remain longer in Argentina without causing suspicion, and we might have to send it back to Israel without using it for the main purpose of its trip. Another consideration was that we ought to complete as much of the operation as possible before the influx of high-ranking delegations from all over the world increased security at the airport, in the capital itself, and on the roads linking the two.

After prolonged discussion between the Foreign Office and the airline, the date of the flight was fixed for May 11. The explanation to the Foreign Affairs Ministry officials was that this was the only suitable date in light of the difficulty involved in taking a large passenger plane out of the regular flight schedules of the company. Only a few people knew that I took an active part in setting the time of the flight.

The earlier flight suited the members of the delegation, for apart from representing Israel at the anniversary celebrations they would have more time for lecture tours and other personal appearances in Argentina.

When all the negotiations were concluded, the special flight was announced in the press, and the public was offered seats to Buenos Aires or intermediate airports. But the company still had to attend to all the official and technical arrangements: obtaining landing clearances, securing agents for servicing the plane, assuring fuel supplies, and setting up a special Telex code for communication between the Argentine capital and Tel Aviv.

At my request, Kedem went on ahead to deal with all these matters and also to try to obtain a permit for taking passengers from Argentina to Israel. In addition, I asked him to survey conditions at the airport so that when the time came he could help us coordinate the plans for secretly taking Eichmann out of Argentina. Kedem suggested, and I agreed, that he should have an assistant in Buenos Aires. He selected Aharon Lazar, manager of one of the larger overseas stations.

And so all the arrangements for the special flight to Buenos Aires were gradually completed, a flight that was much more special than most of the people handling it could ever guess.

# 11

Menashe Talmi would be the first member of the task force to leave for Argentina. Earlier I had questioned him about Argentina in general and Buenos Aires in particular—local customs and characteristics, behavior at cafés, hotels, and restaurants, living conditions, possibilities for renting or buying houses and apartments, transport, roads, prices, traffic licenses, police methods, routine papers and documents, tourism, procedures at harbors and airports, and so on. For here I was, about to go where I knew very little about the country and even less about its people, and Talmi, because he knew Buenos Aires extremely well, could help me with all the information the books and tourist guides don't provide. He gave me as many answers as he could and promised to find out the rest, discreetly, from his Argentine friends.

I explained that we'd have to know everything in advance, because I had made up my mind that from the moment we arrived in Buenos Aires we would never ask for help from any of the locals or from any person or group having any direct or indirect connection with Israel's official representation there. He would have to be our "living encyclopedia" in everything to do with the affairs of the city and the country and the interpreter of local customs for the members of the task force who would be going into action ignorant of the culture or conditions of the place they'd be working in. Talmi agreed without hesitation and went off to make technical and organizational preparations for the operation.

———

Since the force had to be self-sufficient in every sense, and had to provide all its own needs even in the vital matter of documentation, Shalom Dani was an essential member. He was a skilled craftsman in that delicate art, the forging of official documents of all kinds, especially identity papers. But Shalom was more than an expert of rare capability, he was a person of refined character and unusual dedication. His modesty, his willingness to perform any task or service, his courage, and his ability to do his work at any time under any conditions, made him a shining example to all his fellow workers.

Shalom once went out on an arduous and complicated operation in the guise of an artist (painting was his hobby) and while carrying out his assignment he earned quite a name for himself as a talented artist— only the most rigorous search of his studio could have revealed that it contained certain tools and implements that had nothing to do with the usual artist's equipment. That operation entailed very precise work, and every letter, every line, and every signature he drew could have withstood the most stringent examination. His documents were written in the local language, which was foreign to him, and he had to use local aides; but the clandestine nature of the work was too much for the aides and they gave up, leaving Shalom alone with piles of material accumulating on his desk. He was forced to work sixteen to eighteen hours a day, permitting himself no rest, not even for meals; for days on end he didn't change his clothes.

His superior officer on the operation was amazed at how he overcame all obstacles and produced perfect work in a language he didn't understand, a language which Shalom, with wondrous persistence, learned in a few weeks of uninterrupted hard labor to read and write. Perhaps knowing that he was engaged in an operation of great importance encouraged him, for when he finished his job, crushed with exhaustion but glowing with contentment, he said simply, "It was worth the effort."

People who watched him do his delicate work were fascinated by his rare proficiency. He could make the tiniest printed letters indistinguishable from real print, and he could do all this, and even more, not only seated comfortably at his desk but also standing up or rocking from side to side in a car or train.

At the beginning of 1960 Shalom was living in a European capital, doing work which made it possible for him to fulfill one of his longings: to study the art of *vitrage,* the making of stained glass. However, when I called him to take part in a new operation he didn't hesitate. On hearing the nature of the operation and our plan to capture Eichmann and bring him to trial in Israel, his eyes filled with tears. Dani was a survivor of the holocaust. I did not have to explain the special national and humane significance of the undertaking.

Shalom Dani was born in Hungary in 1928 and was still a boy when the Germans took over the country and sent his father to die in Bergen-Belsen. His older brother was conscripted for manual labor, while he, his mother, and his younger brother and sister, were first shut up in a ghetto in their home town and later shunted about from camp to camp, until Shalom decided to run away. The whole family escaped from the transports and remained hidden in an Austrian village until the Allied soldiers arrived. The older brother was found in a hospital, wounded. While they were still making their way to Israel, Shalom helped other war refugees whether they had immigration certificates or not, and he was caught in an "illegal act" and put into an American prison. Later Shalom and his family sailed on an illegal refugee ship which was caught. In the British camp in Cyprus where the passengers were imprisoned, Shalom put his special talents in documentation to good use, advancing the release of many of the refugees and their immigration to Israel. His years in Israel were spent serving in the army and security organizations.

There was no need to tell Shalom Dani what preparations to make for his departure. I have never come

across such a resourceful man. He could do his work
to perfection even with minimal equipment, with primi-
tive means, and under conditions of severe pressure. He
realized what hinged on his preparations and knew,
too, that he was going to have to solve for himself the
problems of transporting his equipment to the target
country without arousing suspicion.

Shortly after I appointed Gabi Eldad to command the
operation, he came back to me with the first outlines of
a plan as well as a suggestion for the composition of the
limited operational team. He had based his rough plan
on the material in our files, on Kenet's reports, and on
the information that had been accumulated in the
meantime about the target area, and I authorized it
on general lines.

And now the team. The success of the operation depended on the character and capability of the people
taking part in it, all excellent operatives, devoted heart
and soul to their work, and completely fearless.

First there was Ehud Revivi, Gabi's personal friend
and, like him, an outstanding operations man, an excellent planner, proficient in several languages, and experienced in actions abroad. Ehud was the son of an as-
similated family in Vienna who led a pleasant easy life
until the day Austria was annexed to Hitler's Third
Reich. For Ehud the change manifested itself when
about thirty of his classmates fell on him and another
Jewish boy in the class and gave them a brutal beating
in the presence of the teacher, who didn't intervene.
Ehud was confined to bed for two weeks, and when he
was well again he didn't go back to school. His father's
business was confiscated, and then the family was
evicted from their apartment. Ehud's childhood mem-
ories were interwoven with visions of the flames from
the synagogues on the "Crystal Night." The day World
War II broke out the persecuted family reached the safe
shores of Israel. Ehud finished high school, joined *Palmach,* and later served in a reconnaissance unit in the
Israeli Defense Force. His commander was Gabi Eldad,
and through Gabi he came to the operations group. The

friendship that had grown up between them in the days of their army service deepened in the daring operations the two of them took part in.

Eli Yuval, the second man to appear on Gabi's list, was born in Poland. He went to Israel with his parents when he was six. His sister and her three children remained in Poland—it was impossible to get immigration certificates for them—and they were murdered by the Nazis. The day the youngster Eli heard about the fate of his sister and her children he swore an oath to avenge their deaths. When Ehud Revivi informed him that he'd been chosen for the operational team and, what's more, according to the preliminary plan he would be the first to come into physical contact with Eichmann at the moment of capture, he regarded it as the fulfillment of his vow. Eli was extremely fit, which was why he was cast in the role of the man to seize Eichmann, but he was also remarkable for his technical skill. After being wounded in the War of Independence and taken out of active service, he wrote one-act plays for the troops and often acted in them. His hobby was make-up and he became so efficient at it that he had succeeded at various times in fooling a watchman in the building where he worked, an old friend, and even his own mother. This talent had also been taken into consideration when he was chosen for the team.

The third member of the small party was Zev Keren, Lithuanian-born, who also came to Israel as a child. A graduate of a technical school, he was known as "the man with the golden hands": he could open any lock and improvise solutions to all kinds of problems that crop up during operations. Zev had a colorful security history. For a year he served with Wingate pursuing Arab marauding gangs, and during the war he fought in the Jewish Brigade on the Italian front. After the defeat of Germany he and some of his friends from the Brigade were engaged in punitive actions against Nazi war criminals. Gabi Eldad had these exploits in mind when he suggested that Zev take part in the capture of Eichmann. Zev was ready to kill Eichmann with his own hands and was deeply disappointed when Gabi informed him that he would be the technician of the team. Gabi soothed him with the promise that he would also be able to do his bit in the capture itself, but he must start attending to technical problems immediately.

Ezra Eshet was still in Europe, keeping the Eichmann family under observation. Gabi suggested including him in the operational team as he was experienced, level-headed, and an extremely capable organizer; he was the natural candidate for handling all organizational matters.

Gabi also kept Kenet in mind. Kenet would have to deal with everything relating to the identification of Eichmann before the capture, and with interrogating him afterward; but Gabi could use him in the limited operational team as well, since he was not only an excellent interrogator but also a first-class operations man.

I knew all these men from various operations I had directed, so I unhesitatingly confirmed the composition of the team and asked Gabi to talk to each of the candidates. I told him he must stress the voluntary nature of the operation. If any of them seemed reluctant, I told him, they must be let off immediately, and nobody would think any the worse of them.

A day or two later Gabi advised me that all the candidates had responded to his offer with great enthusiasm. They were all asked to start work immediately, without attracting attention, on the arrangements for their combined activities, and to devise suitable explanations for their absence. It was decided that the cover story for their families should be different from the one for their colleagues and close friends. They would each tell their friends a different story, but at home they would all say the same thing: they were going to take part in a special mission which must be kept secret from everybody.

Meanwhile the group under the leadership of Ankor went into high gear. They had to attend to hundreds of details in connection with equipment for the members of the task force, including the preparation of personal documentation for the journey to the target country,

the stay there, and the departure on the completion of
the operation. Escape arrangements in case of mishap
had to be very carefully worked out. The group also
gathered all the operational equipment, insofar as it
was possible to prepare it in Israel and take it to the
scene of action without too much difficulty. They prepared itineraries for all the members of the task force
and arranged meeting places for each one of them in
Buenos Aires. Before setting out they all knew where
they would be lodging and how they would establish
the first contact with their friends. Miriam Savyon handled the personal documentation in Israel, and Moshe
Vered, Ankor's assistant, dealt with the organizational
work.

The men could not travel directly from Israel to Argentina, each had to be sent first to someplace outside
of Israel and then from there, equipped with suitable
documentation, to their common destination. Each had
to be provided with permits, character references,
health certificates, travel tickets, and all the rest. We
couldn't go to a travel agent for help—we had to set up
our own "travel agency."

The man to whom I entrusted this important task
was Nahum Amir, Latvian-born and one of the first intelligence men in the *Hagana,* who during his many
years of service excelled at handling complicated problems and getting out of tight spots. His good nature,
kindheartedness, simple ways, and willingness to undertake any task at any time earned him many friends and
admirers. He never asked me why he had to do something; in many cases, I wasn't even sure that he knew
what sort of operation he was taking part in. But he
could always be relied on to respond to a call, even
without any previous warning, and to do his job intelli-
gently and loyally.

On this occasion I explained that we were preparing
to capture Eichmann and make him stand trial in Israel.
At the time I was still considering attaching him to the
task force, and he was very happy when I told him so. I
told him that first he would have to go to Europe to
organize the journeys of the rest of the task force. I

explained to him the special importance of keeping his actions secret, and told him how essential it was to be meticulous in every detail, in view of the possible political complications. There was no room for mistakes in these arrangements, I explained. Every passport and document had to be given separate attention and special thought so that there could be no indication of a combined departure, no hint that these men belonged to one group. I summed up by telling him that, with one exception, all the men would travel separately, by different routes, at different times, and from different airports, so that there should be no possibility of tracing their stay in any particular place, their journey, or their arrival or departure.

Nahum coordinated his work with the group in Israel —Moshe Vered and Miriam Savyon—and took great care that none of the travelers should have to present himself at any consulate to obtain a visa or at any travel office to get a ticket.

When his preparations in Israel were done, Nahum left for Europe to deal with the onward journeys. I told him we'd see each other again in Europe, as I would also be a client of his "travel agency."

Yitzhak Nesher was not an operations man and had no special technical talents, slightly phlegmatic, and slow in his reactions. But he had a rare gift: he could inspire trust in everyone who saw him. He had an innocent face, almost expressionless, but this lack of expression enabled him to assume other identities most convincingly and to implant in everyone's mind an instinctive faith that every word issuing from his mouth was the unadulterated truth. This facility stood him in especially good stead among German- and English-speaking people. Nobody could be as convincing in so many alternating identities and with so many rapidly changing documents as naturally as he could, and the task I assigned to him was to rent or, if necessary, buy everything the team would need—including safe houses, emergency accommodation, cars, and anything else for which a person is obliged to show his papers. He would also have to live with his "wife" in the safe house where we proposed keeping Eichmann after his capture, the idea being to present a natural front to the neighbors.

When I offered him the job he showed no signs of enthusiasm, but then Yitzhak Nesher was never enthusiastic about anything. His full and immediate consent was enough for me, as well as his promise to arrange to be ready at my call.

As a possible "wife" for Yitzhak I chose Dina Ron, who would also "keep house" from the time of Eichmann's capture to the moment of his departure for Israel. Dina was new to the work but had already managed to take part in several complicated operations. She spoke several languages fluently and could assume different identities and adapt herself to different circumstances with ease.

Dina Ron immigrated to Israel with her parents in 1940. Most of their relatives remained in Western Europe and were wiped out by the Nazis. Her family was not particularly religious, yet Dina joined a religious youth movement, founded a yeshiva for girls, and left high school to continue her studies there—the experiment lasted only a year, and Dina went back to high school. Her university studies were interrupted by army service during the War of Independence; when she went back to the university after the war she was active in the Students' Organization and represented it at an international conference overseas. I first met Dina when she was sent to a country which Jews could leave only by secret ways. She was posing as a non-Jew, and it wasn't easy for her in those circumstances to keep up her religious observances—she led a double life: in her social contacts she was the complete gentile while in the privacy of her bachelor apartment she was kosher.

Dina wasn't recruited for the assignment at the same time as the others. I mentioned her to Ankor and told him that if a woman should be needed Dina would be the natural candidate, but the final decision would be made only after I reached Buenos Aires. I thought that if there was not much time between the capture and the departure it might be possible to do without a house-keeper, and I didn't want to include anybody whose presence wasn't vital to the team or who might prove a burden instead of an asset.

Our plan of action necessitated the presence of a doctor to drug Eichmann both at the moment of capture and later when we were transferring him from place to place. We needed a man of courage, willing to bear the heavy responsibility entailed, since the slightest mistake could have fatal results; he had to be well-qualified to give an anesthetic in an emergency, in unusual circumstances, and in unforeseen situations. The doctor would also have to keep Eichmann under constant supervision so that he would reach Israel in good health and fit to stand trial.

There was another factor that made a doctor's participation essential: the members of the task force would be isolated, especially during the period of Eichmann's secret captivity. They obviously wouldn't be able to call for local medical assistance in the event of sickness, injury, or accident. The capture itself might incur casualties. How could strangers in a foreign country, with papers that were not their own and on a mission whose nature they dared not divulge, call on a local doctor who might display too much interest in their identity and their activities in Argentina?

The choice of the right man for such a responsible job didn't present much difficulty. We had a doctor available who might have been born for the job. He was working as anesthetist at a large hospital in Israel and was known to be a man capable of quick decisions, sensible, with more than his fair share of audacity. We had gone to him more than once for medical assistance, sometimes in difficult and complicated circumstances, and we never met with a refusal.

I consulted with Haggai, who knew him well, and also with a doctor who was a good friend of mine and who worked in the same hospital as our candidate. They both recommended him as ideal for our purpose. And he was able to create suitable cover.

I asked Haggai to have a chat with him and find out

if he was prepared to volunteer for the operation. Haggai went to his house and asked him if he'd heard of Eichmann and if he'd be willing to participate in an attempt to capture him. The doctor replied that he knew who Eichmann was and was fully prepared to take part in any action to capture him. At Haggai's request, the director of the hospital released the doctor for several weeks without asking questions.

When I met the doctor later, I saw there was no need to go into long explanations. He understood the tremendous importance of the planned operation and was fully aware of the responsibility he was undertaking, as a man and as a doctor.

I arranged for him to meet Gabi Eldad, and together they prepared a list of the instruments and equipment the doctor would need in the target country in order to be ready for any emergency. They also discussed how best to look after Eichmann at all stages of the action, from the capture itself and the custody in the safe house to the transfer to the plane and the subsequent flight to Israel.

Gabi went to the hospital one day and our doctor gave him a large parcel containing all the requisite medications and equipment, especially all the things that would be difficult to buy at a pharmacy without arousing suspicion or excessive interest. Gabi promised him that when he arrived in Buenos Aires he would find the parcel and all its contents already there.

The men of the task force were busy poring over the details of the plan. They had learned all there was in the files and the reports from Kenet and Talmi. They studied whatever they could find about local conditions, worked over the list of equipment to be transferred to Buenos Aires, and made a note of the things that could be acquired there—they would take only the essential minimum, and buy or install as much as possible in Buenos Aires.

Gabi devoted many hours to discussions of documentation with Ankor's group, since not every member of the task force knew how to operate with fabricated papers.

At a preliminary meeting the task force debated three possible methods of capturing Eichmann: The first was to break into Klement's house in San Fernando, after shadowings and surveillances had confirmed that the man was at home and that conditions in the vicinity were suitable for action. The second method was a "mobile" arrest, while the man was on the move outside the house. The third possibility they explored was to make the capture at a point designated in advance, on his route home. In all three cases the use of a suitable bait was discussed.

Their planning was vulnerable in one respect: it was based on unchecked and even perhaps unrealistic data. To carry out a practical test of the various possibilities the task force had to be on the spot, set up a surveillance of the house, and maintain a prolonged shadowing of Klement himself; it was also necessary to make a thorough reconnaissance of the areas likely to be used as the arena for the capture. Thus the final planning had to wait until the advance party was on the scene and could determine whether reasonably satisfactory operational conditions prevailed. Ehud Revivi was nominated head of the advance party, with Ezra Eshet and Kenet as his associates.

We decided that Yitzhak Nesher would also go with the advance party to start on a search for as many apartments and houses as would be needed. He would also handle car rentals. My intention was that the rest of the men would leave for Argentina only after the advance party had located Klement and reported that conditions were favorable for making the capture.

The question of the timetable also came into the preliminary planning. The crucial point was the date of arrival of the special plane in Buenos Aires. We had already concluded that the capture had to be carried out before the plane arrived—but not so much before that Eichmann would have to be kept longer under house arrest than would be safe. We had to bear in mind that with every day that passed after Klement's disappearance his relatives and friends would become more active in their search for him; and should the Argentine authorities be appealed to, they might, in their efforts to find the missing man, put a strict check on all roads, border stations, and airports.

The date of the Israeli delegation's departure for the anniversary celebrations depended on Argentina's protocol arrangements. The delegates had to be there before the opening of the festivities, and at the same time it wouldn't do for them to come much earlier than the other delegations. The arrival date had to suit the hosts —and besides, if we brought the flight too far forward people would wonder why, including the delegates who were not aware of the plan.

The special flight was still scheduled to leave May 11, 1960, and arrive in Buenos Aires on May 12. It would take off again on May 13 or 14, though the plane could always be held back a little on the pretext of a technical hitch. Once the date of the flight was fixed, all other considerations were subordinate. Eichmann had to be captured before May 11, a few days earlier if possible.

I assumed that, in anticipation of the arrival of official delegations from many countries, the Argentine authorities would intensify their security precautions and keep a strict watch on every stranger entering the country during that time. With this in mind, I had given strict instructions to Nahum Amir to proceed very cautiously with all the consulates, travel agencies, and airline companies he dealt with in making the travel arrangements for the task force. And he did take extraordinary precautions. He scrupulously avoided sending more than one man from any one city, and in many cases did not even let more than two leave from a single country. When he inquired at travel agencies about flights and timetables he took care not to let it be known that the passenger's ultimate destination was Buenos Aires. He would get the clerk at the airline to help him plan tours to South America—Argentina was included as only one of the many countries to be visited. After going into all the possibilities, he would order the tickets from another travel agency. In some cases, he would order combined flight tickets from a travel office and then cancel the superfluous flights at the airline. Sometimes he ordered round-trip tickets for other countries in South America, making Buenos Aires just one of the stops on the route.

Obtaining the visas involved enormous difficulty. It was customary for a traveler leaving on a long journey to obtain all the requisite visas from the consulates in his fixed place of residence, and many consulates demanded that persons requesting visas must be inhabitants of the country or at least have the right to reside there. Some consulates even required character references from the local police, letters of recommendation from employers, and so on. Nahum found out which consulates were less strict about transit visas, and used them wherever possible. Nahum soon realized that all the running around entailed in making travel arrangements for the task force was too much for one man, so he recruited men who ran the strangest errands for him without having a clue as to what it was all about. The health regulations of the various consulates constituted a problem all on their own. Applicants for visas were generally required to be examined by an authorized doctor and to have various inoculations for international vaccination certificates. Nahum and his aides, "representing" the genuine passengers, were obliged to undergo several such examinations and they were sometimes even subjected to a thorough interrogation about the purpose of their journey. However, in spite of the difficulties and adventures, Nahum and his aides managed to produce all the documents and tickets for the whole task force in good time.

# *12*

Menashe Talmi arrived in Buenos Aires on April 22, with a portion of the equipment, and chose a hotel far from the center of the city to avoid running into any of his numerous friends in the Argentine capital. His function was to prepare a base for those coming after him.

He was to lease an apartment for the task force to use for discussions and preparations. The next day he found a place and paid several months' rent in advance. He fixed up the apartment for both work and living purposes and laid in a stock of food, especially canned goods. Later the task force gave it the code name of *Maoz* (Stronghold).

Talmi had been told to go twice a day, every day, to the different prearranged meeting places to receive the newcomers. Each of the other task force members had received a list of hotels to choose from, arranged so that no two of them would stay at the same hotel and that none would be in an unsuitable neighborhood. Top priority, however, was for each of them to appear for his first contact with Talmi. The meeting points were fixed in areas far apart from each other and at different times of day, so that Talmi would not attract undue attention by going to the same place at the same time two days in a row.

Thus, the following day, April 24, Menashe visited the first meeting place to see if any of his associates had arrived. Completely calm on the outside, though in a state of inner tension, he sat in a smart café, a cup of black coffee in front of him. Occasionally he looked up from the magazine spread out before him and glanced at the door. Will anybody come today?—the question repeated itself over and over in his mind. His loneliness was beginning to get him down, even in just these few days; he was fond of company but was forbidden to communicate with friends and acquaintances in the city. He was really looking forward to the arrival of the first member of the advance party and passed the time trying to guess who it would be. He looked at his watch —another four minutes and the time set for the rendezvous would be over.

At that moment the silhouette of a tall slim man appeared in the glass of the revolving door. Ezra Eshet came hurrying in, stopped in the middle of the floor, and looked around at all the people sitting there. Suddenly he saw two smiling eyes gazing at him through the smoke curling upward from a pipe. The smoker rose to greet him and put out his hand.

"I'm pleased to see you. Come, sit here."

"Thanks. How are you?"

They spoke in loud voices, in English. As they sat down they lowered their voices and continued their conversation in Hebrew.

"I've come straight from the airport," Eshet said. "I was pretty sure I wouldn't find you still here."

"And I was already beginning to give up hope. I thought nobody would come today. Let's sit for a while, and then I'll take you to the place I've rented."

A little later they left the café, collected Ezra's baggage, and took a taxi to *Maoz*. There Ezra rested after the strain of the journey, and then the two of them went out to wander around the city.

This was Ezra's opportunity to tell Menashe about the amusing incident that had occurred when he first set foot on Argentinian soil. After passing safely through passport control, he boarded the bus taking passengers to Buenos Aires. He'd been instructed to avoid using taxis. The bus was full, but its departure was delayed for some time and Ezra wondered what the hold-up was. He'd chosen a seat next to the door, in case he had to make a quick getaway at some stage. Suddenly two men came running onto the bus. One was the driver, but the other planted himself in front of Ezra, took a photograph out of a bundle of papers, and held it out to him while showering him with a spate of Spanish, of which Ezra didn't understand a word.

Ezra was literally struck dumb. He looked at the picture and saw himself alighting from the plane on which he'd arrived about half an hour earlier. His blood ran cold. What's happened? he thought. Have they discovered my passport isn't genuine? Were they forewarned of my arrival? Are they going to arrest me?

Confused, bewildered, unable to think what to do next, he looked around. The man was offering another picture to the passenger sitting next to him, and the passenger was paying for it! Ezra breathed a sigh of relief. Obviously the man was a photographer who worked in partnership with the bus driver, and the driver had delayed the bus to give the photographer a chance to finish his pictures of the unsuspecting arrivals and sell them for a modest sum. Ezra thanked the photographer and paid him generously, double the usual price. He still shudders when he thinks back on the incident, and to this day he treasures the photograph.

On April 25 Kenet arrived. This time he had a new identity and had tried to change his appearance as much as possible. On his previous visit he had met a number of people, and he dared not take the chance of stumbling on any of them. He had to be very careful in his choice of accommodation and rendezvous areas.

Kenet's principal role was to identify Ricardo Klement as soon as he was in the hands of the task force. For this purpose the special team had prepared a detailed list of everything known about Eichmann's personal characteristics and identifying marks:

## PERSONAL DESCRIPTION

a) From an SS document dated July 19, 1937: height—5 ft. 10 in.; circumference of head—22″; size of shoe—8½.

b) From an SS document dated January 1939: height—5 ft. 8½ in.; circumference of head—22″; size of shoe—9½; size of clothes—44.

c) From Wisliceny's Nuremberg testimony of October 27, 1946: height—5 ft. 10 in.; shape of head—long and narrow; bowlegged; hair—thin, dark blond in color; nose—long and narrow, large nostrils; eyes—blue-gray; lips—thin and compressed.

d) From an official medical certificate dated November 9, 1934: height—5 ft. 8½ in. (wearing shoes); weight—154 lbs. (clothed); eyes—blue; hair—smooth and blond.

## DISTINGUISHING MARKS

a) From Wisliceny's testimony of October 1946: scarcely visible scar about 1½″ long below the left eyebrow.

b) From Wisliceny's testimony, same date: double fracture of the skull (in 1932); two gold bridges in the top row of teeth, numerous fillings.

c) From an official medical certificate of 1934: appendectomy scar (in 1922).

d) From an official medical certificate of 1937: fracture of the right hand.

e) From a medical certificate of 1937: scar about one inch long in the area of the tenth rib on the left side of the body.

f) From an official medical certificate of 1937: scar above the left elbow.

g) From Wisliceny's testimony of October 1946: blood type tattooed under the left armpit, as was customary with all SS officers.

### VARIOUS PERSONAL PARTICULARS

a) His number in the SS, according to documents from 1932 and 1937—45326; additional SS number, whose nature is not sufficiently clear—63752; membership in the Nazi Party—889895.

b) Wisliceny's testimony of 1946: description of his way of speaking, his accent, languages he knew, etc.

Menashe and Ezra had their first meeting with Kenet on April 26, proving once again that liaison arrangements were working properly. The three of them planned their actions for the day, concluding that the most urgent matter at the moment was to rent a car so they could reconnoiter the San Fernando area and re-establish "contact" with Ricardo Klement.

Kenet had more experience renting cars than the others, but he was afraid to go back in his new identity to the companies where they knew him from before. He even feared that if he went to another firm he might meet a clerk who had switched jobs, or that there was some sort of connection between the various agencies. Admittedly, he had radically changed his way of dressing and even made himself up a little, but the danger was still there. His fears were groundless. The car was rented without mishap, and they promptly set out to buy the equipment on the list prepared in Israel: folding beds, bedding, and kitchen utensils, in case several people had to stay at *Maoz*.

They were careful in their comings and goings not to attract the attention of the neighboring tenants. And it was all done quickly because they still wanted to reconnoiter San Fernando the same evening.

————

By the time of the reconnaissance they were four. Ehud Revivi had received his documentation from Shalom Dani, flown from Israel to Rome, and then gone by train to the city where Nahum Amir was waiting for him. All flights to South America were fully booked, and he could get a seat only from Lisbon. When Ehud boarded the plane he saw that Yitzhak Nesher was also one of the passengers. They pretended not to know each other and didn't exchange a single word throughout the long flight. The plane landed at three o'clock in the afternoon, and each went to his own hotel, following the arrangements made in Israel. The advance party was now complete.

When Ehud arrived at the hotel, the reception clerk was delighted to meet a "fellow countryman" and speak to him in his own language. He asked the visitor what town he lived in, and when it turned out that they both came from the same district, he started chatting about places Ehud had never seen in his life. The clerk was eager to help his "compatriot" and offered to fill out the form for him—all he asked him to do was sign it. Ehud was in a panic; he'd forgotten the name in his passport! His thoughts raced. Here he was, right at the outset of his assignment, and he was already in a mess. He quickly pulled himself together and asked the receptionist to let him have his passport for a minute because he thought he'd left an important paper in it. The paper wasn't there, but he will never again forget the name as long as he lives.

Two meetings were fixed for Ehud that day: eight in the morning at a café, and six in the evening at the corner of Avenida Santa Fe and Avenida Callao. He unpacked and went to the meeting place; he was a stranger to Buenos Aires, but he had no difficulty finding the street corner in the center of the city. Just as he arrived, at six, Kenet and Ezra Eshet came toward him.

The rented car was parked nearby, so they decided not to waste a moment but to go to San Fernando right away. Kenet, who was driving, knew the way by heart, including short cuts.

At seven-forty, on Route 202 near the kiosk which Ezra and Ehud knew well from Kenet's reports, they saw Ricardo Klement walking along the left side of the road, between the kiosk and his house. Ehud identified him immediately from the photograph Kenet had brought with him.

"There he is!" whispered Ehud, and with a start of surprise Kenet jammed on the brakes. The car swerved toward Klement and stopped, but Ehud made Kenet drive on a little farther lest Klement take fright at a car stopping beside him. Ezra got out of the car and shadowed Klement as he walked along Route 202 in the direction of Bancalari, keeping a distance of about a hundred yards between them. He saw Klement leave the main road, turn left onto a dirt road, walk another twenty yards or so, and enter a small isolated house. Ezra recognized the house from Kenet's photographs.

Meanwhile, Ehud and Kenet had continued driving toward Buenos Aires, but a little later they came back and picked up Ezra beside the railway embankment behind Klement's house. They were afraid to go any nearer, even though it was pitch dark.

This was an unexpected bit of luck. About two hours earlier, when they had decided to go to the target area, all they had intended was to give Ezra and Ehud an opportunity to familiarize themselves with the surroundings. It never entered anyone's mind that they would see Klement on their first reconnaissance.

On the way back to Buenos Aires they analyzed the results. It was a Tuesday, and from Klement's presence near home on the evening of an ordinary weekday they deduced that he was no longer working far from home but in Buenos Aires itself or its vicinity. If this was the case, Klement probably walked from the bus stop to his house at a regular hour; and at this time of the year it was already dark at that hour. This meant that the capture could be made in the section of the road between the bus stop and Klement's house.

Although their hypothesis needed to be checked further, Ehud believed—and his companions shared his opinion—that there were good grounds for reporting to Israel that Klement's whereabouts were known and that the operation could be carried out. That same evening, April 26, they sent such a message to Tel Aviv.

Ehud's message was handed to me toward evening, April 27. The next three days I was busier than ever before in my life. In those seventy-two hours I had to complete the coordination of all the actions relating to the operation, make my own preparations for departure, and arrange for all the diverse branches of my work to be done during my absence.

To start with, I gave the immediate "go" signal to the task force. Once again the various arrangements, as well as the equipment, communications, and provisions were re-examined for a possible hitch. I met with all those concerned with the operation—the people of the task force standing by, the special team that remained at home, and all the persons and agencies outside the Service who had any sort of function to perform in the operation.

The head of the operational team, Gabi Eldad, re-checked all the plans and prepared himself and his men for an immediate departure, while I devoted most of my time to confirming the means of Eichmann's transfer from Argentina to Israel. Until then the details of the special flight were not actually confirmed. Now I had to verify that these arrangements would in fact be carried out. I summoned Asher Kedem, and we decided that he would go to Argentina immediately to handle everything involved in the plane's landing and take-off. He repeated his suggestion that his friend Aharon Lazar go along to help him so he would be available to deal with any problem that might arise.

Everything hinged on final confirmation from the board of management of the airline. I saw Moshe Tadmor and then the managing director of the company. They not only expressed their full agreement but also did all that was necessary to ensure that the airline would perform in accordance with the needs of the operation. The captain of the plane would be one of the company's senior pilots—Yoav Meged.

I met with Meged and explained what sort of operation we were undertaking and its possible effect on the preparations for the special flight as well as on the flight itself. I stressed the necessity for Israeli mechanics to be attached to the crew in order to avoid having foreign mechanics service the engines. I asked him to be prepared for a speedy take-off if necessary and a return flight with a minimum of intermediate stops.

Meged struck me as a self-contained person and not much of a talker. Although certain indications of inner excitement could be detected from behind that armor of taciturnity, his verbal reaction was confined to the remark that he understood and appreciated the importance of the affair, was prepared to take part in it, and promised to do all in his power to make it a success.

As he left my office, I said good-by to him with the familiar Hebrew "see you again": *"L'hitraot* in Buenos Aires."

During Kedem's absence Dan Avner was acting as intermediary between me and the airline. I invited him, with Hillel Ankor and Leora Dotan, to my house late in the evening.

Dan became very emotional when he heard about the planned operation, for he too had a score of his own to settle with the Nazis. Dan's father, a well-to-do merchant and a respected member of the Jewish community in the German town where Dan was born, was one of the first Jews to be persecuted when the Nazis came to power. He was led through the streets in a parade of Jews, beaten, and forced to drink large doses of castor oil; he had a heart ailment and died soon after this treatment. Dan learned after World War II that until February 1943 his mother had been imprisoned in a sort of ghetto and then, with the rest of the town's Jews, she was deported to Auschwitz—but she died on the way. Dan himself was rescued by the Youth *Aliya,* and he was taken to Israel in 1935 at the age of sixteen.

It didn't take much in the way of explanation to make Dan aware of the necessity to devote all his energy during the coming weeks to the tasks entrusted to him. I assigned him to put together an aircraft crew we would be able to rely on, with regard to both capability and security, and to obtain documentation and uniforms for a few of the task force men who might have to pose as members of the crew. I also asked him to see to it that all the technical and administrative details customary for regular flights were adhered to meticulously in order to avoid any mishaps. He was to keep in touch with Ankor's group and with Leora.

In a preliminary discussion with Ankor I put into shape my rough plan for transferring Eichmann to the plane in Buenos Aires. I did this with some reservations, because we were a long way from the scene of action and did not have sufficient knowledge of the local conditions. My idea was to bring Eichmann to the plane under cover as a member of the crew who had suddenly taken ill or was injured in an accident. To make Eichmann's papers as a member of the crew appear authentic, I wanted to attach to the plane's crew one of our men who, in general appearance, physical build, and age, resembled Eichmann as he appeared in the photographs and descriptions we received from Kenet. In other words, I wanted a double. Ankor mentioned one of the operators whose physical characteristics might fit the part, but I told him not to put the double idea into effect until he was informed that the capture had taken place. I added that two more operations men must be made ready to join the crew of the plane, their function being to act as escorts of the sick or injured "crew member," to help him board the plane and to watch him on the journey. These two and the double, I said, could be presented to the genuine crew as bodyguards for the official Israeli delegation to the anniversary celebrations.

I told Ankor that once I got to Buenos Aires these ideas might prove to be impractical, and if so I would let him know immediately; I was considering several other possibilities but would know if they were feasible only when I was on the spot. I might be able to make do with some of the men from the task force itself, and it might also be possible to recruit reinforcements from among the Jews or Israelis in countries bordering Argentina. In any event, Ankor was to make all the necessary preparations for putting the various plans into effect and for sending the requisite equipment to Buenos Aires on the special plane.

On April 28 I went to Jerusalem, as I always did before any overseas trip, to receive the Prime Minister's farewell blessings. He shook my hand and asked me when I'd be back. I told him I hoped to return within three or four weeks.

Afterward I went to say good-by to my daughter and her husband, who were studying at Hebrew University. I didn't tell them where I was going, and they, accustomed to my frequent travels, didn't display any special interest in my destination.

My next step was to see the Inspector-General of Police, Yosef Nahmias. I felt the time had come to tell him about the operation—he was, after all, the man to whom we would be handing Eichmann over for arrest and interrogation, if and when we succeeded in bringing him to Israel. We met on the pavement outside his house, as I was in a hurry and he was just going out of town.

"What's it about?" he asked with a smile.

"I've come to say good-by," I said. "I'm going away for several weeks."

"Where to this time?"

"To find Adolf Eichmann."

"Really?" he said still smiling, but the smile vanished a second later, and his face became serious. "Do you really believe you'll be able to find him?"

I nodded. "Naturally there's no complete certainty. In such matters you never know."

Nahmias wished me luck. There was no need to ask him to keep it secret: I knew that until he got a report on the results of the expedition he wouldn't utter a word.

———

There was, in the meantime, a complication. I was busy hosting an eminent personality from overseas, and although I was pressed for time I had to fulfill my social obligations. I dared not in any way disclose that I was engaged on an assignment that was more urgent than the exercise of good manners. The operation itself wasn't likely to be affected if I neglected him, but politically it could be harmful—for once the operation

was successfully concluded and the world knew that
Eichmann had vanished, my guest might put two and
two together and realize too soon that Israelis had carried it out, the proof being that his host was so busy
just before Eichmann's capture that he was unable to
perform the minimal duties of hospitality. At that stage
I couldn't know what the government's policy on publicity would be when it was advised of Operation Eichmann, or how the Eichmann family and the Argentine
authorities would react. I had to bear in mind the possibility that when Eichmann's presence in Israel was
made known his family might decide not to appeal to
the Argentine authorities to demand his return. I believed that in such an eventuality it would be desirable
that even if we were suspected of having a hand in the
affair we should not furnish them with any proof of
this.

On April 28, the eve of my departure, I had to
entertain my guest at my home. From an anecdote he
told me late that night I learned that it was customary
in South America for any stranger changing a hundred-
dollar bill to be required to show identification, in case
the note was counterfeit or stolen. I sent my driver,
Yaki, to find out what banknotes had been prepared
for me; as it turned out, all the money provided for
my travel expenses was in hundred-dollar bills. Yaki
had to go to a great deal of trouble that night and
the following morning to exchange them for smaller
denominations.

The dinner ended close to midnight. After the guest
had gone, a few people came to consult with me about
arrangements during my absence. Only in the wee
hours of the next day was I able to make my personal
preparations for the journey. And, in view of the new
identity I had to assume, these preparations were by
no means easy.

By the time I was ready it was already getting light.
Early that morning I had to see my guest off at the
airport. My only fear was that his plane might not
take off in time, because as soon as it was airborne
I had to dash home, collect my baggage and papers,

and hurry back to the airport to leave for Europe. The slightest delay in my guest's departure was liable to upset my whole timetable. I suppose I could have made my apologies and told him I had an important meeting and couldn't wait with him until the plane left—but how would it look if we met as passengers later at the airport?

Fortunately, the plane left on time. I managed to get home, take what I needed, and return to Lydda. My good-bys to my wife were hurried and routine. She was used to my "disappearances" from time to time, never asked questions about my work, and only in a few cases did she find out afterward where I had been. I told her that this time I'd be away for three or four weeks and wouldn't be able to write to her. I knew she could see how tense I was—but this too had become a routine part of our lives.

---

I arrived at the intermediate airport in Europe at night. Only two people knew I was there: Nahum Amir, who met me at the air terminal in the city, and Efraim, Shalom Dani's immediate superior—and I had arguments with both of them. Efraim complained bitterly that he didn't want me to take Shalom away from the operations they were then engaged in; I expressed my sympathy and understanding, but made clear that I had no choice but to appropriate Shalom even if it meant bringing another man from Israel to replace him. Then, before I was able to go to bed at Efraim's apartment, I had to explain to Nahum why I couldn't let him join the task force as I had originally planned. He was the sole person who knew all about the members of the force—their assumed names, their flight routes, their documentation—so it was vital that he remain in Europe, especially if we failed and the men had to get away from the target area and needed his services to resume their former identities and return to their bases in Israel or abroad.

Early the next morning I traveled to a neighboring country and from there took off for Argentina. Only then, sitting in the plane, did I have time to go over my new papers and memorize the details of my temporary identity.

At one of the stops on the long flight I suddenly heard my name—which I had only just learned—echoing through the lounge. At first I thought I was mistaken, but the loudspeakers repeated that Mr. So-and-So—the name on my passport—was requested to come immediately to the information desk. To make sure, I slipped into a corner and opened my passport: yes, that was the name.

I was in a dilemma. Nobody in the world but Nahum knew what flight I was taking to Buenos Aires, and it was inconceivable that if Nahum wanted to send me an urgent message he would try to get hold of me so publicly. There could be only one explanation: something had happened to make conspiracy unnecessary.

With great unwillingness, but with no alternative, I started walking toward the information desk. I was one step from the counter when a man pushed in front of me and breathlessly introduced himself by the name that appeared on my passport. I waited another few seconds at the desk, until it was clear beyond doubt that the call was for him, not for me. Then I heaved a sigh of relief. The strangest part about this incident was that the name had been picked purely at random. Fate seemed to be playing a practical joke on me, putting a man with the same name on the same plane.

The flight was long and tiring, with many landings on the way, and seemingly endless waits and delays. But after the great strain I had been under lately and the arrears of sleep I had accumulated, the journey was sheer luxury to me. Most of the time I slept.

# 13

One of the first essentials the advance party in Buenos Aires had to think about was finding safe houses. We needed places to hold the prisoner until he could be taken out of Argentina, and also for operational purposes such as lodgings for the task force, storage of equipment, and so on. Although the renting of housing had actually been assigned to Yitzhak Nesher, the others in the advance party decided it was so important that they would give it all their spare time in the mornings since surveillances in the target area were maintained mostly in the afternoons and evenings.

They went to real-estate agents and accumulated lists of houses and buildings in the area between Buenos Aires and San Fernando. And they scrutinized the newspaper advertisements every day, especially in the English and German papers, figuring that anybody who wanted to rent a house would look for potential tenants among foreign visitors.

Yitzhak Nesher started his search on April 27, the day after his arrival, and he spent all his time at it. He started off going from place to place by taxi, but when he realized how much time was lost this way he asked for a rented car.

The same day, April 27, Ehud, Kenet, and Menashe went to see a house about ninety-five miles from the capital; according to the agent's description, it seemed eminently suitable for keeping Klement in custody, but they found they had been misled and the place was unsuitable. Yitzhak's search that day also came to nothing. If he found a house that seemed to conform with their requirements, it usually turned out that the owner wanted to sell not rent it and the prices were inordinately high; the vast majority of places being offered for rent were unsuitable. Another drawback was that most of the houses which were to let for a short period included one or more servants—a gardener and nightwatchman, or a caretaker—and any suggestion to dispense with them was received with displeasure and even excited a certain amount of suspicion.

Before many days had passed the group realized that this problem, to which nobody had given much thought, might turn out to be one of the most difficult of the whole operation.

———

As for surveillance and shadowing, the results were better. On the evening of April 27, at six-forty-five, Kenet and Ezra went to the target area to find observation posts from which it would be possible to watch the Klement house and its surroundings without being discovered. They left the car a long way from the house to avoid arousing the curiosity of the neighborhood residents. They found that the best place was on the railway embankment, about seventy-five yards from the Klements' house. The embankment stood about fifteen feet above the level of the surroundings, and the railroad track crossed the main road by an overpass. Parallel to the track, separating it from the house, ran a stream, a tributary of the Reconquista river. The road crossed the stream over a bridge. There were two sets of tracks on the embankment, and at peak hours trains went by in both directions as frequently as every two or three minutes.

They sat on the embankment and focused their binoculars on the road, with the object of checking if Klement always came home at the same time, and if he usually came alone or with other people. They also wanted to find out if there was much pedestrian and vehicular traffic in the section Klement traversed on foot, between the kiosk on Route 202 and his house.

At seven-forty they saw Klement alight from bus number 203, which came from San Fernando and continued toward Bancalari. He got off at the kiosk, about two hundred yards from the house, and started walking along Route 202, on the same side of the road as his house, holding a flashlight which cast a white beam in front and a red beam at the back. They noticed that he switched on the light whenever a car came along. He left the main road at Garibaldi Street. When he got to his house he didn't go straight in but first walked all around the house, and only after that did he open the door.

The watchers thought that his tour of the grounds was a precautionary measure, to make sure nobody was lying in wait for him inside. But they found out after the operation that all he was doing was examining the plants in the yard.

This surveillance consolidated the team's opinion that Klement was in the habit of returning from work every day at the same time and on the same route from the kiosk on Route 202 to his house.

It was becoming obvious that to operate effectively in a city the size of Buenos Aires they each had to have more private transport, so on April 28 Ehud, Ezra, and Yitzhak went to rent cars. One of them was to be Yitzhak's exclusively, for his house hunting.

Ehud, Kenet, and Ezra bought overalls and set out on a reconnaissance of Buenos Aires harbor. They knew that the intention was to take Eichmann out of Argentina by plane, but I had warned them not to rely on this entirely and to examine operational possibilities at the port, especially with regard to transferring a person to a boat waiting outside the harbor. They had to be satisfied with only one superficial reconnaissance that day, and its only result was to persuade them that many more examinations would be required if it became necessary to transport Eichmann by sea.

Toward evening the three of them returned to the

target area. Ehud and Kenet settled themselves at their observation post on the railway embankment while Ezra waited for them in the car at the Bancalari railway station. An unoccupied car, they reasoned, not only attracts attention but also runs the risk of being stolen.

Sitting on the embankment was a severe strain. Trains kept rushing by with a deafening clatter as if venting their fury on the two peculiar characters who had picked this sooty, uncomfortable, dangerous place to spend their evenings. The trains had glaring headlights, and during the hours of darkness they were switched fully on; the men feared that if they weren't run over one night they'd eventually be discovered by the local residents—who included the Klement family.

Just before seven-forty, bus number 203 arrived and stopped at the kiosk. They both breathed a sigh of relief when once again Klement alighted and started walking along the left side of the road, flashlight in hand. As on both previous occasions, Klement again left the main road and turned into Garibaldi Street, entered the yard, did a preliminary tour of the house, and then went inside. Ehud and Kenet left their uncomfortable perch on the embankment, and Ezra came to pick them up in the car at the prearranged spot.

It was now clear that Eichmann came home from work every day at the same time, but they still didn't know what his work was. They traced the route of the number 203 bus and found that it started from the San Fernando railway station. The most likely deduction was that Eichmann got to the station by train, and from there continued by bus. But where did he come from? They decided that the following day they must try to find out.

Worn-out and filthy, but pleased with the day's achievements, they returned to Buenos Aires. Yitzhak reported that his day's search had yielded a few houses worth considering. They agreed to inspect them the following morning.

———

Ehud and Yitzhak went to see two houses in the San Fernando area which might have been suitable—if not for the fact that the owners were demanding excessive rentals and refusing to lease them for less than a year. They tried in vain to bargain with them, or at least to reduce the period of the lease. Eventually they went away, leaving the way open for further negotiation.

Nor did Kenet and Ezra, busy on a parallel search, manage to find what they wanted. After seeing many houses, they found two that seemed suitable, but they were both for sale only. They tried to persuade the owners that rather than be stuck with the houses it would be worth their while to rent the properties for a few months to people like themselves, who were in Argentina on business and didn't want to stay in hotels. But it was useless—both owners were prepared to negotiate sales but were not interested in renting.

Kenet, Ehud, and Ezra gave up house hunting at four in the afternoon to get ready for their daily surveillance of the target area. This time they were going to attempt to find out what Klement did before he boarded bus number 203. They left Kenet at the San Fernando railway station, next to the bus terminal, and drove on to their usual observation post. A few minutes after seven-thirty Kenet saw a man who looked like Klement sitting in bus 203. He wasn't quite sure that it was Klement and didn't want to take a chance on boarding. He was a little surprised that he hadn't noticed the man getting on, but they found out later that they had made a mistake in assuming that the bus started at the railway station. Klement must have boarded at a previous stop.

Luck was not with Ehud and Ezra either. No sooner had they sat down on the embankment than two men came along and looked at them with curiosity. They had no choice but to leave their observation post. They hurried to the car they'd left standing at the side of the road facing Bancalari and drove back along Route 202, toward San Fernando. When they reached the corner of Garibaldi Street they saw Klement turning off the main road into the street where he lived. They checked the time—it was exactly seven-forty.

They went back to San Fernando and picked up Kenet at the railway station. When they heard his story they went to try again to find the starting point of bus 203. They finally found it outside another railway station, the one at Carupa, and they decided that at the earliest opportunity they would keep an eye on this station to see if this was where Klement boarded the bus.

---

April 30 fell on a Saturday, and the advance party took the whole morning off. They needed rest badly. From the day of arrival in Buenos Aires, after a tiring flight, each had been devoting most of the day to incessant running around looking for houses and the nights to surveillance—under extremely trying conditions. They had sat for hours clinging to the slope of the embankment, and the smart well-pressed tourist clothes they wore on their vigils usually became limp crumpled rags—it was the rainy season—by the time they returned to their lodgings. And then their day generally ended with a recapitulation meeting to draw their conclusions on the day's achievements and plan the morrow's activities.

On Saturday afternoon they were going on a reconnaissance of the roads, to familiarize themselves with the entire area and to look for detours through side streets in order to avoid the heavy traffic of the main roads and the numerous railway crossings with their barriers.

They arranged to meet at a certain spot in Avenida Nueve de Julio, but Ehud, who was the first to arrive, discovered that it wasn't the best place. He had been pacing up and down for a few minutes when a policeman came up to him and asked to see his papers. It seemed they'd chosen to meet in front of the German Embassy—unintentionally of course. As soon as he saw Kenet and Ezra approaching Ehud hurried to meet them and tell them what a mistake they'd made.

Later they reconnoitered the roads for many hours, in the target area itself, between the target area and the center of the city, and similarly between the target area and the areas where they were looking for safe houses. On this and subsequent trips they found quite a few suburban byways where the traffic was light and where police or security agents would be unlikely to search if the hunt was on.

That day and the next, Sunday, May 1, no surveillance was set up at Klement's usual homecoming time. Instead, a reconnaissance of the target area was arranged for Sunday morning, one of its main purposes being to find observation posts other than the one on the railway embankment, which was uncomfortable and unsafe. The results were not encouraging. A few alternatives did present themselves, but in each case conditions were even less favorable than on the embankment.

At about eleven-thirty on Sunday they passed Klement's house and saw him working in his garden. To avoid making him suspicious, they drove past at high speed and were thus unable to form a clear impression of him.

———

That Sunday was the day I arrived in Buenos Aires. The sun had almost set when the plane approached Ezeiza, the international airport, and in the afterglow I could see the delta mouth of the mighty Río de la Plata and its two large tributaries, Paraná and Uruguay, each a couple of miles wide at the estuary. Looking out over the vast city girded by the waters of the sea and the two giant rivers which are themselves like seas, it was easy to understand why they say Buenos Aires is a composite of the sparkle of Paris and Vienna and the hubbub of New York and Chicago. Not for nothing is she called *Puerto de Santa Maria del Buen Aire*. It must have seemed an earthly paradise to the Spanish sailors of bygone centuries.

But I had very little time to spend on the glorious gardens and beautiful boulevards of Buenos Aires, its splendid mansions housing the government offices, or the huge harbor area with its quaysides and anchorages adorned with derricks and silos. After passing through immigration and customs, I approached the bus for the

city. As I left the airport building I saw Ehud waiting
amid the throng of welcomers, but neither of us gave
any hint of recognition. Our rendezvous had been prearranged for the following day, but Ehud's presence
at the airport indicated that he wanted to make it
earlier. I left the initiative to him, and sure enough I
saw him climb onto the same bus I was traveling in.

When the bus arrived at the hotel where I was staying, Ehud and I found an opportunity to exchange a
few words and arrange for a meeting. I registered at
the desk and went up to my room, and Ehud followed
me a little later. He reported briefly on the situation
with regard to Klement, the safe houses, and all the
other activities of the advance party. We fixed a later
meeting at a café near my hotel, and I used the interval to bathe and change.

From the café we went straight to the only safe house
we had at the moment, *Maoz*. Kenet, Ezra, Menashe,
and Yitzhak were waiting there, and I listened to their
detailed report on the surveillances they had maintained for four consecutive days. I concluded that we
could now regard as fact our hypothesis that Klement
was regularly employed, apparently in Buenos Aires,
and returned home every evening at the same hour. I
considered the conditions in the vicinity of his home
favorable for carrying out the capture silently and safely.

I was given further particulars of the efforts to find
houses and the negative results. I decided that this
vital issue must be given top priority and that we
couldn't afford to be too choosy about the location or
interior of the places offered to us nor be put off by
the high prices. It was only where security requirements were at stake that we dared not compromise.

The advance party was also experiencing a great
deal of difficulty renting cars. Argentina seemed to lag
behind European and North American countries in this
respect. The prices of passenger cars were extremely
high; an American car cost as much as fifteen thousand
dollars; and to rent one required a deposit of five
thousand dollars. But the worst part of it all was that

the engine and bodywork were generally dilapidated, the tires so worn that it was impossible to rely on them, the batteries old and liable to run down at crucial moments were at stake that we dared not compromise.

choice of models was extremely limited, thus creating serious problems since we were unwilling to be seen too often in the same places in the same car. Nevertheless, I was confident we could overcome all these difficulties, even if it meant devoting a greater effort to them than we had taken into account in our initial planning.

I told the others about the preparations we had made in Israel after their departure and explained that all the members of the task force were either on their way to Argentina or about to set out within the next few days. Another thing I was able to tell them was that I had completed the final arrangements for the flight. The tentative date for its departure from Israel continued to be May 11. Consequently, I said, we would have to make the capture on May 10 at the very latest, as the plane would be taking off on its return flight on May 13 or 14 and we would have to give ourselves a few days' leeway in case of unavoidable delay or unforeseen difficulties. I told them about the special operational equipment I had ordered for embarking Klement, and said that if it was all ready in time it would be coming on that very plane.

At the end of our talk we planned our future work and means of communication. Menashe was assigned the task of maintaining liaison between me and the rest of the men.

# 14

When Aharon Lazar received the Telex message to leave for Buenos Aires and to meet Asher Kedem there, he was sure there had been a misunderstanding —he had never handled South American matters for the airline. He asked for the message to be repeated —there must be some mistake. A second Telex confirmed that Buenos Aires was indeed to be his destination, and he was even given the number of the Swissair flight on which Kedem would be traveling. Accordingly, he flew to São Paulo, and was already waiting in Rio when Kedem's flight arrived.

Kedem left Israel on May 1, 1960. He flew to Zurich, where he changed to a Swissair plane bound for Argentina. At the first stop, Geneva, he saw Gabi Eldad and Eli Yuval, but they gave no sign that they recognized him. At Rio he was surprised to find Lazar waiting, agitated and anxious for an explanation.

Kedem explained that there was concrete news of Eichmann's whereabouts in Argentina and a plan to apprehend him had been devised. Their assignment, he said, was to make the necessary arrangements for Eichmann's captors to bring him safely to Israel.

Lazar was dumbfounded. His first reaction was that the plan was a figment of someone's imagination. Afterward, once he was persuaded that Kedem was speaking about tangible matters, he was overwhelmed with excitement at the thought of participating in such a secret and daring operation. He couldn't understand why they had picked him of all people.

Throughout the flight from Rio to Buenos Aires dreadful visions of the past floated before his eyes, visions he thought he had long since erased from his mind.

Aharon was about ten when the Munich Pact was signed and the region of Czechoslovakia that he lived in was annexed to Hungary. About a year later World War II broke out, but it did not spread to Hungary until 1943. By then he had finished his first three years of high school in Budapest. It was not long before the German army marched into Hungary, and by the beginning of 1944 all the Jews were concentrated in the ghetto. One night the Lazar family was about to cross the border into Slovakia, but at the last moment the parents had second thoughts and decided to cancel the journey. A few weeks later they were all taken to Auschwitz. There his mother and little brother and sister were sent to one side—and vanished forever. He was led off with his father, who lied in the "selection," saying that his son was seventeen though he was just fourteen. The two of them were shuttled from labor camp to labor camp, and more than once Aharon's life was saved by his father's resourcefulness and boundless self-sacrifice. They worked in Czechoslovakia, then Austria, and finally Germany. There father and son were separated, and the boy was sent to the camp at Mühldorf, on the road to the Austrian frontier, where he was put to work unloading coal and felling trees. After nine months of working—and watching hundreds die around him, he was transferred to the Munich region to repair the railroads bombed by Allied planes. Some weeks later he and the other workers were hustled into a train and started on a long journey whose destination, according to their guards, was an extermination camp in the Tyrol. The train stopped for many hours at a small station on the way and was eventually abandoned by the guards. Somebody said that Hitler had been assassinated and the war was over. A few of the prisoners attacked the food coach and grabbed everything they could lay their hands on, while others scattered in all directions. Aharon Lazar was lucky enough to find a wedge of salt cheese. Then all of a sudden the guards were back and shooting at the runaways. Many were killed, the rest were forced back into the train and the doors locked behind them. This time the crush was worse than before because they were thrust in without any attempt at packing them in tidily. The long journey resumed. Allied planes bombed the crammed train. After five days without food, they felt the train stop, this time for good. It was night, and the dreary hours of darkness passed while they sat caged in their carriages without any idea of what their fate would be. It was only when daylight came that they saw the guards had all vanished. And then tanks appeared, their insignia a white star, and the nightmare was over. An American soldier tossed a can of battle rations to Lazar and he ate and survived; others went to a nearby village where they were given heavy food and they ate and died.

Although he tried desperately to forget—through the years of reunion with his father, return to Czechoslovakia, completion of high school in 1948, emigration to Israel, service in *Zahal* (Israeli Defense Force), and employment by the airline—he never did. Most of all he couldn't forget his mother and the little brother and sister who in one ghastly second were torn from him and his father and sent to die. Nor could he forget the others, the ones who died of starvation and the ones who were mowed down by bullets. And now he, Aharon Lazar, condemned to death and saved by a miracle, would take part in bringing to account for his murderous acts the most bestial of all the Nazi criminals. The very thought was staggering.

When their plane touched down at the Buenos Aires airfield and they descended the first-class gangway— as guests of the airline they traveled first class—a photographer standing on the tarmac snapped them. Lazar shook with fright, sure that everyone knew he and Kedem had come to abduct Eichmann. It was only when the photographer came over and asked them to buy the pictures he had just taken that his mind was set at ease.

They were met at the airport by Esther Rosen and her husband. She had been a senior employee of the airline for many years until her husband moved to Buenos Aires to work for a private firm. The airline had asked her to help in certain matters relating to the special flight, particularly in obtaining permission to take paying passengers from Buenos Aires. One of her functions was to handle accommodations for the company's representatives, and she had reserved rooms for them at a hotel. She was very surprised, and a little offended, when Menashe suddenly turned up, introduced himself to Kedem according to a prearranged formula, and informed the visitors that they were staying at a different hotel.

Menashe gave Kedem the address of a café where someone would be waiting for him that evening after he had registered at the hotel.

———

Later that evening I waited for Kedem in a café. Before long his smiling face appeared in the doorway. He introduced me to his friend, Aharon Lazar. I explained to them that at subsequent meetings I would give them particulars of our special needs for the flight, but for the time being all they needed to know was that their help was required to create favorable conditions for taking Eichmann aboard the plane. We arranged the undercover liaison to be set up between us, and I explained to Lazar that at any meeting other than a previously planned rendezvous he was to behave as if he didn't know me. Kedem was familiar with the procedures, but this was Lazar's first experience in undercover activities—and he was obviously bewildered. One time I did meet him accidentally in the street and I could see it caused him considerable discomfort to have to walk past without greeting me.

Kedem told me about the arrangements made by the airline in Israel during the two days between my departure and his. At the end of our conversation I asked the two of them to get right to work securing all the requisite rights and authorizations for the flight. In addition I instructed them both, Lazar especially, to organize a thorough reconnaissance of the airfield and its various installations and to make a study of customs procedures.

By the time we separated it was already very late. We fixed another meeting the following evening for them to report back to me on their progress during the day and for me to give them further instructions.

---

That day, May 2, Zev Keren reached Buenos Aires after a very tense journey. He had a great deal of baggage—mainly accessories and equipment he had provided for the operation, including instruments he had had to improvise himself for the action—and during the entire flight he was in a state of suspense lest something happen to his precious equipment, knowing that without it the operation was liable to be bungled or delayed. When he changed planes in Europe he never took his eyes off his baggage until he had made certain that it had indeed been unloaded from the one plane and transferred to the next. On his safe arrival with all his equipment in Buenos Aires, he felt that within the framework of the greater operation he had just completed his own little operation. He hurried to his rendezvous at one of the cafés in the city. Menashe was waiting for him there, but all his efforts to make Zev laugh at his jokes were a waste of time—Zev was too impatient to see his beloved equipment transferred to a safe place. They collected everything and drove to *Maoz,* where they decided Zev would live and work. Except for short excursions to buy accessories and materials, Zev was going to be imprisoned there, getting things ready, until the eve of the operation.

---

Meanwhile, members of the advance party renewed their efforts to find more safe houses. Ehud and Kenet set out that morning for a holiday resort in the vicinity of Buenos Aires. For some reason, the agents took them for Germans and sent them to German-speaking landlords. They inspected quite a few houses, but once again the results were not wholly satisfactory. One place was in a good location but was too small to hold the captive and his guards; one house looked ideal in its construction but was too near others in the area; another villa, also appropriate for the purpose, was for sale only and not for rent.

While all this was going on Ezra moved in prearranged sequence from one city café to another, waiting for Gabi Eldad and Eli Yuval, who could be arriving any time from that day on. But his was also a wasted effort—they didn't come that day or the next.

---

It was Monday, and the surveillance of Klement's house had to be renewed. The operational trio set out in the evening for the target area. Their aim this time was to find out where Klement came from before boarding bus number 203 and at which stop he boarded the bus.

Kenet and Ezra went to the San Fernando railway station and chose an observation post beside the rail crossing at Routes 202 and 197. The gates were opened only to let busses pass, so every bus had to stop there. They reached the spot at six-forty-five and stayed there until after the time Klement usually returned home. They were quite let down when he didn't appear.

Ehud was stationed near the embankment, close to the yard of the Klement home. After the encounter with the two strangers on their earlier surveillance they wanted to spend as little time as possible on the embankment itself in order to avoid looking suspicious. So Ehud elected to hang around and allow circumstances to decide if he should climb up the embankment or not. Since nobody was in sight, he thought it would be all right for him to go back to their former observation spot and sit on the slope. Luck was with him—Klement made his daily appearance, but this time later than usual; it was close to eight o'clock when he reached the bus stop at the kiosk.

Later, Kenet and Ezra picked up Ehud and they returned to Buenos Aires. On the way, they were able to sum up that on five successive workdays they saw Klement coming home in the evening, on four occasions at seven-forty and once a few minutes before eight.

———————

On May 3 I went with Kenet on a morning reconnaissance of the target area. We drove past all the places that had any connection with the operation and its preliminary preparations. We reconnoitered the roads in the district, visited all the observation points, and finally drove past Klement's house. Traveling on Route 202, we had a good look at the kiosk and the patch of road between the kiosk and the house.

I must admit that when I saw the neglected appearance of the house and its surroundings I was filled with momentary misgivings—could Adolf Eichmann's home really look like that? Were it not for the considerable evidence we had, I would have started doubting whether Klement was really our man.

The reconnaissance led me to the conclusion that if further surveillances confirmed that we now had a "pattern" for part of Eichmann's daily life, the capture must be planned for the patch of road next to his house.

Ehud and Zev Keren—the latter would be taking part in the capture—were also out on reconnaissance in the target area at the time, because although we intended apprehending the man at night it was important for all participants to see the neighborhood in daylight.

In the afternoon I drove out of town with Menashe to inspect one of the houses offered to him by an agent. Time being short and the lack of safe houses a source of anxiety, I decided to check every likely proposal myself and to decide on the spot about renting the place. The area was suitable though not ideal, and the rent was not excessive. There were other houses near the villa, but this drawback could be handled even though it wasn't in keeping with the principles taught at the school for undercover activities. The house was worth considering for its convenience—travel was easy from the target area to the villa and from there to the airport. Its main shortcomings were the interior construction and lack of possibilities for adaptation as a suitable place of concealment for the captive and his guards. The place we needed would have to accommodate a number of occupants—the prisoner, the doctor, and the guards; it had to be able to stand the test of courtesy visits or simple curiosity on the part of the neighbors. The layout inside had to allow for a safe and suitable hiding place to be contrived—a place where a man might be kept under guard in case of a police search without endangering his health.

The villa didn't come up to these requirements. It stood on a narrow piece of ground, and the inside was not convenient for our needs. Nevertheless, rather than risk not finding something more suitable in time, I decided to take it. I told myself that if our further efforts turned up something better we would keep this one in reserve, but at least we now had something to make do with.

Menashe made the deal on the spot, and the villa became ours. I gave it its code name: *Tira* (Palace).

Toward evening the operational trio went to the target area again in another attempt to discover where Klement boarded bus 203. This time Ehud went to the bus terminal in the township of Carupa, Kenet took up his post at the Carupa railway station, and Ezra watched the station at San Fernando.

When the bus left the Carupa terminal Ehud was sitting inside, watching for the stop where Klement got on. He chose a time that fitted in with their previous observations, but Klement didn't appear anywhere along the journey to San Fernando.

Meanwhile Kenet was waiting for the trains arriving at Carupa. When two trains came and went without a sign of Klement, Kenet boarded the third, the seven-forty-five, and traveled to San Fernando; Klement wasn't on that train either.

Ultimately they took to their cars—Ehud and Ezra in one and Kenet in the other—and drove to Klement's neighborhood. Near the kiosk they saw him walking along Route 202 toward Garibaldi Street, just as he did every day.

This was the sixth time they had seen him coming home the same way.

———

For Kedem and Lazar, too, that May 3 was a day of great activity. In the morning they visited the head offices of Argentina's national airline to ask for assistance in arrangements for the special flight. For example, they inquired about spare parts for Britannia aircraft. The airline people explained that they themselves didn't fly Britannias but that a private Argentine company at the airport did. Kedem and Lazar were given permission to use the Telex to communicate with the directors of their airline in Israel.

They went to Ezeiza airport to meet with the representative of the private company. He welcomed them cordially and told them he had a stock of spare parts and even a reserve Britannia engine, which he was willing to put at the disposal of their company.

The two visitors went next to introduce themselves to the employees of the national airline and the representatives of the airport authorities. Wherever they went they were received with great courtesy, and routine procedures at the airfield were explained to them.

It was all quite straightforward until just before they left the airfield. At the last moment Kedem was informed that the Argentine protocol officials for the anniversary celebration would not be able to receive the Israeli delegation before two o'clock on the afternoon of May 19—indeed, to make things easier and assure a suitable reception, it would be better if the delegation arrived no earlier than five o'clock. This meant that the special flight would have to be delayed a whole week.

Late that evening I was sitting in a café with Ehud and Kenet, waiting for Kedem and Lazar. Before Kedem even reached our table I could see something was wrong. He started talking before he sat down, and as soon as I heard what he had to say I knew we were facning the inevitable. Even if I thought there was any prospect of inducing the Argentine authorities to change their stand I wouldn't do anything about it, because I wanted most of all to avoid drawing attention to the special flight. At the same time, it was clear to me that putting off the operation would involve risks —not to mention the negative psychological effect it would have on the task force. I told Kedem he must inform all who were affected by this turn of events, in Israel and in Argentina, that they must reconcile themselves to the new schedule and see to it that the plane arrived at the hour appointed by the Argentine authorities, even if this meant further inconvenience to the airline in upsetting its timetable once more.

When the others left, I sat alone and thought about the effect the delay would have on the capture operation. It was perfectly justifiable to assume, from the results of the six consecutive surveillances, that there would be no change in Klement's daily routine up to the day set for the operation—exactly one week away. But how could we be sure that Klement's routine would continue for two weeks running? How could we be sure that after a certain period he might not be put on a different shift? And what would happen if he changed jobs altogether or took ill?

And that wasn't all: if we postponed the operation for a week the surveillances would have to be prolonged accordingly, and this meant an increased risk of being spotted by Klement himself, or his neighbors, or other passers-by.

There was still another consideration: our men were nearing the limits of their physical and mental potential, and I knew it would be hard on them to be burdened with another week of such severe strain.

I turned it over and over in my mind, time after time I weighed all the factors, until at last I hammered out a decision: the capture must be carried out on the date planned or we might miss a unique opportunity.

I was all too aware of the psychological stress involved in keeping Eichmann in secret custody for an extra week, while not knowing what was happening outside or how the relatives and friends were reacting. But I had to choose between two evils—the danger of a long drawn-out period of undercover imprisonment in a strange country under difficult security conditions and the danger of missing the one-time chance of bringing the monster in charge of the "Final Solution" to trial in an Israeli court of justice. In short, the choice was between a risk which, no matter how prolonged, was only temporary and a sin for which there could never be any atonement.

The next morning I gave the men of the force instructions to act as if nothing had happened and to make ready for the capture operation on the day we had appointed—May 10, 1960.

On May 4 Ehud and Menashe went out in the morning to see a house recommended by one of the real-estate agents. Judging by the description we were given, it should have been the answer to all our prayers. Even the district was right, for although the house was far from the capture area, the approach to it was easy and the road from the house to the airport was a good one. When they got there Ehud and Menashe saw that the agent hadn't exaggerated the virtues of the place. It was spacious, with several wings, and stood in a large garden which hid it from the eyes of the neighbors. For our requirements it was the peak of perfection—but its perfection included a servant who was both watchman and gardener.

When I heard about it I went with Ehud and Kenet to see it for myself. It was wonderful. It might have been specially planned as a safe house for such an operation as ours. The structure was asymetrical, with a maze of rooms in which a number of persons could disappear; many hiding places would delay even police inspection.

It was awkward that the house was a few hours' drive from Klement's house, but this defect could become an advantage once the captive was brought safely to the new house. I thought that even if there were an immediate hue and cry after the capture, it was doubtful that it would extend to an area so far removed from Klement's home.

Everything was fine, except for the watchman-gardener. Needless to say, we couldn't bring a prisoner to the new house and keep him there without this watchman's knowledge; and even if we did manage to delude him about what was going on under his very nose, we had to anticipate the contingency that he might afterward reconstruct events which seemed peculiar to him at the time and perhaps also be able to identify all or some of the occupants of the house.

This worrisome problem was doubly important in view of the necessity of keeping our prisoner under safe house arrest for a longer period than we had expected before the special flight was postponed, and though I didn't know at that juncture how we were going to solve it, I wasn't prepared to let the house go. I thought it could at least serve as an alternative in case of need. I hoped we might still find a way of getting rid of the watchman somehow, if not for the whole period of the operation then at least for part of it. So I told Menashe to rent the house.

We gave this safe house, about two hours' drive from *Tira,* the code name *Doron* (Gift).

# 15

Kenet and Ezra spent the whole morning of May 4 in another survey of the target area. They checked possible approaches and marked out routes for an orderly retreat—or an emergency getaway, in case of failure.

Toward evening the operational detail went to the target area. On the road between the center of San Fernando and Klement's house two policemen were stopping all cars, inspecting vehicle registrations and drivers' licenses, and searching some of the cars. When they saw that the members of the detail were foreigners they allowed them to continue.

Beginning at six-thirty, Ehud, Kenet, and Ezra boarded three consecutive number 203 busses at their point of origin in Carupa. Ehud and Ezra traveled as far as Bancalari without coming across Klement. When Kenet climbed on the bus at Carupa he found Klement sitting there. So it was now evident that Klement's bus journey started at this point, but the question remained: Where had he come from? Or was he perhaps working in Carupa?

Kenet stayed on the bus as far as the San Fernando stop and then got off. He didn't want to risk continuing to the kiosk with Klement, nor did he want to travel on in the emptying bus right up to the end of the line. He knew he would still have to do more roaming around in the neighborhood and had no desire to call attention to himself.

In the meantime, Ehud and Ezra went back to their

car, which they had parked in the vicinity of Bancalari, and started driving along Route 202 toward the kiosk and the Klement home. When they reached the corner of Garibaldi Street they saw Klement walking toward his house—this was the seventh time.

All the effort expended in tracking Klement's starting point had one aim: to find out if there might be an alternative site of capture, farther from the man's house.

———

For two days we had been waiting for Gabi Eldad and Eli Yuval at the planned meeting places, and their failure to appear was beginning to cause us a certain amount of anxiety—not that we were concerned about their safety; we knew that fellows like that don't "get lost." We were, however, worried that their lateness might affect the timetable of the operation. Furthermore, the men of the advance party were already exhausted and needed reinforcements to share the burden and the responsibility.

This evening, however, Ehud's vigil, at Café Opera, was not in vain. At exactly nine o'clock Gabi and Eli walked into the café. They looked tired and their clothes were a mess, for they had come straight from the airport without changing, but broad smiles spread over their faces as they caught sight of Ehud. They related their adventures in a few sentences: at first Eli had trouble with his documentation, then they had difficulty getting seats on a plane so soon before the anniversary celebrations; and to crown it all Gabi had had an attack of food poisoning and couldn't eat anything but toast for several days.

Still, in spite of their fatigue, they were impatient to hear a full report. They had left Israel immediately on receipt of Ehud's message that Klement's whereabouts were known and conditions were favorable for his capture, and during the journey they had been cut off from all sources of information. Now, listening to Ehud's progress report, their fatigue seemed to vanish, and after a light meal they begged Ehud to take them on an immediate tour of the Klement neighborhood.

He tried to persuade them that they were too exhausted, but they would not be put off. Late at night the three of them went on a reconnaissance of San Fernando, and on the way Gabi told Ehud about the equipment he had prepared which was due to arrive on the special plane.

---

The morning of May 5 was devoted to a thorough discussion at *Maoz,* with all the members of the task force present—except Yitzhak, who was still running around tirelessly looking for houses and cars. This was my first meeting with Gabi and Eli since their arrival.

We analyzed the results of the surveillances and their effect on the detailed planning of the capture. Each man gave a detailed progress report on his own field of competence—equipment, safe houses, cars. As this information was summed up, the task force passed from the preparations stage to the actual planning of the operation.

That afternoon Ehud took Gabi and Eli on a daylight reconnaissance of the target area and afterward visited the two safe houses, *Tira* and *Doron.*

In the evening Eli made his first surveillance on the railway embankment, with Ehud again acting as guide. Once again Klement appeared at the usual time, and Eli had his first view of Ricardo Klement.

---

At this point I turned my attention to the arrangements for Eichmann's prolonged imprisonment. I knew that the difficulties would be many and varied, but we had no choice. We had to be sure that the house appeared to be the home of innocent tourists, that there would be no shortage of food for the prisoner and his guards, and that the external cover could be maintained, especially for the neighbors. This meant having a woman on the premises, so I transmitted an urgent message to Ankor to send us Dina Ron immediately.

---

May 5 was also the day Shalom Dani arrived in Buenos Aires with all his precious equipment. When he

set out he was laden with numerous suitcases, pack-
ages, and boxes marked FRAGILE, and both hands were
full of bags and bundles. The airline employee who
handled the belongings and papers of the thin, be-
spectacled passenger with the refined and somewhat
bashful expression, didn't have to look at his passport
to know his profession: the canvases, paints, brushes,
and an easel protruding from his baggage spoke for
themselves.

The weight was way above the allowance. The clerks
tried to be accommodating but were forced to make
him pay a considerable excess; they were apologetic
when they had to tell him how much it would cost to
freight his baggage such a great distance. But Shalom
wasn't concerned about the expense; he had one concern and only one: that his beloved cargo reach its destination safely.

He'd had a difficult time. With near superhuman effort he had collected the equipment he needed and con-
scientiously packed it all himself. Part of his luggage
consisted of legitimate tools and materials. His problem was how to conceal among them a complete set of
strange and unusual instruments which constituted the
workshop of a forger of documents. Shalom didn't rest
until he had packed his materials in such a way that
they could pass frontier controls and inspections in perfect safety.

From the moment the flight began he did little but
sleep. He knew very well that the success of the operation would depend to a large extent on the success of
his documentation, and this success would have to depend on his physical ability to withstand all the demands that would be made on him. He had experienced
enough operations in faraway lands, cut off from contact with the home base, to know what was in store for
the documentation man in such cases. He was determined to stand up to every test, because this operation
was more important in his eyes than all previous ones.

The crew members were courteous and indulgent to
the young artist. They could see he was very tired and

didn't want to be pestered, so they left him alone when
he was reluctant to get out for a bit of exercise at the
intermediate stations; the plane made stops in Lisbon,
Dakar, Recife, Rio de Janeiro, and Montevideo, but
Shalom mostly preferred to remain in the cabin and
guard his valuable equipment. He got off the plane only
once on the way, and that time took all his hand luggage with him.

The eccentric artist had no trouble clearing his baggage through customs at Buenos Aires. Two hours after the plane landed Shalom Dani was at *Maoz,* with
all his tools and accessories.

------

After cabling the airline in Israel about the unavoidable postponement of the special flight, Kedem and Lazar carried on with their surveillance at the airfield.
Lazar soon became thoroughly familiar with the airfield, its points of access and all its installations. As
an added bonus, he got to be friendly with several of
the men responsible for fueling, ground services, maintenance, loading and unloading—and also with the police and customs people. Following my instructions,
Kedem and Lazar looked for the best place to park the
plane. I explained to them that we required a spot far
from the airport buildings and inquisitive eyes. They
discovered that the maintenance area allotted to the private Argentine airline was relatively far from the center of the field. It was simplicity itself to explain to
the airport authorities that our airline was interested in
leaving the plane in the maintenance area of a company which had Britannia parts available. Our operational team inspected the proposed parking site and
found it suitable.

While Lazar was widening his network of connections at the airfield, Kedem was trying to obtain permission for the special plane to carry passengers on the
homeward journey from Buenos Aires. I thought it
would seem strange to the Argentine authorities if nothing was done about this, as no airline would be content
to have a plane return empty from such a long flight.

For the time being, it was only a question of obtaining permission; the decision to sell tickets for the actual flight could be put off till later.

On the morning of May 5 Kedem received a cable from the airline in Israel saying that the suggested change of schedule would present great difficulties and they were therefore not inclined to authorize it—unless they were told that such an authorization was imperative. Kedem brought the cable to me for instructions. I told him that, in my opinion, there was no hope of influencing the protocol officials to change their decision, and any attempt to press them was liable to put an undesirable strain on our relations with them. I repeated my earlier argument that it was inadvisable for the flight to become the subject of undue discussion. I therefore told Kedem to inform the airline in unmistakable terms that there was no alternative but to arrange the flight in accordance with the wishes of the hosts —to land on May 19. We took it for granted that the directors would understand that the cable was sent with my knowledge and that its contents were dictated by unalterable operational necessity. Sure enough, the afternoon of May 6 Kedem brought me the management's reply confirming the new date of the flight.

---

Meanwhile, Dani had unpacked his baggage at *Maoz* and started setting up his workshop. He hadn't seen a single street or house in Buenos Aires by daylight, but there he was already hunched over a table covered with forms, seals, certificates, and papers.

Zev Keren worked in the next room. His associates never ceased to marvel at his sensible solutions—simple and easy to put into practice—to the technical problems they brought him. Zev would occasionally glance into Shalom's room to see if everything was all right or if he needed anything, and sometimes he would spend a few minutes watching his friend work. He was astounded to see how in a few minutes a piece of paper changed into a document indistinguishable from the original Shalom was copying. Shalom didn't need printed forms, he could draw printed letters so perfectly that only a laboratory inspection could detect that the paper had never been in contact with a printing press.

Gabi Eldad supervised all operational and technical problems at *Maoz*. He checked to see that everything was progressing according to plan and that every detail was being given the requisite attention in the order of precedence which he, as commander of the operation, could decide on better than the others.

Zev and Shalom left *Maoz* only to purchase essential equipment and materials. All who came there brought food for these two, who were so engrossed in their work that they had no thoughts for themselves.

I visited them frequently to see how things were going. Shalom would discuss in detail his problems and explain the solutions he devised. It was impossible not to feel a deep affection for this wonderfully modest man who never asked for anything and who never complained. Although no stray visitors were anticipated, the implements of all kinds scattered throughout the flat established beyond doubt that the place belonged to an artist. The stands, paintings, frames, and palettes lying helter-skelter were better evidence than a hundred witnesses.

———

The morning of May 6 Kenet and Ezra organized a reconnaissance in the vicinity of our new house *Doron* to find a safe route for taking the captive from there to the airport.

That same morning I went to see a building that was for sale in the city itself. Since *Tira* and *Doron* we hadn't had a single decent offer, despite all the efforts of Yitzhak and Menashe, but we hadn't given up trying to find something more suitable. This one was a new residential building consisting of several apartments. It was appropriate only for taking a prisoner into a building in one of the centers of the town and getting him out again later, but during my tour of the place it suddenly struck me that it could prove to be a valuable possession if the operation took an unexpected turn. I walked all over, upstairs and downstairs, inspecting the means of access from floor to floor and from unit to unit, to the astonishment of my companions who couldn't understand why I was so interested in the structure of a building that didn't seem to meet our requirements.

But the idea that flashed through my mind was that if we should have to hold the prisoner in Buenos Aires for a long time, this place could be used as a fortress and secure hiding place. What I thought was that a totally "innocent" family would live in one apartment, and we would install an inside passage from there to another apartment, which would supposedly be unoccupied. In the second apartment we could build a hideout which could be entered only from the first apartment. The size and interior layouts of these apartments made them particularly suitable for the kinds of alterations I had in mind. Through the "innocent" family in the first unit we could get supplies and maintain communication with the outside world. I estimated that in an emergency we would even be able to carry out the alterations while the prisoner was already inside. I also foresaw no difficulty in bringing in an "operational" family who would lead a seemingly normal life and whose presence in Buenos Aires would appear reasonable and natural.

I was planning all this as a form of insurance in case a mishap resulted in pursuit. Furthermore, if a last-minute hitch prevented us from flying Eichmann out on the special plane, we might have to keep him hidden for a few weeks until he could be taken out by sea. In such an eventuality, I thought, it would be easier to hide in a populated area. And I was considering another function for this building: if there was such a massive response to Eichmann's disappearance that roads to the other safe houses became dangerous, this one could be used as an emergency refuge.

To keep the building available for us for several weeks, I told the agents that we liked the place, but before we could make a final decision, we had to get in touch with relatives overseas. In the meantime, we wanted an option to purchase and an exclusive right to make use of the building until the reply came from overseas. The owners agreed, after fixing the amount to be paid in case the sale did not go through.

The keys were handed to us the same day. The code name this time was *Ramim* (Heights).

———

Ehud and Gabi spent their day scouring the city for cars, for it had become obvious that Yitzhak couldn't handle this job alone. The frequency of our reconnaissances in the target area necessitated changing cars often. Since we had to spread our business over several rental agencies, and since we were always afraid that these agencies might be connected in some way, we had to assume different identities each time. This put an added burden on the men and also demanded the preparation of appropriate documents on short notice. Every time a car was rented a large deposit had to be paid. Clients ordinarily arranged this through a bank or the firms they worked for, but we were compelled to pay cash, and generally in foreign currency. The mere fact that we had such large sums to deposit was, of course, enough to make us noticeable.

But still the worst part was the terrible condition of the rented cars. We were forced to minimize the risk of breakdowns by buying tires and spare parts for several of our cars, and some we even had overhauled to make them a little more reliable. But we had to take care to conceal the fact that we had made these repairs at our own expense, for this would seem to be very odd behavior indeed to any of the agencies, and they might become suspicious—or at least begin to doubt our sanity.

———

In the evening Kenet went alone to San Fernando. Since all the others were so overburdened with practical preparations for the operation itself it was difficult to find a second man for the job. Klement again appeared at the regular time and walked along the usual path to his house on Garibaldi Street.

Later, at a session with the operational team, I recapitulated the date we had:

"We have a pattern covering one portion of Ricardo

Klement's daily life," I said. "On nine workdays between April 26 and May 6, he was seen returning home at exactly the same time, seven-forty in the evening. Only once did he depart from his usual habit, and even then he was only ten minutes late. In each case he came by bus number 203 from the direction of San Fernando and alighted at the stop near the kiosk on Route 202. From there he walked to the corner, turned into Garibaldi Street, and went into the house. Not once did he change his route from the bus to the house, a distance of over a hundred yards.

"The whole of that section of the road is thoroughly familiar to the men on surveillance, and it is suitable as the site of the capture. Thus there is no point in looking for other sites, nor any need to continue checking back on Klement's trail to find out where he starts his homeward journey. It's better to concentrate on the section known to us and to prepare an operational plan based on this knowledge."

This approach was accepted unanimously. During our discussion we also decided that if we found nothing better, *Doron* would be used as the primary safe house, and Klement would be taken directly there after the capture. *Tira* was settled on as the secondary safe house. Ezra and Zev would in the meantime move to *Doron*, and Ezra would ostensibly be the tenant who was waiting for a party of guests to join him.

One man was still missing from the operational team: the doctor. Like the rest of the team, he went first to Europe, where Nahum Amir met him and gave him instructions and the necessary papers and flight tickets for his journey. He knew several languages, which made it easy to produce new documentation for him. He took off for South America earlier than originally planned, but a mechanical fault caused a twenty-four-hour delay.

When the doctor arrived at *Maoz*, the morning of May 7, he was amazed to see Shalom and Zev in their workshops. This wasn't at all like his mental picture of undercover activities in a foreign country—the men were working as calmly as they might in their own homes.

———————

Gabi, Kenet, and Ehud went out in the afternoon to find easy motor routes from Klement's house to both *Doron* and *Tira*. The doctor went along to familiarize himself with the scene of action and with the proposed residence after the capture.

The same morning we rented the two cars to be used in the operation. We sought nice-looking cars, which tend to be less suspicious than dilapidated ones. The cars also had to be large enough to hold all the operators—and Klement—comfortably and securely. Needless to say, we tried to find cars in good mechanical condition so that we could be sure there would be no breakdowns during the operation. Getting the cars was indescribably difficult. After many days of canvassing every car-rental agency in Buenos Aires, we felt like giving up when we chanced upon two cars at once. These were suitable but far from ideal, and as soon as the deal was made we surreptitiously put each into a garage for a thorough overhaul.

The deposits we paid amounted to many thousands of dollars in cash, for the owners, apparently afraid that the peculiar tourists who were so enthusiastic about large shiny automobiles might forget to return them, raised the amount. We had no choice, we needed transportation—and now we had it.

Yitzhak Nesher found another car in a small garage. It was an old American one, a 1953 model. In spite of its many shortcomings, the owner of the garage hesitated to rent it; he may have been afraid it would be stolen. In reply to Yitzhak's question as to how much he had to put down as a deposit on the car, the man—obviously trying to get rid of this nuisance of a tourist—mentioned the sum of five thousand dollars. He was flabbergasted when the eccentric tourist returned after a while with a packet of twenty-dollar bills. The incident aroused the man's suspicions; he drove with Yitzhak to one of the banks, where he submitted the packet of bills for inspection. Yitzhak sat like a cat on hot bricks, waiting for the outcome of the lengthy and scrupulous inspection. Half an hour later the garage owner came out of one of the inner offices of the bank and announced that all was in order.

They returned to the garage, where the owner put the dollars into his iron cashbox. Yitzhak took possession of the "old American" we needed so badly and drove away post-haste. This was to be the capture car.

# 16

As the crucial day grew nearer, I became increasingly conscious of the fact that far too many people were passing through *Maoz*. The apartment had already served far too long as the center for our undercover activities, and it was more and more difficult to conceal all the products of the technical workshop and documentation plant. We would be in a very tight spot if for some reason a search were sprung on us during any of the periods when the men were working or during planning sessions when maps and lists were strewn all about. Consequently, I decided to reduce the number of visits to a minimum and to move some of the activities to the other safe houses.

May 7 was a Saturday so there were no surveillances in the target area that day. In the evening I called a meeting at *Maoz* and announced that it was essential for the men to avoid meeting there except when matters concerning documentation and equipment compelled them to appear in person. In every other instance, I said, requests and uncompleted orders would henceforth be passed on by a special liaison man who would be appointed for the purpose. All operational discussion and exercises, I said, would in future take place at *Doron*. Zev Keren would continue to work at *Maoz* for the time being but would move into *Doron* with Ezra. Only two people would stay on at *Maoz*: the "tenants," Menashe Talmi and Shalom Dani.

At that same meeting we resolved that the capture would be carried out on May 10.

From then on we met at various cafés and restaurants. For me this meant a lot of wandering around in the central areas of the city, looking for suitable meeting places. I made lists of the names and addresses of each of my stops for all those who might need to know where I was at any hour of the day.

I would spend the first half of every hour in one of the cafés and use the second half to walk to the next one. If a meeting lasted longer than half an hour I would take a taxi. At restaurants I would spend a full hour and then proceed to the next place by taxi. I tried to work it out for each rendezvous point to be a half-hour walk from the previous one, to allow me time to determine that I wasn't being shadowed, and to make sure that I wouldn't be seen for too long in any one neighborhood. With very few exceptions, each meeting place was used only once.

In Argentina the café is something of an institution. Every neighborhood has its own café, with a drinks counter and a large mirror on the wall behind it, and usually old-fashioned, dark-brown furnishings. Many Argentinians love to sit for hours, sipping hot aromatic drinks and chatting with family and friends. It was thus unlikely that our meetings would attract attention, even if a large group of us were to gather around one table.

At many of the cafés in Buenos Aires an opaque glass partition separates the dining room into two sections. The smaller of these sections, marked FAMILIAS (families), is intended not only for families but also for couples and for unescorted women who don't want to be bothered by men. A man on his own doesn't usually sit there, just as a woman on her own won't sit in the larger public section.

I found out a little too late about this particular custom. In my hunt for a quiet corner as far from the entrance as possible, I instinctively chose the FAMILIAS part of the café, which was generally fairly empty even when the larger section was crowded. As a result, it seemed to me that all the people there, including the waiters, kept turning to look at me a little wonderingly, but I thought this must be because I was a foreigner who didn't understand the language and because I isolated myself in a quiet corner, unusual behavior in a country where everybody is very sociable. However, although my behavior went against convention, no comment was ever made to me. The Argentinians, whose courtesy is almost a reflex, probably realized that my rudeness was inadvertent and would never dream of embarrassing a stranger who wasn't familiar with their customs.

———

Though the lease on *Doron* commenced May 8, Zev had moved in the evening before, with some of his equipment. He was now busy preparing the place for a prisoner and making it soundproof and impervious to a police search. The means at his disposal were limited and time was short; but worse, there was the ever-present fear that the watchman-gardener might enter the house unexpectedly in a desire to be helpful. Now and then we would send him on long errands to keep him away from the house. Another restriction was that we dared not to do any obvious damage to the walls or furniture. Here Zev's resourcefulness stood him in good stead and he always found a solution for every problem. He was actually safeguarding himself to a certain extent, because he was the one elected to stand guard inside the hideout in case of a police search.

In the afternoon Gabi, Ehud, Kenet, and Eli drove to *Doron,* each in a car loaded with equipment and supplies. All but Eli arrived without mishap. They waited some time for him, and when he still didn't turn up they began to think something had gone wrong and decided to go out and look for him. Ehud checked the roads around *Doron* but saw no sign of his missing friend.

Eli wasn't very familiar with the road to *Doron,* so it was decided that he should follow Ehud. At one intersection Ehud crossed, but Eli was held up when the light changed to red, and lost him. While trying to catch up with Ehud he made a wrong turning and had to stop at a police roadblock. His first fears were for his friends—he thought they'd been arrested and now he too was going to be caught, but it was too late to make a run for it.

He soon realized, however, that the inspection had nothing to do with him but concerned some local affair. At that time the opponents of the regime in Argentina were engaging in many acts of violence. When his turn came to show his papers, the police found that his driver's license was torn. There followed a discussion between him and the police inspector in sign language. Eli played the part of an innocent, helpless foreigner with great success and was allowed to proceed. He had to use his natural sense of direction—well developed, fortunately—to find his own way back to *Doron*.

All the members of the task force who would be taking an active part in the capture assembled at *Doron* in the late afternoon. Two possible plans were outlined:

Plan A proposed that the team which was to make the capture would wait for Klement in a car parked on Garibaldi Street about ten yards from where it branched off from Route 202. This vehicle would be facing toward the Klement house. The second car, which would act as escort, was to be parked on Route 202 about thirty yards before the corner of Garibaldi Street. It would face the Garibaldi corner, and during the capture its headlights would be turned on to blind Klement and passing motorists. If there were any complications at all, the men in the second car would rush to the aid of the captors in the first one. After the capture, the second car would follow the first until it was out of the danger area.

While they were discussing Plan A, it struck them that the presence of a car with passengers in it on the road Klement always took when walking from the bus stop to his house was liable to startle and alarm him, and he'd manage somehow to run away under cover of darkness. There were strong grounds for their fears, but Eli took a firm stand. He gave psychological reasons for his insistence on the plan. He maintained that a man who had, over a long period of time, been used to walking along the same paved road to his home wouldn't lightly change his habits, especially if he was a German with a military background.

He also maintained that if Klement became suspicious his self-respect would make him ashamed to flinch from walking some dozen meters to the safety of his house.

Eli was adamant on the full execution of Plan A, and the others decided to accept it, especially since he was the one who would be making the first assault on Eichmann.

Plan B proposed that the first car would wait on Garibaldi Street facing Route 202, and the second car would park on Route 202. They would park in such a way that the men in either car could view the occupants of the other. The driver of the second car would signal with his headlights as soon as Klement alighted from the bus and started walking along Route 202. Simultaneously, the first car would start moving slowly, so that it could stop beside Klement as soon as he left the main road and turned into Garibaldi Street; the captors would leap out, overpower him, and thrust him into the car. While they were doing this those in the second car would again use their headlights to blind the motorists on the highway. They would then catch up with the first one and escort it to the safe house.

Both plans included the staging of a breakdown as the explanation for parking at the side of the road.

We also sketched three possible withdrawal routes:

a) In the direction of Buenos Aires, along Route 202 by way of the intersection at Route 197 and toward *Tira*.

b) Along Route 202 toward Bancalari and from there to *Tira*.

c) Along Route 202, via San Fernando and Vicente Lopez, to Buenos Aires and *Doron*.

It was concluded that if anything went wrong at the moment of capture Klement would be taken to the reserve safe house *Ramim*. This plan was based on the premise that if the capture was immediately discovered and the captors pursued it would be advisable to shorten the journey and to go deeply underground. We had to bear in mind the possibility of a protracted period of concealment.

During the course of that Sunday, Gabi, Ehud, Eli, Zev, and the doctor practiced overpowering a man with maximum speed and efficiency and minimum force, taking care at the same time to avoid inflicting any injury liable to endanger their own safety or their captive's well-being. Gabi was aiming for a very high standard of operational efficiency and perfect coordination among the participants, so the exercise was repeated over and over again until he was satisfied with their speed and coordination.

At an evening briefing the capture plans were reexamined and the withdrawal routes rechecked. We repeated all the various contingency plans. At the end of that long and wearying day the operations men came to the conclusion that the capture would have to be put off from May 10 to May 11. Last-minute investigations revealed that certain items of equipment were still lacking and that it would be difficult to finish all the other complicated preparations before May 10. But these weren't our chief difficulties. The overwhelming problem was that the crushing exertions of the last few days had totally exhausted the men.

The team also decided during that session that *Doron* would not do as a safe house, because there was no way of getting rid of the watchman. If anyone still had hopes of an eleventh-hour solution to this problem, the experience of the past few days had shown that the man simply would not leave the premises. The long distance between the target area and *Doron* could also make the journey from the scene of capture to the safe house extremely risky. All these considerations convinced Gabi and his men that *Tira* was preferable to *Doron,* even though it had fewer structural advantages.

The operational team's decisions were subject to my confirmation, and on May 9 they were brought to me for authorization.

At ten o'clock in the morning, at Café Molino, one of the largest cafés in the city, I received three guests —Gabi, Ehud, and Kenet. They wanted to tell me their reasons for suggesting the postponement of the operation, but I told them that one reason was good enough for me—the exhaustion of the operational team. All the same, I couldn't hide my disappointment. My friends knew my basic attitude: once everything was ready for an operation it should not be postponed even an hour because we could never be sure we weren't missing a one-time opportunity. In this case, things were different. Operators dare not undertake an action that demands supreme physical and mental exertion without every certainty that they are fit to stand up to it.

I therefore authorized a postponement to May 11 and gave my consent to *Tira* as the first choice for a safe house.

———

The race against time started anew. *Tira* had to be made ready, an emergency hiding place prepared, and all the equipment accumulated at *Doron* transferred there. Every journey from one house to the other meant the loss of several precious hours, but Zev undertook the new assignment with determination. *Tira* had fewer possibilities than *Doron,* but at least he could work there without having to watch out for prying eyes.

A new obstacle cropped up at the last moment: serious mechanical faults in the second car developed, and we had to put it into a garage to have the gearbox replaced. At the same time we took the opportunity to change the tires which hadn't been replaced previously. Zev installed the operational equipment in both cars.

In the afternoon Gabi and the doctor reconnoitered the roads between the target area and *Tira*. On the way Gabi explained various operational details that had a bearing on the doctor's functions.

Toward evening Gabi, Ehud, and the doctor raced

to San Fernando to take a look at Klement for the tenth time, but they were held up by the heavy traffic on the roads and must have just missed him.

The same evening Ehud went on a reconnaissance of San Miguel and found a road linking Route 197 to *Tira*, a discovery which might prove most useful at the time of withdrawal.

Late in the evening the whole task force gathered for my last briefing. Since *Tira* had been chosen as the future "prison" for Eichmann and his guards, I wanted as little movement as possible about the house, so we met at *Ramim*. That evening I strove to impress upon the men the unique moral and historical significance of what they were doing. They were chosen by destiny, I said, to guarantee that one of the worst criminals of all time, who for years had succeeded in evading justice, would be made to stand trial in Jerusalem, the capital city of the nation which lost six million of its people to the murder apparatus he controlled. For the first time in history the Jews would judge their assassins; and for the first time the world would hear, and the young generation in Israel would hear, the full story of the edict of annihilation against an entire people. Everything depended, I explained, on the action we were about to take. It was a sad thing that in fulfilling such an exalted moral and national mission we would have to resort to force and strike an indirect blow at a friendly state. We were by no means happy about it, but for us this was a necessity and no censure could be attached to it. We deeply regretted that we were compelled to use such methods, but there was no way of serving morality and justice other than through this specific operation.

After this introduction I told them I had implicit faith in their ability and resourcefulness and was certain of their success. And then I gave them instructions in case of mishap. First, I said, once Eichmann was in our hands we must under no circumstances whatsoever let him go or allow him to escape, even if it should entail the arrest of one individual, or a few, or even the entire team involved in the capture. If anything should go wrong, the team must hold on to Eichmann until he is put into the hands of a competent authority. If the team was caught, all must admit they are Israelis, but they must make it clear that they are acting on their own initiative and that their sole motive is to ensure that the war criminal Adolf Eichmann is brought to trial.

I could sense that the men were all keyed up and that each was engrossed in moral stocktaking.

At this point Ezra Eshet asked a question. "How long do you think we'll have to sit in prison if we're caught?"

"A good few years," I replied.

Ezra then made a request on behalf of all of them: if such a thing happened, would I please give their love to their families and take care of their wives and children. I promised immediately, of course. No further questions were asked, and there was dead silence for a few minutes. Ezra had expressed the wishes of the whole group. It was clear to me that they were determined to continue the operation, come what may.

The rest of the group must get away by train to the interior of the country or to neighboring states. They would act similarly in case of mishap before apprehending Eichmann, or in the event he was able to escape capture by using physical force. If either of these two possibilities should occur, the men would have to find their own way out of Argentina. I presume, I said, that any hunt for us would start in Buenos Aires, at hotels and at the airport. It could quite safely be assumed that for the first few hours after the operation the trains would not be searched.

I was sure I had no need to give these instructions, for I believed, and so did my men, that we would succeed. This was no fantasy. The men had invested their strength, their spirit, and their intelligence in planning and preparing the operation down to its last infinitesimal detail, and I knew their capability could be relied upon.

Those last couple of days before the operation we rented a few more safe houses and apartments. Near *Tira* we found a spacious home that would have been suitable for housing the prisoner and his guards if not for the staff of servants which went with it.

As *Tira* might be too confined to accommodate Kenet, who was to be interrogator, and all the men who would be on guard duty, I thought we had better have another house nearby for those who didn't have to be at *Tira* all the time. The code name for the new house was *Elazar* (one of Aaron's sons).

In addition to the two apartments we had in the city—*Maoz* and *Ramim*—we rented two more as emergency reserves and as substitutes for *Maoz* should we be compelled to remain longer than anticipated. Their code names were *Moledet* (Homeland) and *Kohelet* (Ecclesiastes).

By the time of the operation we had seven places at our disposal. Yitzhak went to live openly at *Tira* on the morning of May 10. He played the role of the foreign businessman in South America who was taking a short holiday in Buenos Aires. He let it be known that he would be bringing a woman to the house who would not necessarily be his wife.

As zero hour drew near, I instructed all the men still lodging at hotels to check out and move into our own safe houses. There were several reasons for this. First of all, their daily program was unusual enough to cause curiosity among the hotel employees. And secondly, leaving now would prevent questions about why they disappeared on the very day of Klement's capture. I wasn't prepared to take a chance that the hotel staff would forget the peculiar habits of the guests who disappeared at the same time as Klement.

And so Gabi, Ehud, and Ezra stayed at *Ramim* the nights of May 9 and 10. The next day Zev, Ezra, and the doctor moved into *Tira,* and Ehud and Kenet settled themselves at *Elazar,* while Menashe Talmi and Shalom Dani remained on at *Maoz.* Gabi was to transfer from *Ramim* to *Tira* on May 11.

At that stage I was meeting Kedem and Lazar almost every day. One day they told me that a different parking spot would have to be found for our plane—the plan to leave it in the private Argentine airline's maintenance area had to be dropped because when Lazar went there he found the place surrounded by soldiers. When he asked what was going on, he was told that a few American U-2 spy planes had arrived. I agreed that we had to find some other place for our plane.

Later, Lazar suggested that the plane be parked at the other end of the airfield, in the area belonging to the Argentine national airline. This area, more than five hundred yards from the main airport building, had very few guards on duty at night. We even found we could approach it from the main road without having to go through the fenced-in section of the airport. After checking his information I approved the change, and Lazar attended to the formalities. The usual procedure at the airfield was for planes to be towed by tractor to the apron in front of the main building prior to take-off, and once there they were handed over to their crews. But, on my instructions, Lazar requested the field authorities to allow us to alter the procedure on the grounds that the tractor might damage the front wheels and that the plane could easily taxi onto the tarmac. There were no objections.

Since Lazar had proved himself to be in command of the situation, I thought Kedem had better return to Israel immediately after the capture to personally supervise all the preparations for the flight. I asked him to send Dan Avner to me as soon as he arrived in Tel Aviv. Kedem had been scheduled to leave on May 10, but when the capture was postponed until May 11 Kedem's departure was also put off for another day. I didn't want him to leave until the date of the capture was definite, but at the same time I wanted him to be out of the country before it was carried out, to avoid any suspicion of his having taken part in it. I told him that on the afternoon prior to his departure he should try to be seen by as many people as possible so that he would have an unshakable alibi. I arranged with Lazar

also that he should make a point of being in some
public place that same afternoon where he couldn't
fail to be seen by all his new friends.

It was May 10. Most of the men were already at *Tira*
completing the preparations for a possible siege after
the capture. Yitzhak, the official tenant of the house,
drove to the city to buy food, household utensils, and
heaters. On his way back, while still some distance
from the house, he collided with another car and both
vehicles were badly damaged—fortunately, both he and
the other driver came out of the accident with only
slight injuries. To avoid police intervention Yitzhak
took all the blame on himself and asked the other man
to give him an estimate of the damage to his car. Without any bargaining Yitzhak paid him the whole
amount in cash. He arrived back without the car and
the supplies. Ehud and Eli drove to the scene of the
accident, unloaded Yitzhak's car, and towed it to the
rental company.

Toward evening Gabi and Ehud went out on a reconnaissance of the roads from *Tira* to the target area.
They wanted to get to know the parallel roads so that
if necessary they could dodge pursuers by passing from
one road to another. They intended winding up their
reconnaissance with a surveillance in the vicinity of the
Klement home in order to obtain one last confirmation
of the man's habits.

The previous day's experience had taught them a
lesson, so they took care to be in the target area ahead
of time. When they arrived in San Fernando, however,
they saw a crowd ahead of them and soon found out
why: a scooter and car had crashed and a man had
been badly injured in the collision. As Gabi and Ehud
sat there, looking on, some of the bystanders opened
the door of their car, carried in the injured man, and
imperiously demanded to be driven to the hospital. By
the time they completed their act of mercy it was too
late to have any hope of seeing Klement.

They took a pretty dim view of this. Since Saturday

and Sunday were not working days, no surveillances had been maintained. On Monday they had come too late, and today, Tuesday, they missed Klement because of the accident. Could they still undertake the action after four consecutive days without surveillance?

Disappointed and disgruntled, they came to meet me at the café where I was scheduled to be at that hour. We went over the facts again: On nine working days Klement was seen arriving home at the same time. Nothing had happened in the last two days to indicate that Klement's habits had changed. It was only because they had arrived late that they had failed to see him.

I was strongly against the idea of putting the operation off for one more day. The advisability of an extra surveillance to confirm that the situation was unchanged didn't justify a postponement. I issued instructions for the capture to be put into effect as planned, on May 11. Gabi and Ehud beamed.

Dina Ron was the last to join the task force. On Friday, May 6, Ankor telephoned her at home and asked her to come to the office at four o'clock. The man who handled the operators' traveling arrangements was with Ankor when she arrived, and he was the first to speak.

"So, you're going?"

"I don't know a thing about it," Dina replied.

Miriam Savyon had joined them by then, and without any preamble she asked Dina, "Are you prepared to go overseas?"

"Yes."

"A cable has come from Isser. He wants you to leave without delay," Miriam said.

"Very well."

Miriam looked at Dina questioningly. "Don't you want to know where?"

"You'll tell me."

"What's your guess?"

Dina hardly paused. "Is it the place I came back from not long ago?" she asked.

"No. It's South America."

"Fine," Dina said without hesitation. "And what should I say at home?"

After some discussion it was decided that she should tell her family she was going to an international conference.

On Sunday, May 8, Miriam informed Dina that she must be in Buenos Aires on the evening of Tuesday, May 10, at the very latest. Someone would meet her in Europe with appropriate documentation and further details; he would be waiting for her in the lobby of a certain hotel and would find her with the help of the hotel staff.

Dina was given her operational instructions in Ankor's office. She was told that the day after her arrival in Buenos Aires she would meet someone she knew at either eleven in the morning or five in the afternoon, at one of four cafés she must go to in specific sequence.

Sunday afternoon she flew to Europe. She left her luggage at the airport and went to the travel agency whose address she had been given. She received a ticket to Santiago, Chile, on a flight which made a stop in Buenos Aires.

She then went to her rendezvous in the hotel lobby. Preferring not to approach the hotel staff, she surveyed the people sitting in the lobby until she noticed a man who appeared to be waiting for somebody. She went up to him and asked, "Are you waiting for somebody from Mrs. Savyon?"

"Yes, I am," the man replied courteously as he rose from his easy chair. "Please sit down." He gave her her papers and said, "I don't know your plans, but to be on the safe side I bought two tickets to the theater. Would you care to join me this evening?"

"I'm sorry," Dina replied, "but I can't. I must fly to Paris today."

Her polite escort went with her to the air terminal in the city. As they walked in, she heard her name—her new name, naturally—over the loudspeaker. The man accompanied her to the information counter and heard the clerk say, "The flight to Buenos Aires will leave on time, madam. There is no change in the schedule."

Dina blushed, but her companion, polite to the end, pretended not to have heard.

Despite the assurances of the clerk at the information desk, the plane was an hour late in taking off. On its arrival in Spain an announcement was made that it would be another four hours late in taking off. In fact she was held up there for twenty-four hours, and the entire journey was a continuous series of delays. At the next intermediate airport there was another two-hour delay, and by the time they reached Buenos Aires they were more than a day late. Instead of arriving on the evening of May 10, Dina arrived on May 11 at night, and when she went to reserve a room at the hotel she'd been instructed to go to, she was told it was full. So she had to go to another hotel.

# 17

During the morning of May 11 Zev completed Eichmann's detention "cell" at *Tira* and built an emergency
hideout. Considering the conditions he was working
under, he did wonders; all agreed that the hideout he
had installed would stand up to any routine police
search.

Then came a final inspection—of equipment, materials, and provisions. A few things were missing which
would be required before the operation and for the
first few days after it, and some of the men went out
to fill the gaps. Time was pressing, and all knew they
must hurry back to the base. At the same time they
were ordered to proceed with the utmost caution, since
on that particular day none of them could afford to
be mixed up in a road accident or even a minor traffic violation. At this stage we couldn't do without one
single person or one single vehicle—each and every
one of them had been taken into account for the operation.

Gabi, Ehud, Kenet, and Ezra drove to the city to
return the rented cars which weren't needed for the
capture itself. The task force kept the two operational
cars, and a third for general use. It was important
for us not to use any vehicle that could have been
seen at any time in the target area and could now be
recognized. The members of the team also changed
their appearance and were given new documents and
papers. From now on there would be no apparent

connection between the men who had been wandering around the target area, staying at hotels, making purchases at various places in the city, renting cars, and those who would be going out in the late afternoon to capture Eichmann.

That morning I left my hotel early, before the day staff came on duty. I didn't announce beforehand that I intended leaving. The night workers who made up my account were very sleepy when they totaled my bill and called a taxi to take me to the "railway station."

I deposited my belongings in a locker and set out, a completely free man, on a long tour of the cafés of Buenos Aires. It was a rainy day and my morning walk refreshed me. This time I directed my steps toward a distant area where I had not had any previous rendezvous, nor had the men of the task force ever had occasion to go to that quarter in spite of their many reconnaissances in its environs.

An hour later I reached the first café on my list. Despite the early hour it was already open—which was not just good fortune. On my list of hundreds of cafés I had noted opening and closing times next to their names and addresses. A single mistake on the list could cause a great deal of confusion and lead to a lot of running around and a great waste of time.

New contact arrangements had gone into effect that morning. The object of these was to make things difficult for anyone who might try to shadow me or any of the men on the operational or auxiliary teams. So far, anyone who needed me could find me in one of the cafés on the list, and they could all find each other in case of need. Now I was running a dual system of communications. I still visited the various cafés in sequence, but now these were closer to each other so that more frequent meetings could take place. Whereas previously I spent only the first half of every hour in a certain café, I could now maintain almost uninterrupted contact as it took me only about five minutes to get from one café to the next.

Also I put a contact man, Meir Lavi, on a "beat" parallel to mine, covering cafés on parallel streets. I knew his itinerary and he knew mine. And the whole task force knew how both of us were moving. They were told that if everything went according to plan they could come straight to me afterward, but if something went wrong they should go to the other man. These safety measures had to be meticulously observed. Similarly, I told them that if I saw that I was being shadowed, I would try to warn the liaison man and then disappear. So if any of them came to meet me and didn't find me they must go immediately to the contact man, who would pass on my warning and tell them where I would be after I had shaken my tail.

The contact man didn't have a clue about what sort of operation he was involved in. He swallowed the cover story I told him to explain why we were going to such lengths to safeguard ourselves, and it didn't take much to make him understand that on no account was he to divulge what he was doing.

For the concluding meeting with the operational team I chose a restaurant, so that we could talk while eating and thus save time. Gabi, Ehud, Kenet, and Menashe sat down to lunch with me. To enjoy a little privacy we put two tables together in a far corner, and to justify occupying such a large table for so long a time we ordered a first-class meal. Between courses we made final arrangements for the operation.

We cleared up the problem of what to do if Klement, on seeing the car, were to try running home across the field instead of taking his usual route. My instructions were that if they felt Klement was not making just a chance departure from his routine but was actually frightened, they must at all costs catch him in the field, even if it meant attracting the attention of passersby. I was sure that if Klement were alarmed by the waiting car, he would give us no further opportunity to take him quietly. And so, I said, only if they were sure that his detour was unconnected with their presence were they to leave him alone, but if it was obvious to them that we had terrified him then they must go into action, come what may. In any event, it must be clearly understood that once they started chasing him across the field they must under no circumstances let him go, even if it meant dragging him out of his house.

Another question we discussed was how to act if the car the captive was in was chased. If that happened, we decided, every effort must be made to get rid of the pursuers by turning suddenly off the road, transferring the prisoner to the second car, and then driving the first car back on to the road to mislead them. This car must then be abandoned at the first opportunity, while the second car drove on to the nearest safe house.

Lunch was over at two. We parted with hand-shakes and good-luck wishes. The men were in good spirits. I felt sure that nothing human could frustrate our high hopes.

After we left the restaurant, the team went to collect the first operational car, which they had parked in the city. When they tried starting the engine they were dismayed to find that the battery was very weak, though they had charged it. They quickly drove to a garage and had it charged again. At three-thirty the car was in order and ready for use.

At four-thirty a final briefing session took place at *Tira*. Then the men changed their clothes and took their new papers and the instruments they would need for the operation.

At six-thirty the two cars set out for *Tira*. The occupants of the first, the capture car, were Gabi as commander of the action, Kenet at the wheel, Zev beside the driver, and Eli next to Gabi on the back seat.

Ehud was driving the second, the escort and reserve car, with Ezra beside him and the doctor in the back. The doctor was carrying an ordinary medical bag, but inside there were special instruments for use in the operation.

The cars drove to the target area by two different routes and met at a prearranged point, on Route 197. Their object in traveling apart was to check out the two routes, since they would have to choose one for the return journey to *Tira*. On neither route was there any change since their last surveillance. There were no

searches or inspections, and no military or police roadblocks had been set up. When they joined up again
they decided that after the operation they would take
the withdrawal route first proposed.

The two cars stopped for a while in the area between Routes 197 and 202 to assemble their special
equipment. Then they moved off toward the target
area—each car to its predetermined position.

———

May is a wintry month in Argentina, something like
a European November. It was cold and stormy at the
time, and just a couple of days earlier I had caught a
heavy cold. I was running a fever, but I didn't want to
worry or distract my companions so I didn't tell them
about it. On the day of the operation I couldn't see a
doctor, or even get away from my routine meetings to
change into warmer clothes or buy medicines. Instead
of my usual coffee I ordered hot tea with brandy, which
made me feel headachy and nauseated. But that wasn't
what was worrying me: I was afraid the liquor would
make me sleepy, so I went back to strong coffee. As
the hours went by, however, I gradually felt better—
my temperature went down and I was as wide awake
as before.

The operation was planned for seven-forty, and I
could expect the first news any time after eight-forty.
By nine o'clock there was still no sign of our men.
Having nothing else to do, I began going over the
schedules in my mind and working out the various
possibilities. I told myself that if the operation had been
canceled, either because Klement had changed his
habits or because he had come home that evening in
the company of other people, someone should have
been here by now to let me know about it. It can only
be, I said to myself, that Klement arrived late and they
had to wait for him.

Another hour went by. The hands of the clock were
approaching ten, and still nobody came. In an effort
to conquer my anxiety, I started analyzing the situation. If a mishap had really occurred and our men
were caught, it was hard to believe that every last one

had been taken; at least one of them would certainly have found some way of escaping and informing me of their failure. And if they weren't caught but had to make a getaway, it was simply impossible that they would neglect to send someone to tell me about it. Which meant that there had been no hitch of that sort.

As time went by and still nobody turned up, I became more and more convinced that the operation was a success but our men had so much on their hands that they just didn't have a spare second to let me know how things had gone. As it got later and later, and there was still no sign of anybody, I told myself that of course they were busy at the safe house confirming Eichmann's identity. I sat waiting and wondering, drinking tea and coffee at rendezvous after rendezvous until it was nearly midnight and the café I was sitting in started to close.

I had paid and was getting ready to move on to the next when Ehud and Kenet appeared in the doorway. They were tired and their clothes were rumpled, but one look at their faces was enough. Before they could open their mouths, I knew that not only was the operation a success but that Klement had been identified as Eichmann.

They sat with me for a few minutes and told me that everything had gone just about as planned. We then went over to the next meeting place, and there they gave me the full story of the capture of Adolf Eichmann.

---

The cars had reached the target area at seven-thirty-five—a little later than planned—two or three minutes before the arrival of bus number 203 at the kiosk, but those few minutes were enough for them to get themselves organized and ready to welcome Klement. And then the bus came—but no Klement.

The first car was standing in Garibaldi Street, about ten yards from the corner of Route 202, its nose facing Klement's house. The hood was raised and Zev was tinkering with the engine, standing where Klement wouldn't notice him as he came along. Eli stationed himself at the left side of the car and also bent over the engine. Kenet, wearing glasses for the occasion, sat behind the wheel, while Gabi slid from the back seat to the floor and, leaning his head against the window, looked around to see what was going on. After a minute or two a man on a bicycle stopped next to them and offered to help fix the car. Never had people "in trouble" been so keen to be left alone with their troubles. They refused the cyclist's help politely but firmly. The man probably thought they were very ungrateful and went away without saying another word.

The second car was parked at the side of the road on Route 202, between the bridge over the river and the corner of Garibaldi Street, about thirty yards from the first car. The passengers lifted the hood and pretended to be repairing a mechanical fault. About a dozen yards behind the car a truck was parked, its driver sitting in the cab eating and drinking. This man remained there throughout the operation and never noticed what was going on under his nose.

The men in the second car were to switch their headlights on full and blind Klement so that he wouldn't see the first car until he was right at it. Seven pairs of eyes were glued to the bus stop in suspense.

Two busses arrived, but Klement didn't alight from either of them. The men lying in wait began to get a little worried. Could it be that he had come back early that day and was home already? Perhaps he wasn't coming at all? After all, four days had elapsed since their last surveillance; wasn't it possible that in the meantime he had changed his routine?

Yet another bus went by, and Klement didn't appear. Doubt began to gnaw at their minds, but nobody said anything. None of them wanted to discourage the others.

They had agreed that if Klement didn't come at his usual time they would wait until eight o'clock. When eight o'clock came Kenet asked Gabi if they shouldn't drive off, because if they stayed there much longer it would begin to look suspicious and they couldn't risk spoiling their chances of putting their plan into action another day. Gabi said they would go on waiting. He didn't tell the others, but he had made up his mind to wait until eight-thirty, even though it was quite clear to him that a subsequent ambush would be made much more difficult by their prolonged presence on the scene.

Ehud, in charge of the second car, felt the same way as Gabi. Neither of them gave the other the slightest hint of what was going on in his mind, but Ehud had also decided to wait. Just before eight o'clock he got out of his car to take a good look around. He was standing a few yards away from the car, very near the corner of Garibaldi Street. When he saw a bus draw up at the kiosk he turned back and began walking slowly to the car. Then suddenly, in the darkness, he caught sight of Klement. It was five minutes after eight. Ehud broke into a run. Ezra saw him running and quickly slammed the hood shut. In a flash Ehud jumped into the car and switched on the headlights. Klement was already at the corner of Garibaldi Street by the time Ehud started the car.

The men in the first car had almost given up hope. They saw the bus stopping but didn't think anything would happen. All of a sudden Kenet noticed someone walking at the side of the road. It was too dark to make out who it was.

"Someone's coming," he said to Gabi, "but I can't see who it is."

A few seconds later, in a whisper that sounded to him like a shout, he exclaimed, "It's him!"

Gabi's heart leapt with excitement. He threw a hurried glance at his men to check that they were all in position. Eli picked out the approaching figure immediately, but it took Gabi another fifteen seconds. Meanwhile, Klement was turning the corner into Garibaldi Street.

Kenet hissed in Gabi's ear, "He's got one hand in his pocket—he may have a revolver. Do I tell Eli?"

"Tell him," Gabi answered.

"Eli," Kenet whispered, "watch out for a gun. He's got his hand in his pocket."

Klement was standing right in front of the car.

"Momentito," Eli said and sprang at him.

Panic-stricken, Klement stepped back.

In their practice exercises Eli had used the method called sentry tackle, seizing the man from behind and dragging him backward, but Kenet's warning about the gun forced him to change his tactics. He pounced on Klement to bring him down, but because Klement had stepped back Eli's leap brought them both crashing to the ground. As he fell, Klement let out a terrible yell, like a wild beast caught in a trap. Zev darted around the car and grabbed his legs. Klement lay as if paralyzed.

Gabi also had to change his tactics on the spur of the moment. He burst out of the car, seized Klement's hand and started pulling him inside, with Eli and Zev pushing from the other side. Within a few seconds the four of them—Gabi, Eli, Zev, and Klement—were jumbled in a heap in the back of the car. Zev climbed over the back of the seat into the front. Kenet slammed down the hood, jumped inside, and started the engine. The whole action had taken less than a minute.

Ehud couldn't see what was happening in the dark, but when he saw the first car move off he drove rapidly past Klement's house, followed the first car to the street where the kiosk was, and caught up with it at the intersection with Route 197. It was only when they passed the kiosk and Ehud saw Kenet at the wheel that he knew everything was all right. He accelerated, overtook the car in front of him, and took the lead along the prearranged route. The two cars stopped for a moment at the spot where they had met before the operation, the dirt road between the two highways. There they confirmed operational plans for the next stage of the action—the journey to the safe house— then set off again.

Everything was fine in the first car. Klement showed no sign of resistance. When the car moved off his head was pressed against Gabi's knees. Gabi and Eli, with the help of Zev leaning over from the front, gagged him, trussed his hands and feet, put a pair of opaque goggles on him, lowered him to the floor, and covered him with a blanket. During the whole procedure Eichmann didn't utter a sound. Kenet spoke one sentence to him in German, using terms which were undoubtedly familiar to the captive: "If you don't keep still, you'll be shot."

As soon as Gabi's hands were free, he shook hands with Eli, who had in the meantime removed the gloves he was wearing for the operation. Gabi took something heavy out of his pocket, something he'd forgotten he had but which was pressing uncomfortably against him—a pair of handcuffs he had brought in case they needed to shackle Eichmann's hands. He looked behind him and couldn't see the second car, but half a minute later, to his relief, there it was; it overtook them and drove on in front of them. During the brief stop on the dirt road he had managed to convey to the occupants of the second car that everything had gone off as planned.

They continued traveling along the chosen withdrawal route. At the railway crossing the barriers were down and they had to stop. Two long lines of cars were standing and waiting for the booms to be raised. Strains of music wafted through the open windows of the car in which Eichmann was lying on the floor. The two cars waited in line for ten minutes, but if anybody had glanced inside he would have seen nothing out of the ordinary; the passengers appeared to be no different from those in the other waiting cars.

Eichmann lay on the floor, absolutely still, breathing heavily. They had originally intended drugging him as soon as they caught him, to prevent him from causing any trouble on the way to the safe house. However, the doctor explained that if the man had had alcohol or a heavy meal prior to his capture, an anesthetic could endanger his life.

They stopped as planned about five minutes before reaching *Tira* and put on new license plates. They arrived at their destination at eight-fifty-five, fifty minutes after Eichmann got off bus number 203—for the last time.

The official tenant of *Tira* was waiting. The perfect

host, he opened wide the gate of the villa and let the
two cars through. The first was driven into the garage,
from which a passage led to the house. The doors of the
garage were closed behind it and Eichmann taken out.
Supported at either side, he walked from the garage to
the room prepared for him. The car was taken out of
the garage right away, to make room for the second
one. They drove the first car to the city; if the incident
at the corner of Garibaldi Street and Route 202 had
been observed, it was the first car that would have
been noticed, so it had to be removed from the safe
house immediately. The second car also had to be hidden from view, as none of the neighboring tenants had
seen it before in the vicinity of *Tira;* at the first
hint of danger it would have to be used to transport
Eichmann somewhere else in a hurry, so it was better
to take no chances that anybody could point it out as
the car they had seen parked in the yard at *Tira.*

Meanwhile, Eichmann had been put down on an
iron bed, with one leg shackled to the bed frame. He
was still wearing the opaque goggles and couldn't see
the room or his captors. They had taken his clothes off
and dressed him in pajamas bought to fit his measurements. When someone began peering and prodding
around in his mouth, he said that after so many years,
they needn't expect him to still be on the alert and to
have poison hidden in his teeth. In spite of his protest,
his false teeth were removed and a thorough search
made of his clothes and shoes.

Gabi, Eli, Ehud, and Kenet were in the room with
him. They examined his body for identifying marks and
checked them with Kenet's data. Acting on their knowledge that SS officers had their blood type tattooed under the armpit, they looked there first, but in place of
the tattoo there was now just a small scar.

With the list of Eichmann's personal characteristics
in front of him, Kenet asked the prisoner a series of
questions:

"What's your hat size?"

"Six and seven-eighths," the prisoner said.

"And your clothes?"

"Forty-four."

"What size shoes do you wear?"

"Nine."

"And what was the number of your membership card in the National Socialist Party?"

"889895," was his unhesitating reply.

There was actually enough in this answer, along with the measurements, to identify Klement as Eichmann with virtual certainty. No other person could know Eichmann's number in the Nazi Party so automatically. Nevertheless, Kenet wanted confirmation from Eichmann's own mouth, so he carried on:

"When did you come to Argentina?"

"1950."

"What is your name?"

"Ricardo Klement."

"Are the scars on your chest from an accident that occurred during the war?"

"Yes," he replied and started to shake all over. Perhaps it had just struck him that he gave himself away when he told his party number.

"So what's your real name?"

"Otto Heninger," he said reluctantly.

Kenet said nothing for a few minutes but looked at his list in silence, giving the prisoner's nerves time to calm down. Then he asked:

"Were your SS numbers 45326 and 63752?"

"Yes."

"Then tell me your name!" Kenet ordered.

"My name is Adolf Eichmann."

A convulsive shiver shook the captive's body. Deep silence reigned in the room. The four Israelis were incapable of putting their feelings into words. They could only exchange mute glances. But Eichmann knew how to express the tumult going on in his mind.

"You can quite easily understand," he said, "that I am agitated at the moment. I would like to ask for a little wine, if it's possible, red wine, to help me control my emotions." When he was told he would get what he wanted, he added, "As soon as you told me to keep quiet, there in the car, I knew I was in the hands of Israelis. I know Hebrew; I learned it from Rabbi Leo Baeck: 'In the beginning God created the heavens and the earth. . . . *Shma Yisrael*. . . .' "

When the four of them heard their holy words coming out of that mouth they were horrified. The obsequious tone he used in addressing his captors was enough in itself to disgust them, but when he pronounced the sacred words that millions of Jewish lips murmured three times a day and at the moment of ultimate dread, they were shaken to the core. It was forbidden to do him any harm, those were their orders. It was forbidden to respond to the inner urgings that prompted them to shut his mouth. There was only one thing they could do: get up and leave the room.

They went out to their friends who were waiting tensely for the results of the first interrogation. When they heard that Klement admitted to being Eichmann, they were filled with satisfaction and relief, though their spirits were somewhat dampened at the prospect of having to live cooped up with this hideous man for many days.

Now, however, there was a lot of work ahead of them: Eichmann's medical examination, the organization of guard duty and security regulations, arrangements for supplies, planning emergency measures, and so on. Emotions were put aside, and they went on with the job.

———

All this was told to me by Ehud and Kenet. When we separated I went to look for Meir Lavi, my liaison man, who had spent the whole day wandering from café to café without knowing why. I reckoned his day hadn't been an easy one and he would certainly be pleased to be released.

I didn't know him and he didn't know me, but when I walked into the café where he was sitting I didn't have much trouble finding him. We had arranged for him to have a certain book lying on the table in front of him, but long before I could see what the book was I saw a pair of eyes glued on me, eyes that were unmistakably saying, Is this the man I've been waiting for all day? I walked straight up to him. The book was right there on the table.

He was very glad to see me and offered me a cup of coffee—but I had drunk such vast quantities of coffee that day that we settled on something else. To my regret, even now I couldn't tell him why we'd made him run around all day. All I could do was ask him to go to Menashe at a certain place and say to him, "The typewriter is in order."

"And that's all?" he asked. The surprise and disappointment on his face made me feel sorry for him. How could he accept the thought that he had waited for seventeen consecutive nerve-racking hours in so many cafés just to deliver this stupid message? He sat for some minutes, thoughtful and perplexed, until at last he stood up and said, with a smile, "Yes, I understand. I'll go to him at once."

Menashe received the message less than an hour later, and he knew that it meant he must transmit an urgent message to Israel to the effect that Ricardo Klement was in our hands and there was no further doubt that he was Adolf Eichmann.

I went out into the chill, damp night. After the twenty hours I had spent in closed smoke-filled cafés, the cold air felt good. I decided to walk to the place where I had left my belongings, and that walk is an enjoyable memory to this day.

I picked up my luggage and took a taxi to a hotel very far from my previous one. Both the reception clerk and the taxi driver had no reason to think I had not just arrived in Buenos Aires.

The instant I stretched out on the bed in my room I fell into a deep sleep. A few short hours later I had to rise to a day of very important work.

# 18

Before I left Israel I made arrangements for my message about Eichmann's capture and identification to be passed on to three people—the Prime Minister, the Foreign Minister, and the Chief of Staff. This was to be done by Gil, one of my most intimate friends, who had spent many years in close contact with me on numerous operations. Gil knew all about the Eichmann affair because he had collected information about him at various stages, and he was personally concerned: his parents, his young sister, and dozens of relatives had perished in Nazi camps.

On May 13, a Friday, Ankor brought the message that Eichmann was in our hands. Gil immediately asked for an appointment with Prime Minister Ben-Gurion but was told that he was out of town at Sde Boker, a kibbutz. His Political Secretary, Yitzhak Navon, asked Gil to postpone the appointment until Sunday, unless the matter demanded urgent action or decision on Ben-Gurion's part. Gil agreed.

As was usual on a Friday, Golda Meir was at Government Offices in Tel Aviv. In spite of her packed schedule, she agreed to grant Gil a short interview, but when he arrived, the secretary told him with obvious embarrassment that one of the ministers had taken his time. Gil asked her to tell Mrs. Meir that he was there. The Foreign Minister came out at once and invited him out onto the balcony; she knew that Gil wouldn't bother her unnecessarily.

"What's happened?" she asked.

"Adolf Eichmann has been found."

"Where is he?"

"All I know at this point is that Eichmann has been captured and identified."

For a second her breath caught. She pressed her hand to her chest and looked for something to lean against. Then she put her other hand on Gil's shoulder and said, "I beg of you, if you hear any more, come and tell me without fail."

From the Foreign Minister's office Gil hurried to Army Headquarters. There were strong ties of personal friendship between General Chaim Laskov and myself. As Gil walked into his office, he asked, "What news? Anything from Isser?"

"There certainly is," Gil replied. "Eichmann has been found and his identity is no longer in doubt."

"Well done!" exclaimed Laskov, his eyes sparkling behind his glasses. "Do you know any of the details?"

"No. And I don't expect to know anything until they come back to Israel."

At five o'clock Sunday morning Gil set out for Sde Boker in a car driven by Yaki. They arrived a few minutes before nine. Ben-Gurion's bodyguards took Gil to his cottage at the kibbutz, where the Prime Minister welcomed him into his study and asked the purpose of his visit.

"I have come to inform you that Eichmann has been found and his identity established beyond doubt."

Ben-Gurion remained silent for a moment and then asked, "When will Isser be back? I need him."

As far as we knew, nobody had noticed anything special about *Tira* on the night Eichmann and his party of guards arrived there. Gabi knew it was vital that the house continue to appear as quiet as it had been before they came, so for the first thirty-six hours nobody was allowed in or out, except to buy provisions. Yitzhak was appointed caterer because he was already accepted as the tenant. He should really have remained in the house to deal with possible visitors, but there were more important things for him to do.

First of all, he had to return the car used for the capture. Some casual passer-by might have noticed it at the scene of action and might remember it when he heard that the police were investigating a disappearance there. The car had to be out of the way before any witness came forward to help the authorities. Admittedly, if the witness had somehow already given his evidence to the police, there was clear risk in the mere act of returning the car, but I considered it more risky not to do so. If we held on to the car, or tried to abandon it somewhere, the rental agency might complain to the police, who might in turn link Klement's disappearance with the theft of a rented car. If that happened, the large unclaimed deposit could increase their suspicions.

Taking all this into account, I had arranged for the car to be returned only on my authorization. The morning after the capture, I still had no idea if a search for Klement had already started or if the police had been called in. My only source of information was the local press. Menashe checked the newspapers thoroughly and told me that there was no mention of what had happened the night before in San Fernando. In that case, I said, the car must be given back without delay.

A few hours later I was told that it had been returned without any complications and the deposit repaid in full. The operational team breathed more freely when they knew that no suspicion was attached to the car.

---

The doctor examined Eichmann and found him to be perfectly healthy. He was a model prisoner and spared no pains in proving himself willing to co-operate. Keeping him in custody would not, it seemed, entail any practical security problems. There were, however, many intangible difficulties which arose primarily from the very fact that we had to be in continual close contact with him, keeping a strict watch on him.

The men took turns doing guard duty in the room itself and at the observation posts inside the house and in the back yard. They were constantly on the lookout for strangers in the neighborhood or for anybody displaying undue interest in what was going on at *Tira*. Special safety regulations were formulated in case of emergency, including making use of the hideout and evacuating the house in a hurry. These maneuvers were practiced over and over again, and each man knew his post and function. The *Tira* group consisted of Gabi, Ezra, Eli, Zev, the doctor, and Yitzhak. Ehud, Kenet, and Menashe, who were not living at *Tira,* attended to the acquisition of supplies.

---

The only one cut off from the rest was Shalom Dani, who was going through one of the most frustrating experiences in his life. On the evening of May 11, while the operational team was preparing to set out for San Fernando to capture Klement, Dani was on his way to *Doron* to put it in order in case they had to bring the captive there. He made all the necessary arrangements for receiving the party and then reconnoitered the surroundings, checking entrances and exits.

The watchman-gardener kept trying to make things pleasant for him in the large house, and Shalom couldn't get rid of him. He told the man that he had been left alone in the house because something unexpected had happened; he claimed he was a friend of the tenant's and had been invited to spend a few days with him, but his host had been called away unexpectedly to see friends who were passing through Buenos Aires. It could happen, Shalom explained, that the friends might be persuaded to come to the villa, but if not his host would have to join them on their tour of Argentina, which would probably take several days. The host had apologized profusely to his guest for possibly having to leave him on his own.

Shalom calculated that if the operational team intended coming there with the prisoner they wouldn't be arriving before nine-thirty, but the watchman would have to be sent away earlier than that. If Shalom could find some excuse to shake the man for several hours, the team would have a chance to settle in properly.

Shortly before nine Shalom started complaining of excruciating pains in his head, and the watchman immediately offered to go and get a doctor. Shalom told him he didn't need a doctor because he knew what was wrong and what medicine to take, but unfortunately he had forgotten to bring it with him. It wasn't a remedy in common use and only the very largest pharmacies would be likely to stock it. The watchman said he couldn't bear Shalom's suffering and would do anything he could to help relieve it. He would go to Buenos Aires at once and scour the city for the medicine. So Shalom wrote down the name of a certain pill that he knew could be bought without a doctor's prescription, and the watchman set off posthaste.

At nine-thirty Shalom stood in front of the house, holding the key to the gate, watching for a pair of headlights to pierce the solid blackness. He mentally reconstructed the course of the operation. He knew every detail of it and longed to take part, but he was relegated to the background while his friends went to accomplish a great and dangerous mission. Had Klement appeared at his usual hour? Had the action gone as planned? If it had, then the team would by now be halfway to *Doron.* But were they coming to *Doron?* After all, the original plan was to go to *Tira.* . . .

After two hours of waiting he assumed they weren't coming. He went inside and sat down with a book he'd bought at the airport in Europe, but he simply couldn't concentrate on it. His eyes were moving over the printed page, but his brain wasn't taking in a word of it. He kept hoping someone would remember him and come to tell him what had happened, even though no one had promised to do so. For many long hours he sat there—but nobody came.

After midnight the watchman returned with the medicine. Willy-nilly, Shalom had to swallow one of the pills and go to bed. He knew there was no likelihood that anyone would come in the middle of the night.

He woke up late in the morning. The huge house was empty. It was nearly noon, and still nobody had come to tell him how the operation had turned out. Anxiety stole slowly into his mind: had the operation failed? Here he was, cut off from everything and everybody: how could he be certain that everything had gone off properly? No, it was inconceivable that they should leave him so long without news.

But an inner voice whispered that if—God forbid —things had gone wrong, someone would have to come to tell him. Unless . . . unless none was left to tell the tale. After all, more than sixteen hours had passed since the time fixed for the capture. Was it possible that everything was all right and yet they never came to tell him so?

He couldn't eat, and he knew he wouldn't be able to eat until he knew, until they came to tell him what had happened at San Fernando the night before. The hands of the clock moved with irritating slowness. It was three o'clock. How long would he have to sit like this, forgotten by all the others, unaware of the fate of his friends?

A car drew up in front of the house. Shalom dashed outside. At last. Ehud came toward him with rapid strides. There was no need to ask questions, Ehud's face spoke volumes.

Shalom impatiently brushed aside Ehud's apologies about all the work they had to do and how the men were tied down at *Tira*. He wanted details, he wanted to know all about it. His gloom vanished, the weight was lifted from his mind. He didn't try to hide the tears that started to his eyes, nor was he ashamed of them.

Ehud drove him to the city, back to his dingy room at *Maoz* and the work that was going to be more copious and vital than ever.

———

I worked out my appointments that day so that at eleven in the morning and five in the afternoon I would be at the meeting places for Dina Ron. The other men were all overburdened with urgent problems of supply and organization and I didn't want to add the chore of waiting for Dina. For two days she hadn't appeared; no one had kept the five-o'clock appointment the day before because we were all too busy preparing for the capture. But now, a few minutes before eleven, I was waiting for Dina in one of the large city cafés.

She left her hotel early that morning and set out with a map to find the rendezvous. She wandered leisurely through the wide streets and made her way slowly to the corner where the meeting was to take place.

At five minutes past eleven I saw her enter the café. When her eyes had adjusted to the dim light and she caught sight of me, a surprised smile spread over her face. She sat down next to me and apologized for the delay in her arrival.

I couldn't wait to break the news. "We've got him!" I said.

"Who? What do you mean?" asked Dina in bewilderment.

Now it was my turn to be surprised. "Don't you know why you were sent here?"

"No," she said. "They told me I'd receive instructions when I got here."

I laughed, and told her what had happened the previous day. Dina was dumfounded. She was new to the work and had no idea that one of our activities was hunting war criminals. She had read about Eichmann in the novel *Exodus,* but she had never thought of him as a living man. The thought that she would have to live in the same house with a mass murderer shocked her.

I explained that she would have to go to *Tira* to pose as the girl friend of the man who had rented the house, Yitzhak, and to make life at *Tira* appear as natural as possible. I arranged a time for Yitzhak to take her to the house.

She went back to her hotel to check out, and a little

later Yitzhak came for her in a taxi. They went to where Yitzhak's car, loaded with supplies for the "besieged" in the safe house, was parked. Close to six-thirty Dina arrived at *Tira*.

# 19

Those first few days after the capture were by no means pleasant. We were isolated from both Argentina and the rest of the world, and thus had no notion of how Klement's family had reacted to his disappearance. They may have decided to look for him themselves, or they may have turned to the Nazi colony in Argentina for help, or they may have appealed to the police. We didn't know whether they were raising an outcry or handling the matter quietly. There was no source of information other than the press, and the press carried not one word about a certain German resident of San Fernando.

Under such circumstances all I could do was try to assess the situation on the basis of known facts and pure logic. I arrived at the following evaluation:

When her husband was late coming home Vera Eichmann would undoubtedly begin to fear for his safety. She wouldn't immediately suspect, however, that he had been abducted by people who knew his true identity. She would first consider that he had been injured in an accident or that something had gone wrong at work. Instead of going to the police right away, she would most likely first try to find out from one of his friends at work if Ricardo had left at the usual time or if he had mentioned that he wasn't going straight home. Once she had learned that everything had been all right at his place of employment, she would probably try to find out whether he had been involved in an accident on the way home. It could be assumed, I told myself, that for a day or two she would make discreet inquiries at the first-aid stations and hospitals in the area to find out if any injured person by the name of Klement had been brought there. She would then try all the friends her husband was likely to turn to if he were suddenly called away or if he were warned that he had better not go home or get in touch with any of his family.

Only if all these inquiries had no results would she consider appealing to the police; even then she wouldn't be in a hurry to turn to them, because the police would treat this as no more than a routine disappearance. They would tell her to try hospitals and friends of the family. They would also surely question her about relations between her husband and herself. This could be embarrassing: Was Klement often drunk? Were there fights? Arguments? Was he mixed up with some other woman? And like police the world over, they would finally tell her that husbands disappear and return and all she had to do was wait patiently until homesickness brought him back.

In any event, there was little likelihood that the police would go rushing off on the trail of some casual citizen who hadn't come home from work at his usual time and had apparently deserted his wife and family. Naturally, they might comply if Mrs. Klement became insistent, or if she hinted that she had grounds for believing that her husband had been kidnaped or was the victim of some other felony. In that case, they would ask her to explain the reasons for her fears, and she would have to disclose that her husband was Adolf Eichmann, a war criminal wanted in several countries, and there was reason to suspect that he had been abducted by Jews or Israelis. The police officers would immediately hand the case over to the highest authorities, and before long the name of Eichmann would become a topic of public discussion all over the world. The upshot of it all would be that Klement would be irrevocably unmasked, and if his captors still had doubts of his true identity they would now have positive confirmation.

I thus reasoned that Vera Eichmann would under no circumstances go to the police before eliminating the possibility of accident or personal involvement; and even then she would first consult all the family friends who knew who Ricardo Klement really was.

I imagined that such friends, and the leaders of the Nazi colony in Argentina, would understand only too well the significance of Klement's disappearance. Nevertheless, they would also be very careful not to appeal to the authorities or make it public that Ricardo Klement was Adolf Eichmann. It was a near certainty that they would try, by unofficial means and with the help of their own connections, to use their influence with reliable people in the police department and in the government. These might perhaps conduct searches and investigations, but in the most discreet manner. There was no way of initiating a widespread hunt without having to reveal the identity of the person they were hunting for. As a result, their actions would necessarily be far from thorough. Only pure chance, or a serious mistake on our part, could lead them to our men or to *Tira*.

Consequently, I felt that we were in pretty good shape, in no danger of planned and extensive action by the local authorities or Eichmann's friends. At the same time, it was clear that the longer we stayed in Buenos Aires the greater the danger, since undercover government agencies might soon join the other searchers. Still, I estimated that for the time being we could put our minds at ease. Of course we continued to scan the local papers every day, but there was nothing pertinent to us.

———

Years later I received confirmation of my hypothesis about the Eichmann family's response to the abduction. His eldest son, Nicolas (Klaus), reported the following in an interview with a correspondent of the German weekly *Quick:*

On May 12 I was standing on a roof scaffolding with a screwdriver in my hand when my brother Dieter came running up, out of breath, and said to me: "The old man's vanished!" The screwdriver dropped from my hand. My first thought was: Israelis! Dieter and I tore through Buenos Aires to San Fernando. On the way we called on an SS officer whose name I can't divulge. He was Father's best friend. He told us we must be practical. There are three possibilities: Father has been arrested by the police for some offense or other, for drunkenness perhaps; he has been hurt in an accident and is lying injured in a hospital, or lifeless in a mortuary; the third possibility is that he is in the hands of the Israelis.

For two days we searched for him at police stations, hospitals, and mortuaries. In vain, needless to say. And then we understood that he was being held captive. A Peronist youth group put themselves at our disposal. There were times when large parties of men, as many as three hundred on motorcycles, were congregated around the house. We combed every square inch of the ground looking for traces of a scuffle. As each hour passed without bringing results we became more bitter. The wildest deeds were planned during those hours. The leader of the group said: "Let's kidnap the Israeli Ambassador. Let's take him out of town and torture him until your father comes home." The plan was rejected. Someone suggested blowing up the Israeli Embassy. This scheme was also rejected.

There were various reactions in various circles. The "big fish" reacted one way and the "small fry" another. My mother and young brother went to live in a house put at their disposal by a friend of ours, a former SS man. One of Father's friends, also a former SS member, organized a network of checks at the harbors and airports. There was no harbor, railway station, airport, or important intersection that did not have one of our men stationed there. This was how the "small fry" came forward to help, while the "big fish" simply ran away. Most of them beat an orderly retreat to Uruguay.

Klaus Eichmann embroidered his story with a few romantic details. He said, for instance, that he was obliged to pawn his watch and other personal effects to buy a revolver to protect his mother and young brother against kidnapers; former SS men told the family that their father was being held in a cellar beneath a synagogue; Klaus and Dieter took turns guarding Klement's house until the Peronist youth group arrived to take over from them. With regard to his father he added:

> We knew for certain that he hadn't yet left Argentina . . . we had reliable information. We tried to force our adversaries' hand. We spread the rumor that Father had been kidnaped by an Israeli army unit. This woke up the Argentine army.

Nicolas went on from there to relate how his father was taken out of Argentina on the plane that brought the Israeli delegation to Argentina's anniversary celebrations.

> We found out about it half an hour too late. Had we known a little earlier we could have prevented the plane from taking off. . . .
> Then another mishap occurred. The plane was making an intermediate landing in Brazil . . . this too we found out too late. Our contact with the Brazilian Security Service wasn't working properly. Nevertheless, we almost succeeded in obstructing the flight. At Rio a medical team boarded the plane. The doctor noticed that one of the passengers was asleep. It was my father. The doctor asked what was wrong with him. The reply was: "He is an Israeli who took ill. . . ." The doctor

lifted the blanket lying over the man's knees and saw that he was handcuffed. Without saying a word he walked straight off the plane. The Brazilians held the plane back for hours. Eventually the take-off was authorized by the Brazilian Minister of the Interior, Tiexeira Lot.

From this welter of unchecked details and speculation (the plane which brought Eichmann to Israel didn't land anywhere in Brazil), one fact does emerge: the family had gone to all extremes short of calling in the police.

———

At *Tira,* someone stood guard in Eichmann's room twenty-four hours a day; not for a second did any guard take his eyes off the prisoner. At first the men changed duty every two hours, then later on every three hours. The window of the detention room was covered with a thick blanket, the electric light burned day and night. The door to the next room was always open, and Gabi slept there. At night there were guards in the yard as well. Zev had installed an alarm bell in the detention room, which rang in one of the living rooms, for the guard to call for help or signal a warning.

In the garage a car was kept in constant readiness. Each day the engine was started and the engine and tires inspected. The guards knew what they had to do in case of an alarm: take Eichmann to the garage, put him into the car, and get away as quickly as possible.

The guards were under strict instructions never to talk to Eichmann except with regard to personal requirements, such as eating and bathing. Gabi insisted that this was an indispensable security measure and must be meticulously observed, for he was sure that Eichmann, who had held such a crucial position in Hitler's Germany, must be a man of unusual craftiness, capable of taking us by surprise with some unexpected stratagem or cunning move.

Gabi was convinced that Eichmann was ceaselessly

plotting either to escape or to take his own life, and he believed that the man had many friends in Argentina, especially among the Nazi immigrants, who would spare no effort to rescue him. This assumption created an atmosphere of great tension at *Tira,* at least during the first few days. The men believed they had to contend with a satanic brain, a brain capable of springing a daring surprise on them.

After several days they began to feel simply that they were dealing with an ordinary criminal of no great intellectual powers. At the beginning of his captivity Eichmann quaked every time anything unusual happened. When he was told to stand up he shook like a leaf. The first time they led him into the patio for his daily exercise he was in a state of abject terror, apparently believing they were taking him outside to kill him. During the first few days he was even afraid that his food was poisoned, and at every meal he broke into a cold sweat. For the most part, however, he simply lay on the bed in his pajamas, one leg shackled to the bedstead and his eyes covered by the opaque goggles. He occasionally asked for permission to take the goggles off because they irritated his skin, but he knew we didn't want him to see the men guarding him and always drew a blanket over his head before removing the goggles. He behaved like a scared, submissive slave whose one aim was to please his new masters.

Still, it wasn't easy for the men to reconcile the actuality of this wretched prisoner with their image of the superman who wielded the baton in the annihilation of millions of Jews. Where had his power and superiority come from? The elegant uniform and the shining boots? Had he possessed a magic cloak, like Siegfried in the legend of the Niebelungen, that gave him the power to perform superhuman actions?

The men's feelings of profound loathing for the prisoner produced yet another kind of tension in the safe house. Having to attend to the most intimate needs of the man they found so despicable became progressively more distasteful. *Tira* became a prison for the guards as well, and they waited impatiently for their release.

———————

Spirits at *Tira* picked up a bit when Dina arrived. Only Gabi and Eli had ever met her before, but the mere presence of a woman gave everyone the hope that the gloomy atmosphere might be dispelled. They also had great hopes for her cooking, since their experiments in that delicate art hadn't been too successful. Unfortunately, it didn't come up to their expectations, but after a few days they had to admit that her culinary efforts were an improvement. At the same time, she gave the place a feeling of domesticity it hadn't had before. If her dishes were not of a *cordon bleu* standard, at least they were served nicely and were planned with precision: every evening she perpared a list of what she needed for the next day and Kenet or Ehud did the shopping the following morning. Dina herself got out in the neighborhood only once: when she discovered that she was out of matches, Gabi had to let her go to the nearest shop to buy some.

As an orthodox Jew, Dina had to endure a great deal regarding food. Dietary restrictions prevented her from tasting even what she was cooking, and she ate mostly eggs and bread and drank Coca-Cola. Somebody told Kenet that Dina would starve to death if she didn't get kosher food, so he brought her some kosher smoked meat—but she wouldn't eat it with non-kosher utensils. Ezra begged me to order Dina to eat what was in the house, but I could see no justification for exerting my authority in the matter.

During the day Dina was kept busier than any of the other members of the team. She got up very early to prepare breakfast for Eichmann and his guards, and then she was busy washing the dishes and cleaning the house until eleven o'clock, when it was time to start again with lunch and more dishes. In the afternoon everyone ate cakes supplied by Kenet, and for supper they generally made do with something cold.

In accordance with the doctor's orders, she prepared light meals for Eichmann—chicken soup, boiled chicken, soft-boiled eggs or omelets, mashed potatoes. One of the men took the prisoner's food to him. After several days, though, it was decided that Eichmann be asked to sign a statement that he was willing to be brought to trial in Israel. Gabi thought that if Eichmann knew there was a woman in the house, heard a female voice, his fears would be lessened and he would be more willing to sign. Dina was told to deliver the captive's meals to the detention room.

When she saw Eichmann for the first time she was as surprised as all the others. He looked so ordinary that she found it difficult to believe he was the man who had pronounced the death sentence on millions of Jews. The consciousness that it was *Eichmann* she was feeding filled her with such a sensation of revulsion that she admitted afterward having played with the idea of poisoning him. But Dina, like the others, was perfectly trained in discipline and responsibility. After all, how else would we have gotten this far?

An air of heavy depression gradually descended over *Tira*. They knew they had to deliver Eichmann in Israel safe and sound and had no option but to take good care of him. But the discrepancy between their actions and the emotions aroused in them by the prisoner gnawed ceaselessly at their minds. The sight of that miserable runt, who had lost every vestige of his former superiority and arrogance the moment he was stripped of his uniform and powers of authority, gave them a feeling of insult and profound scorn. Was *this* the personification of evil? Was *this* the tool used by a diabolic government to slaughter millions of innocent people? This nonentity, devoid of human dignity and pride, was *this* the messenger of death for six million Jews?

# 20

I knew I could leave the guarding of the prisoner in the trained hands of Gabi and turn to the next step in the action—transporting Eichmann from Argentina to Israel. Ehud was made responsible for this stage of the operation and he, with all the men who could be spared for the purpose, set up day and night reconnaissances of the airfield, its surroundings, and the various roads leading to it from *Tira*. I again got in touch with Aharon Lazar, who had in the meantime become so accepted at the airport that he had the run of the place as if he were a veteran worker there.

There were four main categories of information we had to gather in anticipation of the transfer:

a) Exhaustive knowledge of the airport—its workings, its protection, customs inspections, procedures for incoming and outgoing passengers, arrangements for dealing with people coming and going on airport business or for visitors to the areas beyond the customs barrier;

b) Precise details about the plane bringing the Israeli delegation—its time of arrival, the length of its stay at the airfield, procedures for dealing with both the passengers who were brought to Argentina and those who would return to Israel, how to obtain permission to take passengers from Buenos Aires, the arrangements for the sale of tickets if such permission were granted, what sort of people would be allowed on the plane if ordinary passengers were not;

c) The problems involved in transferring Eichmann from the safe house to the airfield—his documentation, his transport, physical and medical matters as well as other preparations needed to keep him safe, precautions in case of police inspection on the roads;

d) Arrangements for cover and for the general behavior of Eichmann and his escorts on the plane to Israel.

I soon formed a complete picture of the whole setup and proceeded to the initial planning.

On May 14 Gabi and Eli appeared at one of our meeting places. (The fact that Gabi could safely leave *Tira* for a few hours demonstrated that security arrangements there had become more or less routine.) I hadn't seen either of them since May 11, just before they went on the operation, and I was struck by the great changes in their appearance during those three days. Their faces were grave and Gabi's expression was clouded, he was evidently troubled. When he started telling me about his problems and anxieties, I realized that this courageous and daring man was bending under the weight of the double responsibility of guarding Eichmann and keeping up the morale of his companions.

That was my first glimpse into the heavy oppression hanging over the guards of our loathsome criminal. I did everything I could to raise the spirits of Gabi and Eli. I fully understood their feelings, I told them, and I was by no means unaware of the mental problems involved in taking care of Eichmann while living under constant tension. I then gave them a review of the situation as I saw it and of the favorable prospects for the ultimate success of the operation. The overriding consideration, I said, was that we must keep our heads and avoid any mistake liable to lead to our failure.

I think I succeeded in making them feel a bit more cheerful. At the same time, I informed Gabi that, in spite of security restrictions, I wanted to examine *Tira* myself and intended visiting the safe house very soon.

The idea appealed to him, and late evening of the following day, Sunday, May 15, was set for my visit. If neighbors saw increased activity about the house on a Sunday, I assumed they would regard it as natural. It would therefore be quite in order for all the people directly concerned with that stage of the operation to convene without exciting undue attention.

Finally, Gabi and I decided to prepare temporary documentation for Eichmann. If a surprise police search were organized, he could then be presented as a house guest who had taken ill. Besides, we needed suitable papers for the prisoner in case we had to make a sudden getaway.

And so, on Saturday evening Eli was given a chance to demonstrate his skill at make-up in preparation for the photograph—he created a "rejuvenated" Eichmann. In fact he looked like the pictures taken at the height of his murderous career. As soon as Eli started his ministrations Eichmann went into a fit of terror and asked if they were going to execute him, but he calmed down when Eli explained what he was doing.

At nightfall Shalom Dani came to the safe house for the first time, with all the equipment required for the photographs and the preparation of the documentation. Shalom's characteristic composure deserted him the minute he crossed the threshold. He was obviously bracing himself for a severe test: not only would he have to come face to face with the destroyer of so many people, but he would also have to scrutinize him closely to choose the best angle for a photograph and to make him look as natural as possible, a prerequisite for foolproof documents. And, who knows, he might even have to act like an ordinary photographer and ask the man to smile for the camera.

By the time he reached the door of Eichmann's room Shalom was trembling all over, but he did manage to regain control. And Eichmann went out of his way to help the photographer. He even understood the precautions Shalom had to take to keep his face hidden and suggested of his own accord that before he took off his goggles someone could switch on the floodlights so that he couldn't see the photographer's face.

But Shalom saw Eichmann; in fact he couldn't take his eyes off him. He stood as if hypnotized in front of this fiend who was so eager to cooperate with his captors.

Shalom never said a word the whole evening. At first he was absorbed in developing the photographs, and later on he sat bowed over the table preparing the documentation. When he eventually completed his work, very late at night, he didn't go over it again to check it as he customarily did. This time only one thing interested him: to be rid of the documents and never to see them again. When he got up to go he even forgot to say good-by to the friends he had always treated with affection. He literally fled from the safe house. Eichmann's physical presence was too much for such a refined and sensitive man.

———

Kenet was the only one I authorized to speak to Eichmann. We had no desire to satisfy Eichmann's curiosity about the men around him, about the circumstances in which he had been brought to the villa, about the area he was living in, and other such matters. Kenet questioned him about everything connected with his life in Argentina, his flight from Europe to South America, and his whole history since the conclusion of World War II. The interrogations usually took place in the early evening and at night because Kenet was busy all day running errands in the city or reporting to me on the progress of the interrogation. Eichmann tended to sleep during the day and wake up at night, anyway, as the twenty-four-hour light burning in his room made him lose all sense of time. At first Kenet took notes, but later on he used a tape recorder.

I asked Kenet to discuss with Eichmann the possible reactions to his disappearance. I wanted to know what steps he thought would be taken by his family, his friends, his employers, and the authorities. Not that

I trusted for one moment that he would be truthful, but I believed I could glean something useful from what he did say and obtain information about those unknown quantities who were then our most dangerous enemies: the Nazis in Argentina. We didn't know a thing about them or their connections with influential state bodies, nor did we have any notion of the extent of solidarity among the exiled criminals. We didn't know if they had an organized system of communications or if their contacts were purely personal. I hoped that Eichmann's replies to Kenet's questions would teach us something about the strength of the Nazis in Argentina; even if he tried to mislead us, it would not be difficult for us to see through his deception and draw correct inferences.

On hearing Kenet's first report, I came to the conclusion that Eichmann was not trying to throw us off the scent. To my great astonishment, his hypothesis about the reaction of his family and friends was absolutely identical with mine. To his way of thinking, they would hesitate to "make a fuss" and would start by looking for him in all the likely places—at his friends' homes, at hospitals, and at casualty clearing stations. He didn't hang any hopes on his friends. He was positive they wouldn't exert themselves particularly in trying to find him, for fear of endangering their own safety. Though he refused at this juncture to disclose the names of his numerous friends, he spoke about them with unconcealed scorn. He even hinted that he was convinced they had a hand in betraying him to us.

Commenting on the special security measures we had taken, he remarked that we need have no cause for concern—the danger of our being traced was extremely slight. His remarks were somewhat obsequious, no doubt, but in the course of time it was proved that they were made with a degree of honesty.

That doesn't mean to say that he identified himself with the interests of his captors. He knew only too well what we had in store for him and had apparently anticipated much worse things than had actually been done to him thus far. I had no doubt that if he saw the slightest chance of slipping through our fingers he would not hesitate for an instant. But he knew he couldn't escape by his own efforts, nor could he expect any practical help from his friends outside. He may also have been afraid that an escape attempt could cost him his life. From the beginning, he showed open appreciation of our capability and great admiration for our efficiency and resourcefulness. Indeed, some time later, from his prison cell in Israel, he went so far as to say, "The thing was done in a sporting fashion and was outstanding for its organization and exemplary planning." His captors, he noted, "took special pains not to hurt me physically." And he knew what he was talking about: "I take the liberty of expressing my opinion on the subject because I have had some experience in police and intelligence matters."

I assume he had no doubt that in the event of any danger whatsoever we would not hesitate to kill him, so he had virtually no hope of escaping. Thus it was in the interests of prolonging his life that he cooperated with us. He appeared to have decided from the very beginning to show no sign of rebellion but to remain passive and to submit completely to his captors. Self-respect did not seem to enter into his calculations.

During the course of his interrogation Kenet asked Eichmann if he had noticed any unusual events in the months preceding his capture. Eichmann enumerated several occurrences which made him suspect that he was being observed—only one of them had any connection with our activities, while the others merely bore witness to the unremitting state of fear in which he must have lived. What had aroused his suspicions were his neighbors' stories about strangers who said they wanted to buy land for a factory. He knew there were no facilities for electricity or water in the area, and therefore he didn't believe anyone could really be interested in setting up a manufacturing plant there. He suspected then that the inquiries were a blind.

When Kenet told me all this I wondered why Eichmann had not acted on his suspicions, why he had stayed on in San Fernando even after Kenet and Kornfeld's activities had awakened these suspicions. A possible explanation was that he had been prey to fears and suspicions for so long that he had eventually made up his mind that life wasn't worth living if every unusual incident and every breath of suspicion drove him to leave his home and find himself a new hiding place, a new identity, and new employment.

Here is a portion of Kenet's interrogation of Eichmann. Kenet opened the questioning by asking Eichmann why he had said his name was Otto Heninger the night he was caught.

EICHMANN: That was my name for more than four years.

KENET: Where was that?

EICHMANN: At Kulmbach in the Province of Celle, in Germany. I worked there as a lumberjack before coming to Argentina.

KENET: How did you get there?

EICHMANN: I made my way there after leaving the American prisoner-of-war camp at Oberdachstetten.

KENET: The Americans released you?

EICHMANN: No, I escaped.

KENET: Did they know who you were?

EICHMANN: No. They didn't know my true identity.

KENET: And did you use the name Otto Heninger in the camp also?

EICHMANN: No. There I was called Otto Eckmann.

KENET: The name Eckmann is similar to Eichmann. Did you choose it?

EICHMANN: Yes, and on purpose. I thought that if anybody should recognize me as Eichmann and address me by my real name, then Eichmann would sound the same as Eckmann to American ears.

KENET: And what did you tell them about your service during the war?

EICHMANN: I told them I was a lieutenant in the 22nd SS Cavalry Division.

KENET: As an SS officer, weren't you interrogated about your past?

EICHMANN: I explained to them that I was serving in a fighting unit of the *Waffen*-SS, the Armed SS. SS officers didn't interest the Americans much. They were interested in members of the Gestapo.

KENET: But why did you have to admit at all that you were an SS officer?

EICHMANN: Because of the blood type tattooed below my armpit, as with all SS officers.

KENET: That tattoo has been obliterated. When was it done?

EICHMANN: Before I ran away from the camp I tried to erase it altogether. The rest of the prisoners helped me, but we didn't succeed in eliminating it completely.

KENET: How long were you in that camp?

EICHMANN: Nearly six months.

KENET: Were there others there from your division?

EICHMANN: Yes, Janisch was there, my adjutant.

KENET: Were you both taken prisoner at the same time?

EICHMANN: Yes.

KENET: Where?

EICHMANN: Not far from Ulm.

KENET: And from there you were transferred to Oberdachstetten?

EICHMANN: No. First we were in another camp, but we stayed there only a few weeks. It wasn't comfortable for us there.

KENET: What do you mean by that? Weren't the conditions good? Were your quarters overcrowded?

EICHMANN: No. But the Americans started looking for tattoos below the armpits of the prisoners.

KENET: Why did that upset you? After all, hadn't you introduced yourself as an officer in the *Waffen*-SS?

EICHMANN: No. There I made myself out to be a corporal in the air force.

KENET: Under the name of Eckmann?

EICHMANN: No. Under another name: Adolf Karl Barth.

KENET: When was that?

EICHMANN: May 1945.

KENET: What were you doing when you were captured?

EICHMANN: By then I wasn't doing anything. Before that I had taken my wife and children to Austria, and I went to Alt Aussee. Kaltenbrunner was there, Chief of the Reich Security Head Office. But none of us knew what to do. Those were days of chaos. It was when I started walking with Janisch, my adjutant, in the direction of Bad Ischl that I was arrested by American soldiers.

KENET: And when were you caught the second time?

EICHMANN: That was at the end of July or beginning of August 1945.

KENET: And that was when you introduced yourself as *Waffen*-SS officer Otto Eckmann.

EICHMANN: Yes.

KENET: Why did you decide to run away from Oberdachstetten?

EICHMANN: Because of the Nuremberg trials. My name was mentioned several times there, and I was afraid there might be more thorough investigations which would reveal my identity. I became particularly alarmed after Dieter Wisliceny's testimony, which leveled all kinds of accusations against me.

KENET: How did you escape?

EICHMANN: I went to the officer in charge of prisoners, Lieutenant Colonel Offenbach, and asked for authority to escape. He called a meeting of officers. They discussed my request and approved it. They also helped me, naturally. They gave me papers in the name of Otto Heninger. One of them gave me a letter of recommendation to his brother in Kulmbach asking him to help me find work in forestry. I arrived in Celle during the first few days of March 1946. I stayed there more than four years.

KENET: And then?

EICHMANN: I was cut off from my family all those years. I wanted to see my wife and children again, and I was getting fed up with the game of hide-and-seek. I knew I had to wait until the storm died down and their attention was diverted from me. But in the newspapers and on the radio, as well as in books, my name was continually being mentioned. I heard about organizations that had helped others to leave Germany. At the beginning of 1950 I made contact with one of those organizations. They arranged for me to go to Italy. A Franciscan monk in Genoa got me a refugee passport in the name of Ricardo Klement, and a visa for Argentina. In the middle of July 1950 I arrived in Buenos Aires.

KENET: And when did your wife and children join you?

EICHMANN: They came about two years later.

# *21*

The nerves of the personnel at *Tira* were being put to a severe test. The initial tight security had been relaxed, which created a comparatively routine atmosphere and within it many idle hours. True, they had been in the house only four days so far, but that can be an exceedingly long time when people are living in isolation with the round-the-clock pressures of watchfulness, fear, uncertainty—and hatred. For what caused the greatest and most constant tension in them was the contradiction between the way they were expected to treat Eichmann and the way they were feeling about him. They had been ordered to ignore as much as possible the identity of their prisoner and to remember that only the judges before whom he would be brought were qualified to pronounce sentence on him.

But how could they control themselves day after day? They had to shave the man because he couldn't be allowed to have a razor. They had to bathe him because he couldn't be permitted freedom of movement. They even had to accompany him to the toilet.

And through it all they had to command their raging hearts to be still. They had to forget their fathers and mothers, their little brothers and sisters, who had been turned into heaps of bones and piles of ash by their prisoner's extermination machine. They had to push out of their minds the humiliations and tortures, the abominable sadism of this man's campaign of genocide. They had to swallow the anger, the contempt, and the disgust that they felt day and night.

Of all the phases and hardships of the operation this was the most difficult. And I knew that I could neither save them from it nor alleviate their suffering. But we did decide that each of them, in rotation, should be allowed out for a day's holiday.

Eli went first. He was given detailed instructions about how to conduct himself in the city, and he was advised that to avoid losing his way in the maze of lavish dishes which constitutes an Argentine restaurant menu, he should order a "baby steak." Eli set out early in the morning and returned toward evening—furious. The instructions for behavior in the city, he said, so hampered him that he was bored stiff all day, and if not for the order that he mustn't set foot in *Tira* in daylight he would have been back after a few hours. As for the "baby steak," he discovered that it wasn't a small steak but a hunk of meat the size of a baby, and, he insisted, no sane person could eat such a slab of meat in less than a week.

Eichmann's guards spent long hours playing chess. Those who knew English could read the few English books they had. Others listened to music on the radio or invented games to kill time. On a few occasions Eli and Zev organized apple-eating competitions and the consumption of apples at *Tira* reached gigantic proportions.

———

The evening of May 15 I visited *Tira*, taking stringent security precautions coming and going. I noticed nothing about the outside appearance of the house to give any indication of the drama being enacted within —it differed in no way from the other houses in the area.

We were all pleased to see each other. I hadn't seen most of the men since the day of the operation, and this was my first opportunity to congratulate them on their achievement. I told them I intended to take Eichmann to Israel by plane, but promptly added that if my plan failed we would be forced to hold him until we could transport him by sea. I felt I could almost touch their shock and dismay.

Before I went into Eichmann's room I listened to Kenet's detailed report on his latest talks with the prisoner. Lately, he said, Eichmann had begun expressing regret for all he had done to the Jews during the war. He described himself as a small cog in the mighty and tyrannical machinery of the Nazi regime, and he claimed that he was unable to exert any influence on its decisions; but now he realized that serious crimes had been committed against the Jewish people, and he was prepared to do all he could to prevent any recurrence of such things. He was prepared, consequently, to report to the world all the atrocities perpetrated during the war, as a warning and deterrent to the rest of humanity.

Since Eichmann didn't deny his crimes but merely sought to minimize their importance, I asked Kenet to question him about his attitude toward standing trial. It was at this point that I suggested that we try to obtain his written consent to travel to Israel and stand trial there. Not for an instant did I suppose that such a document would have any legal validity when the question was raised of our right to try a man after abducting him to Israel. Nevertheless, I attached a certain ethical importance to such a statement.

Eichmann told Kenet he was ready in principle to stand trial for his part in the crimes committed under Nazi rule, but he wanted the trial to take place in Germany, since he was a German citizen. When he was told that he had to rule out any such possibility he made a slight concession and agreed to be tried in Austria, the country of his birth. Kenet explained that we would consider no country but Israel as the venue for his trial, because that was now the home of the majority of those who had suffered from his actions, as well as most of the witnesses who would appear at his trial. Israel, he was told, is the legitimate representative of the Jewish people, and as the point at issue deals with crimes against the Jewish people only Israel is qualified to pass judgment. I promised that he would have a proper trial according to all the rules of law, and that he could be represented by counsel and de-fend himself by all legal means. After a long discus-sion, in which Eichmann was told repeatedly and em-phatically that we wanted him to sign the document of his own free will and would not use coercion to make him sign it, he asked for twenty-four hours to con-sider his reply. His request was granted.

When I actually saw Eichmann for the first time, I was amazed at my reaction. I didn't respond to the sight of him with the loathing and hatred my people had described to me. My first thought was, Well now, doesn't he look just like any other man! I don't know how I imagined a man who had massacred mil-lions would look. All I know is that I kept saying to myself, If I met him in the street I would see no dif-ference between him and the thousands of other men passing by. And I kept asking myself, What makes such a creature, created in the likeness of man, into a monster? Is there no outward sign that distinguishes him from normal men? Or is the difference only in the corrupt soul?

---

Later that evening all the members of the task force were Dina's guests at a dinner party. At the table I said again that if all went well with the operation it would be over in five days. This put everybody in great spirits—especially Eli, who was bubbling with humor and kept the others entertained all through the meal.

In a more serious vein, however, Gabi said a few things over dinner that made a profound impression on me. What troubled him was that in capturing Eich-mann we were indirectly harming innocent people, since we had left his wife and children without a breadwinner. Gabi believed that the murderer had to be punished with the full severity of the law, but he felt it was incumbent on the Jewish people to show their generosity by providing for Eichmann's family.

I told Gabi that if such a moral obligation existed it would apply to the family of every ordinary criminal, but I had never heard of any countries behaving in such a way toward the families of their own criminals. And in fact we didn't know to what degree Vera Eichmann approved her husband's crimes, as there was no doubt that throughout the war she knew all about his position in the upper ranks of the Nazi Party and his responsibility for carrying out the "Final Solution." For all that, I said, we had never harmed her or her children and had no intention of doing so in the future. But it was a far cry from this to our subsidizing her or the others in the family. Had Eichmann and his associates displayed any concern about the material needs of their victim's families?

Gabi didn't give up easily, and the argument was lively and prolonged. Although I rejected his stand categorically, I was proud of him for holding it. To me it was wonderful that at the height of that period of tension and danger a person like Gabi should consider it necessary to examine his actions and put their humanity and morality to the test. What a contrast between the pitiless murderer and his merciful captors.

We sat there for hours, talking and arguing in that little house in Argentina, while the man who had managed the slaughter of millions of people lay in one of the rooms. The tensions that had been building up for days relaxed a little, and for a while it didn't feel as though we were undergoing "emergency imprisonment" in a foreign country but were sitting with friends at a social gathering somewhere in Israel.

Before leaving *Tira* I talked with Gabi alone to review the instructions about how the men were to act in an emergency. All necessary arrangements must be made to eliminate any possibility of escape or attempted suicide by the prisoner. His health must be assiduously guarded to keep him physically fit for the strain of embarkation and the subsequent flight to Israel; thus he must be under the doctor's constant supervision. The household must be managed in such a way that the neighbors do not notice the large number of people living in the house; it must at all times appear as if the only occupants are the couple renting the house, with an occasional visitor or two. The men must talk in whispers and not leave the house except during the hours of darkness or on urgent business, and then only if they took special precautionary measures. Our reserve houses were always ready for use so that the prisoner and his guards could be taken there in an emergency. If the police or representatives of any other official body came along, the house must be evacuated by all who didn't have emergency functions to perform, while Eichmann must be put into the "cache" with one guard. If it should turn out to be not a routine inspection but a thorough search, then the searchers must be delayed on some pretext to allow time for Eichmann to be moved with the fewest possible guards through a side exit prepared in advance. The others must steal away one by one as best they could. All must act with the clear understanding that the paramount consideration was to get Eichmann out of the house, even if this spelled danger for those keeping the searchers at bay and putting them off the scent of the prisoner and his guards.

If they were taken by surprise by a large body of police and had no chance of getting Eichmann out of the house in time, the majority of the men must do their utmost to break through the cordon and escape in any way possible. Those remaining inside must hand themselves over to the police, disclose the identity of the prisoner, explain the grave responsibility that would rest on the shoulders of whoever let him get away, and demand to be brought before high-ranking civil or police officials.

However, now that Eichmann's identity was no longer in doubt, and the significance of our action stood out in all its clarity, I felt we had to extend these security regulations. More had to be done to safeguard ourselves against losing Eichmann through lack of understanding or carelessness on the part of the authorities, or through interference by circles close to the Nazis. Consequently, I told Gabi that if the worst happened and a large force of police surrounded the house, and if he saw that he couldn't possibly get the prisoner away from *Tira,* he must handcuff one of his

wrists to one of Eichmann's and get rid of the key so
that the two could not immediately be separated. The
rest of the men must scatter with only one or two of
them remaining in the neighborhood to report on what
had occurred and to assure themselves that Gabi was
all right.

Once Gabi—still handcuffed to Eichmann—was under arrest, he would explain that he and a few
friends of his had captured the war criminal Adolf
Eichmann who had murdered millions of their people.
Their plan, he would say, was to establish Eichmann's
identity and then take him to the authorities for trial.
Gabi would then demand that they take him, and the
war criminal handcuffed to him, to the most senior
official within reach, so that he could present further
details and reveal the background of the affair.

I thought that in this way we could prevent Eichmann's release by parties hostile to us and ensure both
that his capture would be made public and that his fate
would be decided at the highest level. I knew that, although it was clear that his captors would be brought to
trial, there was no assurance that Eichmann would also. Still, I believed that at the trial of these kidnapers
the story of the holocaust could be unfolded as the
background to the kidnaping and thus bring the attention of the entire world to the Nazi crimes against the
Jewish people.

I also thought, however, that I had no right to subject Gabi to the ordeal of interrogation and trial all
alone, so I said to him, "When you're caught with Eichmann and brought before a senior police officer or a
high-ranking civilian government official, you will disclose that you are an Israeli and explain that you were
acting under the instructions of another Israeli, the
leader of a group of volunteers you belong to." Gabi
listened quietly. "This group, you will tell them, received information that a resident of Argentina known
as Ricardo Klement was actually Adolf Eichmann, the
man in charge of the extermination of the Jews in
Europe during World War II. The group came to
Buenos Aires to check the truth of the information.

If they found that the man was really Eichmann they intended capturing him and handing him over to the Argentine authorities to be judged for his crimes against humanity and the Jewish people." Still Gabi was silent, taking in all I said. "You will tell them," I went on, "that the name of the leader of the volunteer group is Isser Harel." Now he became impatient but I motioned him to wait. "You will give them the address of the hotel I am staying at and the name under which I am registered there."

Gabi could not contain himself. "You can't do a thing like that," he interrupted.

"Let me finish," I said. "When you've given them my name and the address of my hotel, you will tell them the following: Isser Harel ordered me to give his name and address to the Argentine authorities. He will explain to you himself the motives for the actions of the group he heads, and he will take upon himself full responsibility for their activities, in accordance with the laws of the state and the principles of justice and morality."

"Look here, Isser," said Gabi, "when you tell me I must handcuff myself to Eichmann and go to jail with him, that's natural and understandable; but with all my heart and soul I beg you not to order me to hand you over to the authorities. A man in your position can't allow himself to be arrested."

I tried to make him understand how I felt. "This operation, Gabi, has nothing in common with anything we have ever done before," I said. "As far as I am concerned, it is a humane and national mission that transcends all others, and its success is more important in my eyes than any other consideration. I am acting in this matter according to the dictates of my conscience, and the least I can do is free you of the necessity to struggle with yours." He still looked dubious, so I went on emphatically. "What I have told you is an order, and you must carry out both its letter and its spirit."

Even though our argument raged over a contingency that appeared to us both to be extremely remote, it gave Gabi a severe shock. Clearly, he could not bring himself to agree with me. But I knew I could rely on him to carry out my orders.

———

The long interval between Eichmann's capture and the plane's arrival involved a certain amount of danger —it gave our hidden enemies time to see the connection between those two events and to take action to stop us from putting the prisoner on the plane. Though I had complete faith in our ability to overcome all obstacles, I nevertheless had to examine other ways of getting Eichmann out of Argentina. So I gave instructions to renew the exploration of the Buenos Aires waterfront for the possibilities of putting a man secretly on board a ship anchored in the harbor or offshore.

The harbor of Buenos Aires is divided into two principal sections: the south quay and the north quay. Between them lies Avenida Costanera, one of the favorite summer haunts of residents of Buenos Aires. Then the whole length of the boulevard is lined with carts selling hot delicacies. But this was winter.

The south quay is situated near Riachuelo, one of the tributaries of the La Plata, which is used mainly for small ships sailing along the Uruguay and Paraná rivers. It serves large ships coming from overseas. The area is always teeming with life and activity. Enormous cranes rise far above the heads of the people swarming over the piers. This section of the harbor didn't enter into our plans. Our men were interested mainly in the anchorages where the large cruise ships were docked. They also explored the possibility of hiring a boat that could sail out to sea to meet one of our own ships.

Naturally the reconnaissance of the harbor constituted only a small part of our activities in connection with transporting Eichmann to Israel. The work at the airfield was divided between Dan Avner and Aharon Lazar. When Avner came to meet me the day after his arrival, I explained that he must devote his time solely to making friends with all the airport employees and accustoming the guards to his presence. I told him that first and foremost he must concentrate on learning the procedures used in police and customs inspection.

Before he was properly acclimated to Buenos Aires, Dan Avner had occasion to experience what rented cars in Argentina were like. He had to push his car along the main street of the city to get it started, and no sooner had he done so when one of the tires collapsed and he had to stop in the middle of the roaring traffic to change it. From then on he was all sympathy whenever the painful subject of rented cars in the capital of Argentina cropped up. -

On the basis of the reports from the airfield, I outlined six plans for putting Eichmann on the plane. The choice of which plan to employ would depend on circumstances, naturally, but all were devised in such a way that we could change over instantaneously from one to another to suit changing conditions.

Of the six, three were simple and easy to carry out, and I hoped to be able to follow one of these. The remaining three were designed for use in the event of unforeseen complications.

The first three plans were based on the assumption that Eichmann's family and friends wouldn't make a public outcry to call in the police for a thorough investigation. If my hypothesis was correct, nobody would have any reason to be suspicious of a plane coming from Israel or even display special interest in it. What's more, while the plane was parked at the airfield the security services and airport authorities would be preoccupied with urgent matters relating to the arrival of numerous delegations for the anniversary celebrations, and our plane would be handled in a perfectly routine manner.

We had already obtained permission to skip the usual towing and to be allowed to taxi the plane onto the tarmac ourselves. Thus we were sure that the team, or at least part of it, could board the plane while it was still standing in the Argentine national airline's maintenance area. All six plans included this feature.

The first plan was that Eichmann, wearing an air-line uniform, would be taken to the plane along with the crew needed for manning the aircraft in the maintenance area. He would therefore be inside the plane by the time it was taken onto the tarmac. If an inspection took place there, we would say that Eichmann was one of the relief crew who was lying down because he wasn't feeling well. If there was any reason to anticipate a stricter check, we would hide him from the inspectors by stowing him away somewhere inside the plane.

Plan number two would be put into action if the crew was not permitted to board the plane at its parking place or if the inspection at the entrance to the national airline's section was particularly rigorous. Then Eichmann would be taken openly to the plane as one of the crew—sick or injured in a road accident—and pass through all the usual formalities with a group of genuine crew members.

The third plan was identical with the first except in one detail: Eichmann would be an Israeli who had suddenly taken ill and had to return home immediately. Naturally, he would have to undergo the customary passenger inspections, but to make the story plausible he would be accompanied by a doctor who would be taking care of him on the journey. We would use this plan if the authorities appeared to be unduly interested in the crew.

Since it was impossible to foresee what would happen after the plane arrived in Buenos Aires and what the circumstances would be during the decisive moments before take-off, I decided to work out all the plans down to the last detail and start concrete preparations for carrying them out, including the assembling of all the necessary equipment and documentation.

———

The period of waiting was worse for the doctor than for any of the others at *Tira*. Because his attendance on the prisoner didn't consume much of his time, he read all the books in the house, listened to music, experi-

mented with the tape recorder, and even tried his hand
—without much success—at cooking. So he was very
pleased when I invited him to meet me in the city.

He knew enough about the nature of our activities
not to be surprised at any of our requests, so he took
it quite calmly when I asked him to teach me the
practice of medicine while standing on one foot, in a
Buenos Aires café. I showered him with question after
question about the possible types of injury in a road
accident, about diseases of the heart, about brain concussion, loss of consciousness, and so on. He answered my questions patiently, even when I asked if a
person could falsify symptoms and fool the doctors.
I also wanted to know if a person who had suffered a
heart attack or brain concussion would, from the medical point of view, be allowed to travel by plane, and
at what stage of the illness he would ordinarily be released from the hospital.

He apparently knew what I was driving at, because
he advised the hypothetical malingerer to feign symptoms of brain concussion, as a doctor would be unable
to prove that the patient wasn't really injured. So I took
his advice—concussion of the brain as the result of an
accident would answer all our requirements, especially
since the patient would continue to need medical care
and attention even after his release from the hospital.
The best thing for a man suffering from concussion
would be to recuperate in the comfort of his own home,
even if this entailed a long plane journey. However, it
would be important for the flight to be as comfortable
as possible and not have too many intermediate stops.

And so Operation Road Accident came into being,
to be followed by Operation Flying the Accident Victim
Home.

------

Rafael Arnon was born in one of the original kib-
butzim in Israel and is still a member of its community. He served in *Zahal* and fought in the War of
Independence. In fact, from the moment he first knew
his own mind, he had never failed to respond immediately to any appeal to help his country.

By pure chance he happened to be in Argentina in 1960. About a year earlier he had suffered a head injury in a tractor accident and was hospitalized for many months. He left the hospital with a souvenir in the form of a large scar from his forehead to the top of his head. When he recovered he decided to realize an old dream—a long overseas tour; all his associates agreed that he was entitled to it after his years of hard work, and the months of discomfort he had just undergone. Relatives in South America invited him to stay with them and saw to it that Rafael had an interesting and eventful trip. When he left his hosts he figured that, having come so far, he might as well take the opportunity to visit a few more Latin American countries, and that's how he happened to be in Buenos Aires. One day he met an old acquaintance in the street—none other than Menashe Talmi. With a lot of careful and evasive maneuvering, Menashe managed to avoid revealing what he was doing in Argentina and where he was staying, but he made a note of Rafael's address and asked him how long he would be in the city. Menashe was on his way to an appointment with me, so he arranged to meet Rafael again later in the day at a neighborhood café.

Menashe didn't want to lose contact with Rafael, because I had told him we were going to need more men —either Israelis or Jews from South American countries other than Argentina—who spoke Spanish and had a good knowledge of the people and customs of the continent. Rafael was a likely candidate as one of the Israeli aides in our operation.

Menashe was right about Rafael's willingness to respond to every call. Before very long, the fellow was sitting at my table in the café. After looking him over, I asked if he would be prepared to do something I described as "not difficult, but at the same time not pleasant." I explained that the assignment itself might seem trivial to him but would actually serve a very important purpose, even if I couldn't tell what that purpose was.

Rafael had no idea who I was, but he didn't ask

questions. He trusted his friend Menashe when he said, "It's O.K." Without a second's hesitation, he said he was ready to do anything he was told.

I was sorry I had to give such a passive role to such a husky fellow, but I told him I hoped to find him a more active assignment some other time. All he had to do now, I said, was to go to a hospital and ask to be admitted. He would say he had had a road accident and was suffering from a concussion. I told him our doctor would brief him on what to say to the doctors at the hospital and how he should act while he was there. Rafael grinned and, pointing to his scar, said he was an expert on hospitals.

When he arrived at the hospital, I explained, he was to tell the doctors that he had come to Buenos Aires to fly back to Israel on the plane bringing the Israeli delegation to the anniversary celebrations. He was to harp on the fact that he wanted to return to Israel on that plane, regardless of his state of health. It was because of the accident that he was so eager to get home quickly, and the special plane was providential for him because it would get him there without unnecessary moving around and long intermediate stops. The doctor who would be briefing him, I said, would also tell him how to stage a recovery step by step, so that the hospital doctors would allow him to travel by plane when the time came. All the time he was in the hospital he would be briefed on what to do.

Our doctor spent the day in town because security regulations forbade him to return to *Tira* before dark, so he took the opportunity to meet Rafael and describe the symptoms of brain concussion. "At the hospital," the doctor said, "you must say you were in the back seat of a car at the time of an accident and that all you can remember is that the car stopped suddenly and you lost consciousness. When you opened your eyes, you found yourself at your hotel. From then on, you'll claim, you have suffered from vertigo and a general feeling of malaise." The doctor went on to tell how these symptoms could gradually disappear. Rafael said that he understood and promised that his illness would proceed along the lines of his instructions.

After the meeting, Menashe took Rafael back to his hotel, where Rafael told the staff about the "accident" he had just been involved in and asked them to call a doctor. With Menashe's help, Rafael described the circumstances of the imaginary accident, and the doctor ordered him into the nearest hospital immediately. After the doctor in the casualty ward had heard the story of the accident, he insisted that the patient be kept under observation and given a series of tests.

Soon a professor with his entourage of students appeared in the ward, and one by one the pupils examined the patient under their teacher's instructions. In the evening there were blood tests, and the next morning his head was X-rayed. Rafael's only fear was that during the course of these exhaustive tests his doctors might discover some real sickness he hadn't reckoned on.

# 22

While Rafael was receiving the best of care and attention at the Argentine hospital, Ehud and his detail organized frequent reconnaissances of the roads to determine the best route for transferring Eichmann from *Tira* to the airfield. Dozens of times they drove over the various roads between the two points, at all hours of the day and night, to choose the most convenient time and the safest route.

The city was beginning to show signs of the approaching festivities. The police and other security agencies were taking every precaution to maintain quiet and order in the country and to insure the safety of the honored guests at the anniversary ceremonies. On all roads in and around the capital, and especially those leading from the airport to the city, police patrols were making frequent appearances. Police escorted the foreign visitors into the city and the local celebrities to the airport to welcome the new arrivals. Here and there roadblocks were set up and cars were searched.

Since we didn't know what the police were looking for, we had to be prepared for anything. Thus, for our own travels, we chose side streets and secondary intersections which were not on routes used for the visiting dignitaries and their reception committees. As we got closer to the airport on our reconnaissances our choice of alternatives narrowed, and near the entrance to the field we had to return to the main road and travel in the company of visitors' cars, the police, and the army.

Because of the volume of traffic on the roads and the preparations at the airfield itself, we decided Eichmann would have to be drugged when we took him to the airport. Although he had been cooperative from the first, we couldn't trust him among strangers, especially during a security check. So he would have to be anesthetized, the dosage to be adjusted according to road conditions and the various stages of the operation. We discussed it fully with the doctor, and he undertook to handle this aspect of the transfer and to assume responsibility for the prisoner's welfare.

At the safe house an unusual relationship had developed between the prisoner and Eli, who attended to his personal needs during his captivity. Eichmann seemed to sense that this warden was particularly kindhearted. Perhaps the attraction was deeper because Eli was the man who tackled him on that fateful night outside his house in San Fernando.

Anyway, they began to chat—the captor in piquant Yiddish and the captive in Austrian-accented German —and their talks grew longer and eventually filled the time that Eli spent with the prisoner. It soon became clear that it was impossible to make Eli observe the regulation against holding conversations with the prisoner.

Eichmann, in his blind adulation of force, seemed to look upon the man who had brought him down as a person whose authority must be submitted to, and he never missed an opportunity of fawning on him and groveling to obey every order. He made no attempt to escape, and even dared to express concern about the fate of his family.

"I didn't leave them any money," he said. "How will my wife and sons live?"

"No harm will come to them," Eli replied. "They'll manage all right without you. But tell me, please, you who worry so much about your children, how could you and your colleagues murder little children in the tens and hundreds of thousands?"

Eichmann almost sobbed. "Today I can't understand how we could have done such things," he said. "I was always on the side of the Jews. I was striving to find a satisfactory solution to their problem. I did what everybody else was doing. I was conscripted like everyone else—I wanted to get on in life."

Contempt and pity were intermingled in Eli's attitude to the man. He tried in vain to imagine him dressed in uniform, arrogant and cruel, as he had been in the past. He simply couldn't. He still saw the wretched, despicable, pitiable creature in front of him. Now and then he would accede to his requests for wine, even though this annoyed Gabi.

"I can't understand how you can treat me so decently," Eichmann used to say.

Once, when Eli brought Eichmann a small record player, Yitzhak burst angrily into the room, shut off the music, and took the machine away with him.

It was therefore not surprising that Eichmann felt he could consult Eli about signing the statement that he was willing to be tried in Israel, and it was on Eli's advice that he announced he would sign it. The text we offered him contained nothing but his agreement in principle to travel to Israel and stand trial there, but Eichmann wasn't satisfied with it; he preferred to compose his own version:

I, the undersigned, Adolf Eichmann, declare of my own free will that, since my true identity has been discovered, I realize that it is futile for me to attempt to go on evading justice. I state that I am prepared to travel to Israel to stand trial in that country before a competent court. I understand that I shall receive legal aid, and I shall endeavor to give a straightforward account of the facts of my last years of service in Germany so that a true picture of the facts may be passed on to future generations. I make this declaration of my own free will. I have been promised nothing

nor have any threats been made against me. I
wish at last to achieve inner peace. As I am unable to remember all the details and may be confused about certain facts, I ask to be granted
assistance in my endeavors to establish the truth
by being given access to documents and evidence.

                              (Signed) *Adolf Eichmann*
Buenos Aires, May, 1960

All along we kept following the Argentine press, but
it contained not even the slightest reference to Klement's disappearance. Menashe devoted a considerable
portion of his time to reading the Spanish newspapers,
while the others—including the men at large in Buenos
Aires as well as those in the safe house—shared the
German and English papers. No item of news or small
announcement escaped the eyes of the readers, but every day the newspaper check ended with the same
result: not even a hint, not even a sign.

The men at *Tira* regarded this as cause for anxiety.
They supposed that Klement's disappearance would
have repercussions in the country and expected at
the very least to find notices requesting the public
to assist in the search for him. They would have inter-
preted such notices as evidence of failure of the search,
whereas the absence of any mention of disappearance
seemed to them a bad sign—it led them to conclude
that their opponents were acting in secret and didn't
want to show their cards.

My opinion, as I have said, differed from theirs.
Not only did the silence not cause me any concern,
but I even regarded it as a confirmation of my first
hypothesis that Eichmann's family and his friends
among the Nazi exiles would be in no hurry to share
with the authorities their concern about the missing
man. I regarded the complete silence surrounding
Klement's disappearance as proof of fear on the part
of his Nazi cohorts, and of their unwillingness to risk
any danger to themselves by making an effort on behalf of their friend.

Our men at the airfield were another source of information. I instructed Lazar and Dan to inform me immediately about any unusual occurrences there, any tightening of inspection, or any departure from routine. Their regular reports demonstrated that there were neither special supervision nor searches of departing planes. Everything was normal, another indication that the authorities were not looking for Eichmann.

———

During those last feverish days in Israel I had looked through the files of all the war criminals who were believed to have escaped to South America. In particular, I delved into the dossier of Josef Mengele, the Auschwitz doctor whose frightful cruelty was described by all survivors of the death camp. He was in charge of the selections, the sorting out of the new arrivals at the camp; with a casual wave of the hand, he decreed who would go to the gas chambers immediately and who would be sent to die a slower death by forced labor. The horrifying acts of brutality he perpetrated on the sick, the women, the children, were notorious; of all the evil figures who played principal parts in the macabre drama of the attempt to wipe out the Jewish people, he was conspicuous for his abominable enjoyment of his role as death's messenger.

Our information had never been checked, but it was reported that Mengele was living at present—or in the not too distant past—in Argentina, in a suburb of Buenos Aires. I had resolved from the very beginning that if I had the chance I would try to check up on this archbutcher. In fact, when Nahum Amir, our "travel agent" in Europe, had told me that, by his calculation, it would cost a fortune to send a special plane to take Eichmann to Israel, I had said, "To make the investment more worthwhile, we'll try to bring Mengele with us as well."

Everything we knew about this man was written in my notebook, in a personal code which only I could decipher (and even I had some difficulty). Now, during that unenterprising—though by no means inactive —period preceding the arrival of the plane, with all the preparations for transporting Eichmann at an advanced stage, I decided to do something about Mengele.

Circumstances were not particularly favorable. Most of my men were tied to the safe house, and even during their free time they could leave the place only after dark. The others were busy with the flight operation, while I was spending seventeen or eighteen hours a day in Buenos Aires cafés, keeping appointments with the tenants of *Tira,* listening to reports from the road-reconnaissance detail, briefing our representatives at the airfield, and giving directions to the documentation workers and newspaper readers. But the thought that Mengele might be hiding not far from us wouldn't let me rest. It was clear from the outset, however, that I had to stick to one principle: notwithstanding my strong desire to trace Mengele, I dared not take a step that might endanger our primary objective, Operation Eichmann.

The day I visited the safe house I asked Kenet to question Eichmann about Mengele. I told him not to ask if he knew Mengele or where he was hiding, but to tell him that we knew the man was in Buenos Aires and that he must give us the exact address.

Eichmann's response wasn't very encouraging. He didn't disclaim acquaintance with Mengele, but he said he didn't know where he was and had never heard whether he was in Argentina or anywhere else in South America. Eichmann simply refused to say more, and to justify his refusal he told Kenet he didn't want to betray his friends. I regarded his reply as confirmation of two things: that Mengele was not far away and that he and Eichmann had been in contact.

When Kenet continued to press him, Eichmann brought up another argument in support of his refusal: he was afraid, he said, of what might happen to his wife and children. We didn't quite know what he meant by this remark. Was he afraid that if he gave Mengele away revenge would be taken on his wife and children? Or was it that he feared no one would be left to take care of them financially?

I told Kenet to promise Eichmann that we would

undertake his family's support if he would give us Mengele's address. But all our urgings and promises were of no avail. My impression was that he went into a panic when we demanded Mengele's location, and I felt that his obduracy stemmed not from any sense of loyalty but from sheer funk.

We put no further pressure on him, as I was interested in securing his maximum cooperation during the departure from Argentina and flight to Israel. Consequently, we confined ourselves to persuasion and material promises. Eventually Eichmann revealed that Mengele had been in Buenos Aires until a little while ago and that he had been living in a boardinghouse run by a German woman named Jurmann.

I needed more men if I wanted to deal with Mengele. Of the members of the task force only Menashe might be able to give me part of his time; and when Shalom Dani heard about the new assignment he demanded that I allow him to take part in it. But these two were not enough—I had to have more, especially people who spoke Spanish.

I asked Menashe to send me Meir Lavi, the man who had acted as our liaison the night of the capture. Meir and his wife had emigrated from North Africa to Israel in 1955. They joined a kibbutz, and from there he was sent to the Hebrew University for a bachelor's degree in Hebrew literature and Jewish history. In 1958 some close relatives invited them to one of Argentina's neighboring countries, and they had stayed on to live there. Menashe had met Meir when they were both in Buenos Aires before and had suggested him for the liaison job. After that night I had asked Meir to stand by in Buenos Aires in case we needed him again, and he and his wife were waiting for a message from Menashe that they were free to go. But I decided to mobilize them again.

He came to meet me at a café and I asked him how much Spanish he and his wife knew and if he thought they could get away with posing as natives. I was thinking of having them rent a room at Mrs. Jurmann's boardinghouse.

Meir impressed me as being an intelligent person who would undoubtedly be able to carry out the assignment successfully. Unfortunately, neither he nor his wife had sufficient command of Spanish to convince anybody they were Argentines. I wanted them, with the help of photographs I would give them, to find out at the boardinghouse—which was apparently considered a safe refuge for wanted Nazis—if Mengele still visited there. However, I was afraid that the appearance of a foreign couple on the scene might look suspicious.

I asked Meir if he knew another couple who could stay at Pensión Jurmann and give the impression of being authentic Argentinians. He did—an Israeli couple, Ada and Binyamin Efrat, also kibbutzniks, whom he had met on several occasions in the country where he lived. They had been given long leave to enable Binyamin to attend to family affairs after his father took ill. Ada was born in Buenos Aires and Binyamin in the country where he was spending his leave. After they were married they had lived in the Argentine capital until they emigrated to Israel.

Meir said that his friends were absolutely trustworthy and reliable. I asked him to fetch them. I explained that the affair couldn't wait and they must come at once, regardless of family or business considerations.

The following morning Binyamin Efrat was sitting opposite me in my "on duty" café. One look was enough to tell me he was the man I wanted. He spoke Spanish fluently and looked exactly like an average Argentinian. He had heard of Mengele but didn't know much about him. I told him we had information that this sadist was in Buenos Aires, and we were trying to locate him. He said he was prepared—without any reservations—to undertake any assignment that had to do with Mengele.

I introduced him to Shalom Dani, who would be giving him his instructions. That day Shalom reconnoitered the well-to-do district, Vicente López, where the house Mengele was reported to be living in was situated. Using only a map, asking no one for directions, he found the place. It was an isolated villa on a narrow lane, with a well-tended lawn surrounded by a white picket fence. At one side there was an entrance for vehicles and at the other steps for pedestrians.

In the evening Shalom took the Efrats to Vicente López and showed them the house. He told them to roam around the area and try to find out, in a careful roundabout way, who lived there and what sort of people they were.

Ada and Binyamin came up with a feasible excuse for their inquiries and went to one of the neighboring villas to ask their questions. They were told that the tenants of the house they were interested in were North Americans.

When I heard this a little later I thought it quite possible that the neighbors were telling the truth and Americans were indeed living there now, but it didn't rule out the possibility that Mengele was living there too, under cover as an American. I asked Shalom to go there himself early the next morning to watch the house, take a look at the tenants, and see if he could determine from their appearance if they were Americans or Germans. I asked him, of course, to take particular notice if any of them in any way resembled Mengele.

To lend an air of plausibility to his presence in the neighborhood, Shalom asked Ada Efrat to go with him. Their surveillance lasted from six to ten A.M. Ada whiled away the time telling Shalom, in fluent Spanish, all about a film she had seen. He knew only a few words of Spanish, but he tried his best to comment on her story with his meager vocabulary. The surveillance itself was somewhat disappointing—nobody who looked even remotely like Mengele entered or left the house. Fairly early they saw two children leave the house, but they didn't know if the children had anything to do with Mengele.

The following day Meir and Binyamin went out on surveillance. Shalom provided Meir with a briefcase camera and showed him how to use it. They were instructed to photograph everybody who went in or came out. That day too all they saw were the children leaving the house early, apparently on their way to school. Meir took a photograph of them, which did not come out well when it was developed.

I was getting impatient. Time was short, I explained to Binyamin, and we had to make an urgent effort to discover who the occupants of the villa were. I decided to try a shorter and more direct method of identifying them.

Binyamin went to Vicente López the next morning. He strolled through the streets for about two hours until he met a postman. He went over and asked very politely, "Excuse me, but could you help me? I'm looking for my uncle, he's a doctor. I lost touch with him a long time ago. I know that he used to live in this neighborhood but I don't know his exact address."

"And what's your uncle's name?" asked the postman.

"Dr. Menelle."

"Dr. Menelle? Oh yes, there was a person by that name in the neighborhood. He lived over there"—the postman pointed to the suspect house—"until a few weeks ago, maybe a month."

"Oh, bad luck," said Binyamin, "so I've come just a little too late. Didn't he leave his new address? Where do you forward his letters?"

The postman shrugged. "I don't know. They've given me no instructions about a new address."

"Maybe the new tenants in the house know," Binyamin suggested. "Do you know who's living there now?"

"The new tenant is an engineer from South Africa," the postman said. "Why don't you ask him."

Binyamin said, "Thanks very much," and came to report to me.

The fact that Dr. "Menelle" hadn't left a forwarding address helped confirm my belief that it was indeed Mengele's trail we were on. It could be, I thought, that something frightened him enough to change his hiding place. The question was, had he left Buenos Aires and Argentina altogether, or had he just moved to another part of the city?

I presumed anyway that the postman was telling the truth, and I attached great importance to the discovery of fresh tracks of the killer-doctor. It remained for us merely to find out if Mengele had requested that the postman keep his new address a secret, and we could find this out at the local branch of the post office. I briefed Binyamin on the questions he should ask there, reminding him to be careful to avoid the postman he had spoken to before.

Binyamin went to the post office about four hundred yards from the villa—choosing the time when the postmen set out on their rounds—and asked the chief clerk if the Dr. Mengele (I had told him not to distort the name this time) who used to live nearby had left his new address. The clerk said Mengele had lived there until a month ago, but he was sorry to say they didn't have his new address and all the letters that came for him were "returned to sender."

---

In my notes on Mengele was another item that gave me grounds for hoping to find his new hiding place: Mengele occasionally called himself Gregor and he kept two or three lathes at a service garage. We knew the address of the garage, also in Vicente López. There was always the hope that Mengele had not severed his connections with the garage when he moved out of his house a month ago.

When briefing Binyamin for his visit to the garage, I started out with the assumption that the owners would know the Gregor whose lathes were kept there. I reasoned that they couldn't possibly have done business with him for any length of time without discovering that he used different names for different purposes, especially since he had lately been living in the vicinity of the garage and was known to the neighbors by his real name. It could thus be inferred that the garage owners were allies of his, or would at any rate keep his secret. Obviously Binyamin would have to proceed with great caution when he went to the garage, and he must have a credible cover story.

We finally came up with the idea that he should go there to order a large quantity of left-hand screws. He would say that it had taken him a whole day of running around the city to find a single left-hand screw, and that when he tried to buy more at hardware stores, he was told that ready-made left-hand screws were unobtainable except from workshops that did lathe work. He got hold of a visiting card of one of the big garages in the city to give the impression that he was their representative.

At the workshop where Gregor supposedly kept his lathes, he spoke to the secretary and explained that he represented a big garage and he needed a large quantity of left-hand screws. Mr. Gregor's lathe workshop had been recommended to him, and he asked to see the gentleman in question. The secretary asked him to sit down and left the room. Binyamin heard her talking to somebody outside, though he couldn't catch the drift of their conversation. She came back, scrutinized him without saying a word, and went out again. Several minutes later she appeared and told him that they had nobody there by the name of Gregor and they didn't do lathe work.

When I heard Binyamin's story about what happened at the garage, I was positive that our second item of information also had a solid foundation. It was obvious that if the people at the garage didn't know Gregor the secretary would have told Binyamin so at once. There would have been no need to consult with somebody about what answer she should give. Even if she were new to the job, the natural thing to do was to tell Benyamin she would go and ask if they had anybody by the name of Gregor there. But her behavior proved without a doubt that she wasn't surprised at his inquiry about Gregor and that she had heard the name before. She had obviously been told to go back, have a look at him, describe him to her employers, and eventually inform him that there was no such person at the workshop.

So it was reasonable to suppose that Mengele did have some connection with the garage, but if he still maintained this connection he was taking great care to keep it quiet. I was sure that the people at the workshop would lead us to Mengele if we had a team of professionals—like the task force at present occupied with Eichmann—who could invest the necessary time, patience, and skill. But I had at my disposal—and for a few days only—a handful of people lacking experience in undercover activities. I had no choice but to give up trying to find Mengele that way.

There was only one thing for us to do: a straightforward inspection of the villa in Vicente López to check if the neighbors, the postman, and the post-office clerk had misled us, either willfully or out of ignorance. Before I left Argentina, I wanted to be sure that I had done all I could to locate the unmerciful Angel of Death of Auschwitz and bring him to trial in Israel together with Adolf Eichmann. I decided, therefore, to make one last attempt to find out if Mengele was still at the house.

# 23

Asher Kedem had expected to leave for Israel on May 10 to supervise personally the final preparations for the special flight. When, at the last minute, his departure was postponed to May 11, he assumed it had something to do with the capture operation, and he was worried sick until he was told that the delay was purely technical.

The day he was to leave he went to the airport well in advance of his departure time and made a special point of seeing as many people as possible to make sure they would remember him. He tried to look gay and unconcerned, but he was under great stress. I had told him not to leave until he received final instructions from me, and he could hardly conceal his impatience. He knew that the most critical stage of the operation had been reached, and he waited for hours for a signal that all was well.

After what seemed to Asher an endless wait, Menashe appeared, perfectly calm. The expression on his face gave nothing away.

"Have you got a message for me?" asked Kedem.

"Yes, you can leave according to plan."

"That's all?"

"Yes, that's all."

Kedem couldn't for the life of him make out what was the matter with chatterbox Menashe, who chose this of all moments to be sparing with his words. But he didn't have the nerve to ask questions. He had to content himself with the thought that if a hitch had occurred I would certainly not be sending him to Israel to get the special flight ready. So he said a cheerful good-by to Menashe and left for New York at eleven o'clock that night. The following afternoon he continued his journey on an El Al plane. The nearer he got to Israel the more tense he became. He knew that he was the first to leave Argentina after Eichmann's capture, and he should have been in a position to bring the news to Israel—but there he was, unable to tell a soul. Even he actually knew nothing about it.

As the plane was about to take off from Rome on the last lap to Israel, he saw Haggai join the passengers. Without stopping to think, Kedem went up to him and said, "Mazel tov." Haggai looked at him a little surprised and made no response to his congratulations. Thinking it over, Kedem realized that if Haggai was just returning to Israel from Europe he couldn't know that Eichmann had been captured the night before, and he had the uncomfortable sensation that Haggai must have thought him a little peculiar. But when the plane landed at Lydda, Hillel Ankor and Leora Dotan were waiting for him. Haggai joined them, and Kedem was then able to break the news to all three: "Eichmann is in Israeli hands!"

---

A few days before the special flight was scheduled, Hillel Ankor called Yoram Golan in for a talk.

"I want to let you in on a secret," he began. He knew, actually, that his disclosure wouldn't come as a complete surprise to Yoram, because circles close to the operations group had already grasped the connection between the sudden disappearance of several outstanding operators, the interest displayed lately in specific files of Nazi war criminals, and the rumor current in the most restricted circles about the capture of Eichmann. No, Yoram Golan wasn't at all surprised when Hillel said, "Adolf Eichmann is in our hands, and you may have to go to Argentina to help in transporting him to Israel. Would you be prepared to go?"

"How can there be any doubt about such a thing?" said Yoram.

"Good. You must get ready to leave at once. And bring with you all the photographs you have of yourself."

Yoram had reason to be eager to take part in Operation Eichmann: his parents, his brothers, and his 107-year-old grandfather had been murdered by the Germans.

The next day, Hillel and another man spread out several pictures of Eichmann in uniform and in civilian dress, and next to these they put photographs Yoram had brought. Yoram shuddered as he watched the others comparing the two sets of photographs. He heard them say there was some resemblance but that fresh photographs of Yoram would have to be taken after applying suitable make-up. He was astonished to realize that he had been chosen to act as Eichmann's double. He felt a momentary but fleeting reluctance. After all, he said to himself, the part has to be played by somebody, and actually what did it matter what his role was as long as he had the privilege to be one of the men bringing Eichmann to Israel.

It took a laborious process of photographing from various angles and with various types of make-up to achieve a picture of Yoram that was completely satisfactory. A few days later he was sent to the airline to be fitted with a crew uniform. Hillel explained that he would be flying to Argentina as a crew member by the name of Zichroni. On the return flight to Israel, Eichmann might travel with the documentation prepared for Yoram, while Yoram would leave Argentina by another route.

Also on Yoram's flight, under cover as airline employees, were two other operators—Yoel Goren, who reconnoitered 4261 Chacabuco Street in 1958, and Elisha Naor. They were to be the escorts and guards of the "sick" crew member Zichroni on his "return" to Israel. They would have to handle any and all situations arising on the way, searches at intermediate stops, forced landings, or anything else.

Leora dealt with the documentation for the three new airline employees. No one knew how she managed to get the necessary papers, but in the end she brought Hillel Ankor documents that were in no respect different from those of the rest of the crew. The three of them packed their uniforms in suitcases and boarded the plane in civilian clothes. The delegation thought they were ordinary passengers, while the crew thought they were security men who would be guarding the delegation during its stay in Buenos Aires.

I had yet another task in mind for Yoel and Elisha: I was considering them for a last-minute commando operation, with the object of including Mengele among the plane's passengers—if we succeeded in locating him in time.

The schedule for the special flight had been changed twice. The original date, May 11, was postponed to May 14 because of the difficulty of taking a plane off the regular route at the height of the season. Then, in deference to the request from the Argentine protocol officials, it was put off again, this time to May 18. The airline advertised the change, stating that the flight from Lydda to Buenos Aires would take off at eleven A.M. May 18, landing en route at Rome, Dakar, and Recife, Brazil, with an estimated time of arrival at Buenos Aires of five P.M. May 19. The plane would take off again from Buenos Aires at five A.M. May 21, arriving at Recife at twelve-twenty P.M.; it would spend one hour at Recife and then fly to Dakar, arriving at seven-thirty P.M.; another hour at Dakar, and it would take off for Rome, landing at four-forty-five A.M. May 22; finally, after an hour in Rome, it would take off on the last lap to Lydda, due in at nine-forty-five A.M.

The responsibility for all the airline's activities in the Western Hemisphere, including South America, had always rested with its New York office. When the people there found out about the special flight they were extremely annoyed—and learning about it from the newspapers was considered a severe blow to their

authority. The manager of the New York office complained bitterly to Moshe Tadmor, claiming that they
had missed an excellent opportunity for a widespread
publicity campaign on behalf of the company in
Buenos Aires. He was also upset that he had lost the
chance to sell tickets in New York to passengers wish-
ing to go to Israel via South America. Tadmor apologized, explaining that the company was not in complete
control of the flight because its purpose was mainly
political, and for political reasons the date of the flight
had been postponed several times; consequently, all
the official announcements were under the authority
of the political departments. Tadmor wrote to his New
York friends,

> We were not aware of the possibilities mentioned
> in your letter, but, for compelling reasons which
> cannot be detailed here, it was not in our power
> to exploit them as we could have wished. . . .
> You are kindly requested to refrain from any in-
> tervention, conversation, or remarks pertinent to
> this flight, either at the office or outside, and to
> leave matters in the hands of the Head Office,
> except where you are explicitly requested to han-
> dle them.

Needless to say, the manager of the New York office
later apologized for his interference.

————

Asher Kedem went through five difficult days before
the plane took off from Lydda, but he could eventually
be proud of what he had accomplished. The air crew
was made up of the company's best employees: Captain
Yoav Meged was the pilot, with Captain Gad Nishri
joining him at Dakar; two excellent aircraft mechanics
were attached to the crew, with all the tools and spare
parts they could possibly take; the special equipment
was loaded according to instructions, and the three
crew members we had contributed were supplied with
everything they needed.

The official delegation was composed of people who

would enhance Israel's prestige; it included one of the
army's most eminent officers, Brigadier Zorea, who was
then Chief of Northern Command. The delegates knew
absolutely nothing about the drama of their flight.
Among the passengers were the Ambassador-designate
to Uruguay, with his family; another Israel diplomat
going to South America, with his family; and Rabbi
Efrati, who was going to Buenos Aires on behalf of
the Chief Rabbi to supervise kashruth. The delegation
was seen off at Lydda Airport by the Argentine Ambassador to Israel, the Director-General of the Foreign
Ministry, directors of the airline, and newspaper cor-
respondents.

———

Despite all the secrecy about our part in the special
flight, it was impossible to prevent a few people, particularly the flight crew, from noticing various oddities
and drawing their own conclusions. Gad Nishri, for
example, said he was positive from the moment he
was told he would be acting as copilot that a special
operation was involved in this special flight. A glance
at the list of the others flying with him only strengthened his suspicion. Gad was a veteran of *Palmach*
and served as a pilot in the War of Independence. He
was shot in the face when the "Primus" (a rickety
little Piper Cub) in which he flew was airlifting arms
to the famous Nebi Samwil convoy, encircled by Arabs.
Later he went overseas to graduate as a pilot, and for
several years he commanded a transport and parachute
squadron in the Air Force. Perhaps it was his *Hagana*
experience that led him to guess that the flight had some
connection with Nazi war criminals. Maybe he remembered the *Hagana*'s "Security Blacklist" No. 8, of
October 1947, warning the men against Adolf Eichmann: "speaks German, Hebrew and Yiddish . . . it is
not inconceivable that he may have succeeded in in-
filtrating into Israel."

Whatever prompted him, the fact is that, at Dakar,
Gad greeted Kedem with "Who are they bringing,
Mengele or Eichmann?"

Kedem drew back in amazement. How had the news

reached Dakar? How did Nishri know the best kept secret in the world? He promptly realized that his surprised look must have confirmed Nishri's shot in the dark, so he decided it would be better to tell him the truth and ask him to keep the secret than to let him go on with his questions and guesses. He asked, "Who told you that?"

"Not a soul."

"Look," Kedem said, "they're taking Eichmann. It's a dead secret, and if it's disclosed the operation will fail. You've got to promise me you won't open your mouth."

"Don't worry, Asher, don't worry," Gad said, and with great glee he kissed Asher on both cheeks.

Gad relieved Meged in the pilot's seat and probably spent the long journey from Dakar to Recife recalling the time he first heard Eichmann's name. He was a youngster, in Vienna in the thirties, when a rumor spread through the city that Eichmann, the commissar for Jewish affairs, had promised Hitler a birthday present—a *Judenrein* (Jew-free) Vienna.

Nishri was fourteen when Austria was annexed to Germany. For him this event meant expulsion from school and his family's eviction from their apartment. Of all the dreadful sights during those days one in particular was engraved on his memory: He saw a German mob fall upon an old rabbi, force a piece of pork fat into his mouth, and, with a victorious yell, set fire to his beard. A crowd of people stood by, but no one uttered a word of protest.

After the "Crystal Night" Gad's father managed to escape to Antwerp, and the rest of the Nishris joined him a little later. In 1940, under the auspices of Youth *Aliya,* Gad went to Israel, but his family was stuck in Belgium during the Nazi conquest. All were sent to Auschwitz, never to come out. About twenty of Gad's relatives perished in the Nazi death camps. Now the man who directed it all, the foreman of the murder factory, was going to be brought to Israel on this plane, to be judged for his crimes.

Nishri wasn't the only one who sensed something

unusual about the special flight. Fritz Shefer of the
airlines service department also understood that something was in the wind when he was told he would be
attached to the crew of the plane flying the official Israeli delegation to Argentina. He told his friend Yoav
Meged about his surmise. Yoav didn't go into detail
about Fritz's conjectures but merely told him he
wouldn't be sorry he'd been chosen to participate in
the flight. This cryptic remark heightened Fritz's curiosity even more. And then when he saw three crew
members he didn't know, he went to Meged and asked,
"Those three . . . are they O.K.?"

Yoav smiled his mysterious smile and said to Fritz,
"They're a hundred per cent. And don't be surprised if
on the way back we pick up another one you don't
know." And he left Fritz alone with his thoughts—
thoughts which no doubt recalled his childhood in Germany. Twice he had evaded the Nazis: first in 1938
when he fled to Denmark with the help of Youth *Aliya*
and again when his country of refuge was conquered.
At the height of the war he succeeded in reaching
Israel, through Sweden, Turkey, and Syria. Eichmann's
long arm hadn't caught up with him—but his father
perished in a Nazi concentration camp.

Leo Barkai, one of the airline's veteran stewards,
who had gone to Dakar ahead of the plane to obtain
provisions for the onward journey, also noticed the
three strangers among the passengers, but he thought
they were security men guarding the official delegation. However, before the landing at Buenos Aires
he saw them dressed in airline uniform, and that
started him thinking. He thought about the extensive
preparations that had preceded the take-off, the special
composition of the crew, the mechanics, and all these
things took on a new significance in his mind. Something was going to happen on this flight, he said to
himself. He detected an air of tension about his colleagues, but he saw them going on with their work in
a formal fashion, so he decided he'd better keep quiet.

Zvi Gutman, the airline's hangar foreman at Lydda,
reacted the same way. On May 16 the departmental

manager instructed Zvi to get a Britannia ready for a special flight. Zvi and his companions were extraordinarily meticulous about preparing the aircraft bound for Buenos Aires. Because the plane would be undertaking a longer journey than usual, and as it had to be presumed that good maintenance stations on the way might not be available, their preparations had to be painstaking over and above even their usual high standards. Several times during the next few days the departmental manager came to ask if everything was progressing according to plan, and Zvi gathered that even the company's management attributed special importance to this flight. One afternoon he was summoned to the office of the departmental manager.

"Zvi," he said, "we have decided to send a mechanic and an electrician on the flight." He noted the surprised expression on Zvi's face and hastened to explain, "It's a very long flight, and in that part of the world there are few Britannias, so we have reason to fear that in the event of a technical hitch on the way personnel familiar with this type of plane might be hard to find. The management is anxious to have the delegation arrive without any delays, and we have therefore decided to attach two aircraft mechanics to the flight. Whom do you suggest?"

"As electrician," said Zvi, "I suggest Negbi. As for the mechanic . . ."

Suddenly a thought flashed through his mind: why not himself? After all, it would be an opportunity to see South America. He had relatives there. Who knew when he would get another chance like that?

"As mechanic, I suggest myself," he said at last, amazed at his own audacity.

The departmental manager had some reservations about accepting his suggestion. Since Zvi was the ruling spirit at the hangars, his absence, even for a few days, would be hard to bear. But he quickly thought it over, perhaps because of the eagerness plainly displayed on Zvi's face. He agreed—and Zvi was the happiest of men.

Zvi worked long hours before he was satisfied with

the mechanical condition of the plane. It was only after
they took off that he had a chance to rest. Before long
he sat up and began looking at the members of the
official delegation. After all, it wasn't every day that
he had a chance to be at close quarters with a diplomat and brigadier. He also noticed the three strangers
who were neither delegates nor company employees,
and he came to the conclusion that they must be security men guarding the delegation.

A little overdone, he mused. A special plane and
special bodyguards for a flight from Lydda to Buenos
Aires. . . . But then, who am I to judge?

During the flight, Zvi had occasion to go down into
the freight compartment and was surprised to see several items that were unfamiliar to him. When he
climbed back into the cabin, he started making inquiries among the crew to find out if any of them
knew what their peculiar freight was. They didn't, but
Zvi noticed that one of the security men appeared to
be interested in his questions. He decided he'd better
put the whole thing out of his mind.

The last straw for him in this series of unusual happenings was the sight of the three security men in airline uniform just before the landing at Beunos Aires.
Zvi decided to pretend he hadn't noticed them.

————

The plane landed at Recife at five o'clock in the
morning. In spite of the early hour, the Israeli Ambassador to Brazil, Yosef Tekoa, was waiting for them at
the airport, and thousands of Jews had given up their
sleep just to welcome the Israeli delegation. The delegates were greeted with excited cheers from the assembled crowd, and the crew members handed out
everything they could find on the plane that could be
considered a souvenir of Israel. The head of the Jewish community and the local rabbi invited the delegation on a tour of the city.

Meanwhile, as was customary, Meged and Kedem
had presented themselves to the airfield authorities to
register the flight plan. They were stunned when the
airport controller told them they had no flight authori-

zation from the Brazilian authorities. Kedem claimed in exasperation that he himself had arranged the flight clearance when he was in Argentina, but the controller stood his ground and declared that they would not be allowed to take off until they had the requisite authorization. He added that it would take them not less than two hours to obtain the authorization, and maybe as much as six hours.

Meged asked him how come he had allowed the plane to land at Recife without a clearance, to which the controller replied that they had permission to land but not to fly over Brazilian territory. Kedem promptly suggested that they could turn toward the sea again on their take-off and in that way avoid flying in Brazilian air space. The controller said that actually they had the right to fly in Brazilian air space—but not to take off. The head of the delegation and Ambassador Tekoa tried to intervene, but the controller stuck to his guns.

The man's behavior seemed suspicious to Yoav. He wondered if something had leaked out to the Brazilian authorities, since otherwise it was hard to understand what made the fellow put obstacles in their way. Kedem and Tekoa went to the Israeli consulate in the city to try to communicate with the central air authorities in Rio de Janeiro, but they couldn't get a connection. When they returned to the airfield, they saw Meged in the distance waving a piece of paper—it was the authorization to fly in Brazilian air space. Meged had solved the problem by applying to the representative of the Argentine national airline, who obtained telegraphic confirmation from Buenos Aires that the clearance for transit over Brazilian territory had been sent to Recife the day before.

Then, when the passengers were already seated in the plane, the airport controller found another excuse to delay the take-off. He demanded that Meged sign a statement of wide legal significance in connection with the flight—something that was contrary to all airport usage. Meged rejected his demand, and only after a long dispute did the controller agree to be content with a statement about the place of departure, the purpose of the flight, and its destination.

The incident at Recife cast a gloom over the spirits of those members of the crew who knew the true purpose of the flight, and the controller's obstinacy had a depressing effect on the others as well. Yoav Meged was more worried than any of them, and Gad Nishri was afraid there had been some hitch in the capture of Eichmann.

# 24

The confusion in Recife had delayed the plane's arrival in Buenos Aires by two and a half hours, but the reception was not affected. A red carpet was spread, a band played national anthems, and children were waving flags and cheering the visitors. In addition to Argentine protocol officials, the Israeli Embassy staff and Jewish community leaders were there to welcome them. The atmosphere was solemn yet friendly.

Dan Avner had no time to watch the ceremonies. As soon as the delegation left the plane he boarded it to inform the two mechanics that they were not allowed to leave the airfield to go into the city, they had to guard the plane during the night. He explained that there was reason to suspect that hostile agencies might try to damage the plane.

They were extremely disappointed. Was it for this that they had taken the long journey from Lydda? To be confined to the airport and not see Buenos Aires, so famous for its beauty? Zvi thought about the relatives he wouldn't be able to visit. How was he going to explain to his father that he had been in Argentina and yet hadn't seen any of them?

Aharon Lazar and Esther Rosen were among the airlines people welcoming the plane. Esther was surprised at the way the special flight had been handled. First we had asked her to help get permission to fly passengers from Buenos Aires. She had come up against innumerable difficulties and had devised all kinds of ruses to overcome them. Yet when she thought she was finally within reach of her goal, Lazar suddenly announced that she must stop all further activity in the matter. She simply couldn't understand this strange decision. Every single ticket sold in Buenos Aires was clear profit for the company. She tried protesting, but nobody paid any attention to her complaints. Now she was determined to appeal to Kedem, who had given her the job of getting the permit to carry passengers, and demand to know the reason for the sudden change in policy. She wasn't to know that I was responsible for the order to do nothing further about passengers from Buenos Aires.

That night a few of the crew stayed at the airport hotel, while the rest, including the two captains, put up at a large hotel in the center of the city.

In anticipation of the plane's arrival, I moved my roving headquarters to cafés nearer the airport, and shortly after it landed I received a report about the initial arrangements for guarding, parking, and preparing the aircraft for the return flight to Israel. The delegates would not be returning the way they had come. The head of the delegation intended going from Argentina to visit the United States, and the others also wanted to spend a little time in the Western Hemisphere. So the plane had only two things to wait for: a thorough technical checkup, and the compulsory rest period for the crew as laid down in international regulations.

I gave instructions that throughout the waiting time the plane had to be under the continuous supervision of the crew. The cover story for these security measures was that enemies of Israel might attempt to damage the aircraft in their rage at the warm reception given to the delegation by the Argentine government, press, and public. My real object was to be on constant watch for anybody who had thought of connecting Klement's disappearance with the arrival of the plane and would certainly try to check up on the plane and its crew. Also, I believed that this was one way of finding out if there was any government agency, officially or unofficially, taking an active interest in Eichmann's fate.

Yoav Meged and Asher Kedem came into the café shortly after the plane arrived. They looked tired, which I attributed to the long flight, but they allowed that their condition was due to extreme tension and not just fatigue—they couldn't rest because of the incident at Recife. Meged firmly declared that he was prepared to do whatever I ordered him to do, except one thing: he would never land at Recife again. Kedem explained that it wasn't his fault; before he left Buenos Aires for Israel, he had attended to the clearance for transit in Brazilian air space and the right to land, and he couldn't understand what the Brazilian airport controller's motives were.

I calmed him down and told him that logically no link was possible between the incident at Recife and the operation itself, since if there had been any mishap in the operation the first repercussions would be felt in Buenos Aires and not in Brazil. Furthermore, if anybody had any suspicions about what the plane would be used for, he would presumably try to test these suspicions before it took off from Buenos Aires, and not while it was still on its way to Argentina. All these considerations apart, I said, it was an accomplished fact that the operation had gone off without a hitch, and there was no sign of any change in the situation. Naturally, we would have to exercise constant vigilance to safeguard Eichmann during his transfer to the plane. I hoped, however, that the plans we had made would enable us to bring this stage, too, to a successful conclusion.

Before long, they had both relaxed, but Meged repeated that he would not fly by way of Brazil. He considered our first plan the most workable—putting Eichmann on board in the maintenance area under cover as a crew member who was sick or had been injured in an accident. It was decided that the whole crew would come to the maintenance area together, so that our special passenger could be brought in as one of a large group. All those who had no tasks to perform at take-off would remain in their seats on the plane, together with Eichmann, and take a nap to be fresh for the last portion of the flight when they would take up their duties as members of the crew. They were to have the use of the first-class compartment.

I wanted to bring the departure time as far forward as possible, but Meged explained that for safety reasons it was essential to allow the crew substantial rest before the plane set off again. He finally fixed midnight of the following day, May 20, 1960, as the time for the take-off. I suggested announcing the time of departure as later than it really was—two hours after midnight—in order to mislead any hostile agencies who might be planning a surprise inspection of the aircraft at the last minute. There was nothing to stop us from doing so, I said, because the flight was not included in the regular timetable and there were no passengers to be called to the airport beforehand.

The day before our plane arrived the army had set up roadblocks on the roads leading to the airport. There were at the time American air-force planes and a British plane on the field. Lazar believed they had brought official guests to the anniversary celebrations. The inspection at the checkpoints next to the airfield was very scrupulous, and even Lazar wasn't allowed to pass until he proved that he was the representative of a foreign airline.

Our aircraft was parked, as planned, in the Argentine national airline's maintenance area, which we were able to approach without going through the fenced-in section of the airfield. We intentionally created a constant traffic of people passing through the checkpoint at the Argentine company's maintenance area. The two aircraft mechanics were ordered to get busy without delay on preparations for take-off, so that the plane would be in flight condition should circumstances compel its departure before the appointed hour.

Zvi was now certain that all the strange happenings since they took off from Lydda were part of a pattern, but he didn't talk to anyone about it. When he finished servicing the plane, he again asked Dan for permission to visit his relatives in the city. Dan said yes and even gave him money and a car with a driver. However, his relatives were not at home, so Zvi left a note asking them to come and see him at the airport hotel. Negbi took advantage of Zvi's early return to treat himself to a tour of the city.

———

At *Tira,* the tension was again rising. In the oppressive atmosphere of the safe house, impatience, disgust, and boredom were all mixed up together. Everyone had read all the books in the languages he understood; each knew all the popular Argentine tunes broadcast over the radio; there had been endless games of chess; and newspapers were read from beginning to end. All were waiting, on edge, in suspense, for the arrival of the liberating plane.

Shortly before the aircraft was due, Gabi increased the guard and stiffened the security regulations. Any departure from the house for any reason whatsoever was absolutely forbidden, and severe limitations were placed on traffic even inside the house, in case the neighbors should notice too much activity in a house which as far as they knew was occupied by only two persons.

Several nights Gabi thought there were strangers moving around outside the house. He was no longer apprehensive of a visit from the police, but he had fears about the Nazis and their sympathizers who were probably combing the entire city for Eichmann.

When the plane arrived, Gabi and Ehud were at the airport. They stood to one side among the waiting crowd, their sharp eyes registering every person who came down the gangway. Three of the new arrivals they knew very well, and they would be meeting them shortly in the city, at a prearranged rendezvous.

The disembarkation was a little embarrassing for Yoram. Rabbi Efrati was an acquaintance of his. When they met at Lydda, the Rabbi asked Yoram if he was also one of the delegation. Yoram said yes—what else could he say? Now, descending the steps dressed in the uniform of the crew, he met the Rabbi again, despite all his efforts to avoid him. Rabbi Efrati didn't ask any questions this time; he just looked at him with a meaningful smile, and for a moment Yoram thought he saw the highly respected man of the cloth wink at him. Later, after consulting with his two companions, he decided he needn't ask the Rabbi to keep quiet: all three were sure the Rabbi would realize that he mustn't mention the transformation from "delegate" to "crew."

Yoram, tired from the journey, lay down to sleep as soon as he arrived at his hotel. But he had barely dozed off when Ehud came and woke him. He had come for the uniform and documentation to be used by Eichmann.

Late that evening I held a long series of discussions with the men of the task force. All the plans for the next day were reexamined and various modifications made. The timetable for each stage of the operation was compiled, with each man's function clearly defined and meeting places fixed for the various groups.

During those last hours before the decisive day I made up my mind that it was still worthwhile detaching a couple of men for one last try at the Mengele plan. The object was to check the identity of all the tenants of the house where, until a month ago, Mengele had lived. As part of my final plans, I took into consideration the contingency that we might have to make a last-minute attempt to capture Mengele and put him on the plane.

I settled all the operational arrangements with Gabi and Ehud: the dismantling of the installations in the safe house, the concealing of the equipment, the returning of the cars, and the procedure for the departure of our men from Argentina on completion of the operation.

The plan we had finally settled on was that Eichmann be taken from *Tira* to the plane dressed in airline uniform. He would have with him the documents in the name of Zichroni which had been taken from Yoram. Eichmann would pass, we hoped, as an air-

plane crew member whose head had been injured in an
auto accident. The doctor would make all the necessary preparations to drug him during the transfer.
From morning on, reconnaissance of the roads leading from the safe house to the airfield would be
organized. The last reconnaissance would be made by
Yitzhak, whose arrival at the airport would be the
signal for the car to leave the airport to collect Eichmann from *Tira*. It would proceed to the safe house,
pick him up, and then return to the airport carrying
Eichmann and his escorts  Kenet would drive this
car, and Eichmann would be placed on the back seat
between the doctor and one of the escorts. The other
escort would sit next to Kenet. If, after the car arrived at the airport, it was for some reason impossible for Eichmann to embark with the crew at the
plane's parking spot, we would try to put him on
board when the plane was standing on the runway. In
that case, the "injured" man would pass through all
the conventional border controls.

We decided further that the security cleanup of the
safe house would be done by Gabi, Ehud, Eli, Shalom,
and Dina. They would set to work immediately after
the departure of the plane and then they would leave
Argentina immediately, as soon as they were sure they
had left behind them no sign of what had gone on at
*Tira*.

Ehud was given the task of delivering all the instructions to the persons concerned, as Gabi had in the
meantime returned to the safe house and couldn't participate in the summing up. Menashe was ordered to
make sure that the car taking Eichmann to the airport was in perfect condition. He would also be the
one to take it to the airport and hand it over to Kenet.
Menashe was put at the disposal of the group which
was to inspect Mengele's former home, and he was
also asked to help Rafael Arnon obtain a quick release
from the hospital. Menashe would deliver Rafael's
papers to Shalom Dani, who would quickly adapt
them to suit Eichmann's personal description. These
papers would be used in case Eichmann could not be

embarked with the crew and proof of his injury would
be needed. Menashe was requested to make himself
available to me at the airfield, with another rented
car, from early afternoon on.

The last one I spoke to that night was Shalom Dani.
I stressed that his most urgent task was to complete
the documentation for crew member Zichroni. We
also made sure that the documentation for all the men
of the task force was in order. And finally we discussed the disposition of his equipment and the manner of his leaving the country. We decided that after
he finished his work in the laboratory he would come
to me at the airport. I told him he should put together
a set of essential tools so that he could still do any
indispensable last-minute work that might crop up. I
warned him that such work would have to be carried
out under difficult operational conditions—sitting at
a table in one of the airport lounges, for instance, or in
a car in the parking lot.

It was late when we parted. Shalom didn't go to
bed that night—he went straight to work.

---

It was a sleepless night for most of the people at
*Tira,* too. Until the early hours of the morning there
was feverish activity in the house. Each of the temporary tenants was studying his assignment for the next
day and going over Gabi's instructions for "liquidation
of personal matter," concentration of belongings in
one spot, security inspections of personal luggage, and
a thorough check of documentation.

A great deal of work also went into restoring the
house to its former condition. Everything that was in
it when we rented it was put back in its place, and
everything that was added during our tenancy was
destroyed or put aside to be taken away. Another inspection would be held the next day, and then a final
check while Eichmann was on the way to the airfield.
The inspectors worked with exact lists in their hands
to make sure they wouldn't forget even the most minute detail.

Similar arrangements were made for the other safe

houses and operational apartments. Gabi was put in charge of both the removal of all traces of our activities in the Argentine capital and the disposal of the entire inventory of items we had bought or rented.

# 25

It finally came, the twentieth of May—the last day and, for me, the longest and most dramatic day of Operation Eichmann. Early in the morning, after snatching a few hours of sleep, I got up, packed my things, paid my hotel bill, and took a taxi to the railway station. I deposited my luggage at the station and went to my first rendezvous of the day. I intended picking up my luggage sometime during the day so that I would have it with me when I decided how I was going to leave Buenos Aires.

The first to meet me that day were Binyamin Efrat and Meir Lavi. I knew that there was only a very remote chance that Mengele was still at the house in Vicente López, but I wanted the facts checked thoroughly. If he was there, my plan was to mount a surveillance near the house throughout the day, and if nothing important or unusual happened we would try to get into the house in the evening and take Mengele forcibly to the car waiting nearby. To be sure the police were not called in, I would leave two men watching his family until the plane left. I had also devised a plan for putting Mengele on board the aircraft. It was a plan which involved a certain amount of risk, but I estimated that it wouldn't endanger our main operation. What I had in mind was to bring Mengele to the plane just before take-off, once our first "client" was already safely inside. I was working on the assumption that there would otherwise be no special reason for the police to make a search at the airfield—and even if they did catch our men, it could be taken for granted that they would reveal nothing about Eichmann.

But all this depended, naturally, on what Binyamin and Meir found at the house. I told Meir he should gain entry to the house on the pretext of delivering a parcel; Binyamin was to claim that he had been summoned a few weeks before to inspect and repair the water heater. I fixed a timetable for each of their visits to the house—Meir was to go there first, in the morning, and Binyamin would go late in the afternoon.

Shortly after Meir and Binyamin left, Yoav Meged and Asher Kedem came along. They requested permission to tell the senior members of the crew about the operation, so that they could act with full understanding of the situation. I agreed, and it was decided that Meged would tell the copilot Nishri, the two navigators, two flight engineers, two stewards, and the air hostess. We also arranged the schedule for the crew. The captain and those members of the crew required for starting the aircraft would leave their hotel in Buenos Aires at eight-thirty in the evening and arrive at the plane at nine-thirty. The rest of the crew members, apart from those staying at the airport hotel, would leave the city at nine-thirty and arrive at the airfield at ten-thirty, where they would immediately join their colleagues at the airport hotel.

The car with Eichmann would arrive at eleven o'clock. After a final check of the situation the car would proceed to where the plane was parked, accompanied by a minibus containing the crew that was not already at the aircraft. The car should be at the plane by eleven-ten. As soon as Eichmann was embarked, the plane's engines would be started and it would taxi onto the apron—the time would then be about eleven-fifteen. After that, every effort would be made to take off at the earliest possible moment.

That morning Meged assembled all the members of the crew who were to be let in on the secret. He told them that their plane would be taking a passenger who would be introduced as a member of the crew and would be wearing company uniform. Though the man would look ill, the illness would be due to a drug injected into him a little earlier. Without mentioning the name of the mysterious passenger, Meged said that the operation was of paramount national importance. His listeners—except Nishri—were flabbergasted. Now all the strange incidents and obscure activities they had witnessed began to make sense. Meged told them what they had to do and explained the assignments they would be carrying out under his orders.

Meged sat with Nishri and the navigator Giladi and plotted a direct flight from Buenos Aires to Dakar. The flight would put the Britannia to a severe test, as it was slightly beyond the aircraft's range and there might be a shortage of fuel. Weather conditions, however, were favorable, and they decided that the flight could be undertaken if these conditions remained stable.

Back at the hospital, Rafael's condition improved steadily. Every day his friend Menashe came to visit him and pass on our doctor's latest instructions. Rafael saw to it that the course of his recovery followed the doctor's instructions to the letter. He was a model patient, and despite his ignorance of Spanish he won over all the hospital workers with his pleasant behavior. The doctors regarded the fact that he wasn't vomiting as a good sign, and when he heard them say there was an improvement in his condition Rafael started showing an interest in the date of his release from hospital. He explained that he had come to Buenos Aires in order to fly home on the plane that had brought the delegation. All the lines to Europe, he said, were fully booked and it was almost impossible to get a seat on a plane, and his best prospect of getting home without too many transfers on the way was by the special plane. Since tickets for the flight were not offered for sale, he said, he hoped he could save a considerable sum of money since the airline might take into account his state of health and accept him as a nonpaying passenger. His friend had already spoken to the airline about this and had assured him that the airline would approve, as long as the doctors gave him permission for the flight.

The hospital staff sympathized with Rafael's problem, but the doctors said that it would of course depend on his condition. They couldn't take the responsibility of releasing him too soon, especially as he intended taking such a long journey. They assured him, however, that he was making steady progress, and that his prospects were good.

Menashe visited Rafael on the evening of May 19 with a large box of candy and gave him the doctor's instructions for his symptoms that evening and the following morning. Menashe told him to tell the doctors that because of his illness, the airline was prepared to take him but the airline officials wanted written confirmation from the doctors that he was in a fit state to travel. The doctors said that if there was no deterioration in his condition, and if the results of further tests in the morning were satisfactory, then they would give him the confirmation.

The next morning Menashe brought me a report on the patient's condition. He had a quiet night, it said, and woke up fresh and full of energy. Now everything depended on the results of the tests— if they were favorable the patient would be released in time.

———

Yoram Golan also came to see me that morning. I told him that if everything went well Eichmann would be using Yoram's documentation to leave Argentina as a member of the crew; but as the details of the plan had not yet been finally settled, I suggested that he have a look around the city and meet me again in the afternoon.

The report from *Tira* was encouraging. The night had passed quietly and no suspicious movement was noticed near the house. The people imprisoned there were in cheerful spirits. Eichmann had slept well, and his meals were planned—under doctor's instructions—

to suit the various quantities of anesthetic he would be given during the course of the day. The doctor gave him another thorough examination and stated that he was in fine health and would be able to withstand the long flight.

The information from the airfield was also satisfactory. The plane was in excellent condition. No special interest in our Britannia had been displayed by the authorities or by anyone else during the night.

Menashe reported that, according to the newspapers, the anniversary celebrations were in full swing, and the authorities were apprehensive about demonstrations or outbreaks on the part of groups hostile to the regime. All the security establishments were therefore on the alert, and police and army units were patrolling the roads. As for Klement—still no word about him in the press.

———

In the afternoon I moved my mobile headquarters nearer to the scene of the critical stage of the operation, the airport itself.

The place was teeming with planes and swarming with people. Soldiers and police awaited the arrival of the important guests gathering to convey the good wishes of their governments to the people of Argentina. Senior members of the government went out to welcome the VIPs, and a large concentration of security forces guarded the guests and their reception committees.

My first idea was to settle myself in one of the passenger lounges, but I was certain that among the huge crowd there were bound to be quite a few security men on the alert to anything out of the ordinary; and even though it was not unusual for people to spend a few hours in the passenger lounge at an airport, I still considered it inadvisable to risk attracting attention, especially since the security men would be under unaccustomed strain. I toured the airfield installations, looking for a suitable place to hold my meetings—a reasonable place from the point of view of security. In all the lounges set aside for passengers it was the same: throngs of passengers and other people coming to meet or see them off. Eventually, in one of the side wings of the complex of buildings, I found a large hall which served as a kind of canteen for airfield employees. It was more plainly constructed and furnished than the reception halls for passengers, and the food served there was simple and cheap.

The canteen was filled to capacity with civilians, soldiers, and police, most of them taking a breather between tours of duty, having something to eat or drink, and sheltering from the cold, rainy weather outside. The air in the hall was heavy and full of smoke, and the din was deafening. I looked in vain for an empty table—all were occupied, and numbers of people were standing around waiting for chairs to become vacant. There was a constant stream of people moving between the tables and the exit.

I decided that this was the ideal place to establish my operational headquarters. In that constant turmoil nobody would pay attention to several people coming in, sitting down at a table, then getting up and giving their seats to others. But how to get a table here? I joined the long line of people in uniform, in office clothes, in overalls, who were wandering around the hall in search of unoccupied or emptying tables. A few of them were lined up next to tables which showed imminent signs of being vacated. The minute anybody got up one of those on the waiting line grabbed the empty chair. I did the same and found myself sitting with a group of soldiers eating with hearty appetites. My table companions were in high spirits, and their courtesy was exemplary.

The first person who came to see me at my new location had to stand stooping over me so that we could hear each other through the general uproar. Nobody took any notice. As time went on, more and more of our men came to stand around me. When one of the places at the table was vacated we didn't give an outsider the chance to take it but grabbed it quickly for ourselves. Ultimately, the table was all ours, and from then on we were very careful not to leave a seat empty. We contributed several chairs to a neighboring table and saw to it that nobody from our table got up unless he could give a chair to another of our men. It was from this place that I directed the operation to its conclusion.

———

Asher Kedem was one of the first to come to the new headquarters I had set up. I asked him how the crew had reacted when the nature of our operation was explained to them. He said a few of them had guessed that the flight had something to do with Nazi war criminals, and they were all filled with anticipation about the final action. There's no doubt, he said, that they will now work with twice as much devotion. When I asked if we could rely on the punctuality of the crew, Kedem replied that I need have no fears about late arrivals, personal complications, or anything similar which might upset the course of the operation, since the entire crew had been carefully selected.

Once again we examined the plans I had drawn up, and Kedem gave his opinion that under existing conditions all of them were workable.

I asked him about the normal inspection procedures for those on the crew who started the aircraft's engines and taxied the plane onto the apron. I wanted to know at what stage these men passed through customs and border control.

We decided finally that the car and the minibus carrying the rest of the crew to the plane would wait in the parking lot until the car with Eichmann in it joined them, and all three would proceed together to the checkpoint in the area where the plane was parked. The car with the crew members would head the procession to test the reaction and alertness of the sentries. The men must be noisy and gay, I said, as if they were still in holiday spirits. The technical inspection and fueling must be completed before the arrival of the crew, and all the provisions to be loaded on to the plane from the apron must be ready in good time, so that not a single second should be lost.

Only one problem remained to be cleared up, one that was actually only indirectly connected with the operation. The local branch of the airline company had received quite a few requests from Israelis—ill or stranded in Buenos Aires—to be flown to Israel free of charge, and Kedem wanted to know how to deal with them. With great regret, particularly for the sick applicants, I had to refuse them. I was afraid such passengers might hamper the speed of take-off and cause other delays; furthermore, accepting them would be likely to raise procedural problems, not to mention the security risk of taking just anybody on an operational flight. To avoid unfair criticism of the airline for hardheartedness, I advised Kedem to explain to all the applicants that, according to directives from Tel Aviv, the plane might have to change its flight direction at the last moment and proceed to some airport other than Lydda.

———

Zvi and Negbi were busy the entire day preparing the aircraft for its long flight. They checked and rechecked time after time, but they found no malfunctions. In the afternoon Zev Keren joined them. They had been told he was authorized to come and go as he pleased and that they could trust him and must give him all the help he asked for. Zev asked a lot of questions, and Zvi could see they were all to the point. But he couldn't make out what this reticent man, who displayed such professional skill in technical matters, was trying to accomplish.

Toward evening Zvi was told to wander around the aircraft and to leave and return a number of times, so the guards at the checkpoint would get used to the constant traffic of company men to and from the plane. After he had gone through the gate a few times he was no longer asked to show his papers.

These peculiar instructions finally convinced Zvi that something out of the ordinary was cooking, but still

Zev's activities provided no key to the mystery. Zev went on asking questions and showing great interest in the plane's construction, but he kept his mouth shut about the important matters. Zvi decided to ignore him and start fueling the plane.

———

Rafael Arnon waited impatiently for the results of the final medical tests which would decide his fate. He had no idea why it was so important for him to be released from the hospital on that particular day, but he was intelligent enough to comprehend that the success or failure of a vitally important action might depend on his ability to convince the doctors that he was completely recovered. When he was summoned to the doctor's office, he was still trying to remember if he had done exactly as Menashe had told him. Judging by the smile with which he was greeted, he understood everything was in order. The doctor patted him on the shoulder and told him that the tests were satisfactory, and the hospital was prepared to let him go and to give permission for him to fly to Israel. The doctor even had a medical certificate ready for him:

### SUMMARY OF CLINICAL PICTURE
### OF RAFAEL ARNON

On May 17, 1960, the above mentioned was injured in a car accident while sitting on the rear seat of a moving car, when the car braked suddenly and he was thrown against the front seat. There was no visible injury to the head. Nevertheless, he lost consciousness for several minutes. For twenty-four hours after that he suffered from vertigo, but he had no nausea and did not vomit. The neurological test carried out the following day (May 18) was normal. Skull X-rays showed no fracture or other abnormality. He was released on May 20. The neurological test is normal. In our opinion, there is nothing to prevent the patient from traveling by air. It is advisable that medical supervision be continued in order to diagnose rapidly any possible complications following the blow.

Rafael promptly telephoned Menashe, who was waiting at a large café in the vicinity, and asked him to come and pick him up from the hospital. He said goodby to the staff and the friends he had made among the patients, and they all wished him a speedy recovery and a pleasant journey.

Menashe arrived shortly afterward. They drove to the safe house *Ramim,* and as soon as they were inside Menashe took away Rafael's papers and forbade him under any circumstances whatsoever to set foot out of the building until the papers were given back to him or until he was supplied with other documentation. Menashe hurried off to *Maoz,* to Shalom Dani. Eichmann's photographs were already lying on the table, and Shalom quickly attached them to Rafael's documents.

From *Maoz,* Menashe dashed off to meet me. He found me surrounded by people standing and waiting to talk to me—and to sit down. He reported Rafael's release and showed me his doctor's certificate. I told Menashe that Rafael must remain at *Ramim* until further instructions. If we used his papers, Menashe would bring him fresh ones prepared by Shalom Dani so that he could leave Argentina without delay. But even if his documents were not used, Rafael must take care not to linger on in Argentina, since there was always the likelihood of his meeting one of the doctors who had attended him. In the meantime, Menashe must go to see Rafael in his "prison" to explain the circumstances and to see that he had enough food and everything else he would need until he could leave.

Meir Lavi, who was handling Operation Mengele, was two hours late. I had already begun to fear that this delay might force us to make serious changes in our arrangements for a final briefing. And the diversion of personnel for Mengele's capture—presuming, of course, that he was still in the house—would create an even greater disruption.

When Meir eventually appeared, the expression of his face showed that he'd had no luck. He explained quite candidly that he hadn't managed to arrange a parcel delivery as a plausible pretext for entering the house. He could see he was wasting valuable time so he decided to do something else. By looking through the telephone directory until he came across the address of the house, he was able to find the name and number of the owner. He promptly dialed the number and asked to speak to the owner of the house. The woman who answered the phone could hardly speak Spanish. She asked him if he spoke English, and they switched to that language. From her accent and idiom Meir gathered that she was American, new to the place, and definitely not of German origin. She had no hesitation in giving her name, and when he asked about the previous tenants, she said she knew nothing about them.

I reprimanded Meir for not having followed instructions, and then I set him at ease and told him that he'd caused no harm and had even achieved certain results. He was very relieved, though he was still positive he'd made a serious mistake. I asked him to sit and wait for further instructions.

About an hour later Binyamin Efrat appeared. He was wearing overalls and looked tired and depressed. Equipped with electrician's tools, he had gone to the house in Vicente López and rung the doorbell. He explained in Spanish to the woman who opened the door that he had come to repair the hot-water heater. She replied in halting Spanish with an English or American accent, and it was obvious she hadn't fully understood him. Very patiently he explained again what he had come for, and she said she hadn't ordered any repairs. Binyamin told her the workshop had been asked to send somebody. He admitted that this was quite a few days ago, but nobody had telephoned since then to cancel the order. She tried to explain that it must be a misunderstanding, or that maybe the former tenants had asked for the heater to be repaired. In any case, she didn't know anything about any repair orders.

During the course of the conversation, Binyamin asked for her name and she gave it without hesitation —the same name the postman had mentioned earlier. Clearly the woman wasn't German and she wasn't trying to hide anything. It was quite obvious that Mengele had in fact moved out of the house.

I thanked Meir and Binyamin for their conscientiousness and asked them to convey my thanks to their wives as well. I told them that they had better leave Argentina the next day—unless Menashe told them to wait—but that I'd like them to stand by until midnight. They knew nothing about what was going to happen that night.

Their findings came as a bitter disappointment. Though I knew that the prospects of finding Mengele at his old address were pretty poor, I nevertheless hoped that luck might be on our side. It was hard to reconcile myself to the fact that we had missed the opportunity of capturing the murderous doctor by as little as a couple of weeks. However, there was nothing to do but continue with the work ahead of us.

---

For the next few hours reports on various details of the operation continued to pour in. The safe house *Doron,* I was told, had been evacuated and was ready to be handed back to the owners the next morning. At *Tira* everything was in order. From midday they had stopped giving Eichmann food or drink in preparation for his partial drugging. Eli made up the prisoner's face as he had for Shalom Dani's photographs, and he did a perfect job—even Eichmann's best friends in Argentina wouldn't have been able to identify him.

Conditions on the roads weren't ideal, but there was no particular cause for anxiety. The security forces were out on patrol, but it was possible to avoid running into them. If nothing unexpected happened, there was every reason to assume that private cars wouldn't be held up in the vicinity of the airfield.

The airport itself and the approach roads were full of all kinds of security men, but they were not conducting searches at either the airport itself or its entrances. In the departure lounge there was no extraordinary bustle and no sign of abnormal tension. The security men seemed too busy with the important incoming visitors to pay much attention to departing passengers.

In the maintenance area where our plane was standing there was no undue commotion. The afternoon and evening papers were well scrutinized: still no mention of Klement's disappearance.

# 26

At seven-thirty I was waiting for Yitzhak's final re-connaissance report. Since I had only until eight o'clock to dispatch the car to *Tira* to pick up Eich-mann, the results of Yitzhak's latest reconnaissance were really vital. But he was late.

Kenet, who was to drive the car, sat at my table, awaiting instructions. By seven-fifty-five he was showing signs of anxiety—Yitzhak wasn't there yet. If I knew that his car had broken down I wouldn't have worried; I could send Kenet out to look for him at the side of the road. Or Kenet could still have made a final check of the roads himself. But what if Yitzhak had been stopped? I knew that even in that case he would hold his tongue and win the confidence of the guards, for no one was more capable of looking con-vincingly innocent.

At eight o'clock precisely I told Kenet and the other man with him that we couldn't wait any longer and they must get going. I told them that if the high-ways seemed more or less safe they should bring Eich-mann and his escorts without awaiting further word from Yitzhak. I reminded them that they should ar-rive at the airfield by eleven o'clock. I would arrange for reconnaissance of the airfield itself, and if any-thing went wrong I would send a courier by car to stop them and give them fresh instructions. If they didn't come across any of our men on the road it would mean that the way was clear, and they would then go straight to the spot on the parking lot previously agreed on by Kenet and Ehud. They were to wait there for further instructions from me.

Yoav Meged fixed seven o'clock as the time for the crew's evening meal and told his men that as soon as they had finished eating they must leave the hotel and drive to the airport. He and the men who had to prepare the aircraft for take-off left Buenos Aires at eight-thirty. Neither on the way nor when they entered the airfield were they stopped or asked to show their papers. It was only when they got to the checkpoint at the Argentine national airline's maintenance area that they were asked to identify themselves, but the inspection was perfectly routine. By nine-thirty they were at the plane. A final check showed that everything was in order, so there was nothing more for them to do except wait for the convoy of cars bringing Eichmann. While waiting, they noted once again that all was quiet in their vicinity.

Shalom Dani also arrived at the airport in the evening, having completed all his work in the laboratory. He was carrying a briefcase and looked like any passenger waiting for a plane. I gave him some last-minute work, and he sat down at a table in a corner and got busy with his "correspondence," just like a tourist with time on his hands. Letters were strewn over his table and he himself wrote many "letters" that evening—filling in various official forms, extending the expiration date of one passport, changing the photograph on another. The waiters who went over to him from time to time, serving him drinks or clearing the table, didn't notice anything out of the ordinary.

Dan Avner came to tell me that all the crew who had been lodging in the city had arrived; none of them had been held up or had experienced any difficulties whatsoever when they entered the airport. As for the plane, it was ready for take-off and waiting only for its chief passenger.

The hands of the clock stood at ten-thirty. If every-thing is all right, I told myself, the Eichmann con-voy will be at the airfield in half an hour. Ehud came to report that the latest reconnaissance at the field and at the entrances revealed no cause for suspicion or anxiety. There was much traffic of security forces, but there were no roadblocks and no searches. I agreed with Ehud that there was no need to send anyone out to the convoy. It was better to let it proceed on its own. But Ehud must go at once to the spot where the plane was parked to check that everything was in order and come straight back to give me the results of his inspection. Afterward he would go out to meet the convoy and inform me as soon as it arrived. The minute he got the order to move he would lead the convoy through the checkpoint and up to the plane.

Meanwhile, Dan Avner assembled all the crew at the airport hotel and addressed them: "Gentleman, you are participating in a great event. Don't ask me what it is. Just do exactly as I tell you. We are taking someone with us to Israel. I will tell you his identity later on."

Even those members of the crew who had not yet been let in on the secret were not very surprised when they heard the disclosure. They had already sensed from all the activity that something out-of-the-ordinary was taking place. When Dan told them to get into the car and minibus standing at the edge of the hotel parking ground, they did so without further ques-tion.

Ehud had in the meantime carried out a quick in-spection near the plane and found everything as it should be. He drove immediately to the main entrance of the airport and sent a courier to tell me that the road to the aircraft was open and safe.

Ehud made his way to the parking lot and found Dan and the crew waiting there. He told them that from then on none of them would be allowed to leave the cars. He instructed the drivers to start the engines and wait for a signal. Turning to the crew, he told them that when they were passing through the checkpoint before our parking area they must act loud and boisterous to draw the attention of the sentries away from the occupants of the third car that would be joining them. When they reached the plane they must form a tight cordon to cover up a most important security action. Ehud then returned to the main entrance of the airfield to wait for the convoy and direct it to the parking lot.

———

While all this was going on I never moved from my seat in the employees' canteen. I calculated that almost three hours had passed since the car had left to pick up Eichmann and his guards. I hadn't made any reporting arrangements in connection with the car's departure from the safe house because I knew that if anything went wrong I would be powerless to help. Nor had there been any word from Yitzhak yet. Two things could have happened: either he had run into trouble or he had met his colleagues on the way and joined the convoy.

After a long drawn-out wait—I felt that time had never crawled as it did that evening—I saw one of our men elbowing his way toward my table through the packed crowd. I looked at my watch. It was exactly eleven o'clock. Eichmann, he told me, had arrived a few minutes before, and four men were with him, including the doctor. They were all wearing crew uniforms. An escort car driven by Gabi had followed them all the way. The journey and the entry through the main gate had passed off safely. At the moment they were parked at the edge of the parking lot, waiting for further instructions.

I got up and went there. I had no difficulty finding the two cars at the spot described to me. I exchanged a few words with Gabi and Ehud and turned toward the car in which Eichmann was sitting. He was wearing a crew uniform and looked fast asleep. I asked the doctor about his patient's condition. He replied that Eichmann was capable of standing on his feet and walking, provided he was supported on both sides, but he was incapable of acting on his own initiative and it was doubtful that he could answer questions. It was possible that he could see and hear, but it was a virtual certainty that he understood nothing of what was happening around him or what was being done to him. In any event, he was incapable of interfering with what was going on. The doctor judged that we could proceed to the next stage—passing through the checkpoint and boarding the plane.

The three cars moved off, Dan driving the first one, Eichmann and his guards in the second, and the remainder of the crew in the minibus. The convoy drove back through the main gate, continued along the highway for a few hundred yards, and turned right onto the side road leading to the Argentine national airline's maintenance area.

As the little procession approached the gate, the sentry went to the first car. Dan called out to him, as he had done dozens of times during the last few days, "Hi, Israel!" All the guards knew Dan well, and they all liked him for being cheerful and polite. The sentry glanced at the car's passengers and saw that they were wearing the uniform of the company whose plane was parked in that area. Some of them were noisy and jolly, as if reluctant to leave the gaiety of Buenos Aires. Some looked tired, and a few were even dozing. The three men sitting in the back of the second car were really asleep. The sentry raised the barrier and the three cars drove in. They didn't go straight to the plane but made a wide circle to avoid the lighted hangars on the way.

Several minutes earlier a few men from the night shift of the Argentine company had turned up to see the Britannia. Zvi Gutman gave them a friendly welcome and answered all their questions. When he saw the cars approaching, he quickly drew the visitors around to the other side of the plane. He saw a large party of crew members get out of the cars and walk toward the plane. Before turning back to his visitors, he noticed that one of the crew was supported by his companions. He must be ill, he thought. Zvi's guests didn't appear to notice anything unusual. When he saw the crew arriving, he hastened to take leave of them.

As instructed, the crew formed themselves into a tight bunch at the foot of the steps. Eichmann walked in the middle, held up by Ezra Eshet and Yoel Goren. Gad Nishri, standing beside the plane, saw a man in company uniform leaning on two crew members who were strangers to him and guessed immediately who it was.

As the three of them started walking up the steps, the neighboring searchlights lit up the gangway and the men standing on it. To speed things up, Nishri supported Eichmann from behind, and when his hand touched Eichmann's back he was astonished at his own lack of response—he felt no more than a slight revulsion at the contact.

Fritz Shefer was waiting in the doorway of the plane. The steps were a little too low for the Britannia, and Fritz was standing at the top to help the crew up. He lifted Eichmann a little and pulled him inside. They took him straight to first class and sat him down in the forward seat, at the side next to the window. There were eight seats in all in the first-class compartment and, in accordance with instructions, these were taken by the crew. They were all told to feign sleep, so that if questions were asked the answer could be that they were the relief crew having a rest prior to taking over their duties on the second lap of the flight. So as not to disturb their slumbers, the lights weren't switched on in that compartment.

With Eichmann safely installed, the two captains went into the cockpit. Within a few seconds the engines started up. The aircraft began to move, turned around, and taxied toward the tarmac. It reached the apron at exactly eleven-fifteen.

It was only afterward, of course, that I was told all about what was happening while I sat and waited for the news of the convoy's arrival at the plane.

Kenet and his companion had arrived at the safe house as planned, at nine o'clock. The roads were empty. As they drove along, they kept a lookout at the side of the road for Yitzhak's car, but it wasn't there, nor was there any sign of an accident. They were still hoping to find him waiting at *Tira,* but no one there knew anything about him either.

Kenet and the other man found themselves plunged into a veritable hive of feverish activity. Eichmann had been bathed, and Eli had finished shaving him and was now putting the finishing touches on his make-up. Then they dressed him in company uniform. Eichmann had known for a few hours that they were about to take him away from Buenos Aires and, without being asked, offered his full cooperation.

When the doctor began preparing him for the injection of the drug, he remarked that it wasn't necessary, they could trust him to behave quietly. When he realized that they obviously had no intention of relying on his promises, he helped as best he could with the injection. The doctor used a special needle which could be left in the vein, so that he could administer small additional doses of the drug without the blood coagulating. His object was to keep Eichmann's senses blurred without actually putting him to sleep, having in mind that if the necessity should arise to put him out completely the dose could be increased without anybody noticing. This could be done even in a moving car without endangering the prisoner's life.

By the time they took Eichmann out of the house the injection had already started working, and they had to help him walk. All the same, he noticed that they hadn't put a jacket on him, and he asked them to dress him exactly like the others so that he wouldn't be conspicuous.

His cooperation during those last few hours went so far that he began taking an active interest in the conspiracy and finally even showed concern for the success of the operation. Was it his slave mentality coming to the fore? Or could it be the hope that pleasing his captors would help save his life? Nobody had time to give it any thought.

Eichmann was put into the back of the car, between the doctor and Ezra Eshet, who were both wearing company uniforms. The doctor sat in such a position that he could give Eichmann more of the drug should he show any signs of increased wakefulness. This was, of course, the reason why they hadn't put on Eichmann's jacket. When they were already seated in the car, he asked Kenet if they would please bring him his glasses, as he "would need them in Tel Aviv."

He dozed throughout the journey. The car he was in and the one escorting it had to stop only once, at the railway crossing. The whole journey went off without a hitch.

———

After taking leave of the convoy driving Eichmann to the plane, I returned to my command post. Asher Kedem was waiting at my table. As we sat, wondering what was happening at the plane, the roar of motors blasting the air gave us our answer. Kedem recognized the Britannia engines immediately. For me it was a signal to move my headquarters to a more forward post.

A few minutes later I was established in the lounge for departing passengers. I found a quiet corner where I could keep an eye on what was happening. I didn't want to maintain overt contact with Kedem in this lounge where there was so little traffic. We agreed that he should go to Aharon Lazar and Dan Avner for their report on developments and then give me a prearranged signal. Shortly afterward I saw him come in—his beaming face made signals superfluous.

In the distance I could see Dan Avner and some of the crew who had earlier boarded the plane with Eichmann; I imagined they had disembarked to pass through emigration. I noticed that the task force men who had escorted Eichmann were not among the group waiting in the passenger lounge, and I gathered that they had decided to stay on the plane along with some of the genuine crew, so that the latter could provide cover for Eichmann and his guards. I deduced that everything was going according to plan and assumed that it was in order for some of the crew to remain on the plane while the others attended to formalities on their behalf.

I got up and walked out of the lounge to talk to Gabi and Ehud. We arranged then for some of the task force at the airport to join the flight. I thought that if a few of my people could go back to Israel this way it would make it much easier for the others to scatter and get out of Argentina. I told Gabi and Ehud that the ones we had chosen should wait in the vicinity of the passenger lounge for a signal from me.

I arranged with Gabi that those remaining in Buenos Aires should go out and look for Yitzhak, whose prolonged absence had me very worried. And I said that if he was not found right away one man would have to be left behind to continue the search while all the rest departed from Argentina as planned.

I reminded Menashe that as soon as the plane took off he was to return to Buenos Aires and release Rafael Arnon.

I didn't tell anybody what I was going to do myself. I had my papers and luggage all ready with me, and I was free to make my decision at the last minute.

When I returned to the passenger lounge, nothing had changed. The crew was still crowded around the customs platform. I beckoned to Kedem and asked him to hasten matters as much as he could so that we could advance the take-off time. He explained that the holdup had nothing to do with the plane but with the procedure that had to be undergone by the crew and the few passengers who were joining the flight. The customs men hadn't turned up yet, he said, and that's why everybody was waiting at the platform.

It was eleven-forty. I asked Kedem to involve Lazar in a last effort to make the proceedings move faster. Kedem called Lazar, who immediately went in search

of a customs official. After five minutes he returned
with an official who apologized for the delay and arranged the inspection quickly and efficiently. Less than
five minutes later the men were at liberty to leave with
their luggage. The porter hurried the suitcases and
bags out to the plane waiting on the apron.

Now it was the turn of the men waiting near the
lounge. At a signal from me they came and walked
up to the control counter. They looked tense, probably because they didn't quite know what was happening. I said, "Attach yourselves immediately to the
group going out to board the plane," and off they
went.

Just then Yitzhak appeared. He was perspiring and
looked exhausted, strained, and worried. His eyes
were not yet accustomed to the bright lights of the
lounge, but I went right over and told him to join the
others boarding the plane.

He wasn't the last to walk out onto the tarmac. At
the final moment I also joined the line, and within a
few seconds I was on the plane. The doors were closed,
the engines started their slow roar, and the huge aircraft began moving toward the runway.

It seemed we had overcome all obstacles and luck
was with us till the end. And yet I wasn't completely
at ease. When the crew members had passed through
customs control and were about to go toward the exit,
I noticed a man in civilian clothes who was evidently
at home in the airport and even looked as though he
might hold an important official position there. He
crossed the lounge with quick strides, walked through
the exit door without being stopped, and almost ran
toward the apron where our plane was standing. Another man ran after him. When I walked out onto the
apron, the two of them were standing next to the plane.

My peace of mind was seriously disturbed and I
couldn't relax even when I was seated on the plane
and it was already moving off. It reached the end of
the runway, where it made a slow turn prior to taking
off. The engines revved faster. Let them get going, let
them take off! I was silently praying. But the aircraft

remained on the spot for long, agonizing moments, as if gathering strength for the take-off. What was happening in the cockpit? Had they radioed the captain not to leave, or was he just waiting for a signal from the control tower?

The engines revved still faster, and it felt as if the plane was making a desperate effort to break an invisible chain shackling it to the ground. The equanimity that had stood me in such good stead even in the most difficult of situations suddenly deserted me. I couldn't understand what was going on. Why didn't we take off? Had our luck betrayed us inches before the finish line?

Then, with startling suddenness, the plane leapt forward with a deafening roar. It glided along the runway and a few seconds later rose effortlessly into the air. We soon left behind us the lights of the airport and the boundaries of Argentina's sovereignty. Only then did I relax.

The time was five minutes after midnight on May 21, 1960.

# 27

It was only after we were airborne that I found out what had delayed Yitzhak. The car he was driving broke down, and after desperate attempts to get it started again he was forced to leave it at the side of the road. He had to walk a long way before finding a taxi to take him to the city. He didn't dare drive up to *Tira,* so he told the taxi to wait and he set off again on foot. When he reached the safe house, only Dina and Eli were there, dismantling the hideout and getting rid of all signs that a number of persons had been living there. They were waiting for Gabi and Ehud to bring news and hoping that everything had gone according to plan at the airport.

Yitzhak sketched a rough map of where he had left the car and asked them to have it repaired and returned to the rental agency. Then he dashed back to his waiting taxi to rush off to the airport.

---

Aharon Lazar was the one person who knew why the plane was held back on the verge of departure. Those last fifteen minutes before take-off were the worst Lazar had experienced during his entire stay in Argentina. All day long he had hustled around, sparing no pains to guarantee that everything would be ready in time and that the flight wouldn't be delayed.

As midnight drew near and he knew Eichmann was already on the plane, he realized that these were the decisive moments. He mentally recapitulated all the arrangements made that day, lest he had forgotten something, but he could think of nothing left undone. Not a thing. Everything was in order, and in a few minutes the plane would be in the air. There, they were already closing the doors. And look, the plane was moving on the runway. But what was happening over there? Why were they stopping? What were they waiting for?

Lazar got in touch with the control tower to find out what was detaining them. He was told that there was a slight holdup, a triviality, some little technicality missing from the flight plan.

Is that the genuine reason for the delay or is it only an excuse? Lazar wondered. In his mind's eye he saw the anxious faces of the men on the plane, probably no less tense than he was himself. He rushed off at top speed to fill in the missing detail. He knew that if the aircraft was still delayed after that, then it meant that everything had been discovered. . . .

But now the plane started racing along the runway and a few seconds later it was in the air. Lazar was dizzy with the happiness that flooded him in those few seconds.

He was still standing and watching the plane which had become a tiny dot of light in the night sky when his happiness was rudely dispelled. A passenger who had expected to be on the flight had just walked into the lounge and been told that the plane had left without him. He was Aharon Dovrat from the Ministry of Commerce and Industry. He had come to Buenos Aires on the special flight to visit relatives and to transact certain business on behalf of the ministry. When he heard that there was a chance for him to leave Argentina within two days, he made up his mind not to miss it. Naturally, he had inquired about the plane's departure time and was told explicitly that it was two A.M. And now, having arrived nearly two hours ahead of schedule, he found the plane had gone. What sort of nonsense was this? How could they have misled him so? Where was the person in charge?

Since there was nobody else to make his complaints

to, he poured out all his wrath on poor Lazar, who knew very well that officially the man was right. Lazar apologized, but there was one thing he couldn't do—he couldn't explain to Dovrat why the plane had to leave before time. Without knowing this, Dovrat couldn't be expected to put up with Lazar's inadequate explanations. He demanded that Lazar communicate with the control tower and order the plane back. Lazar said this was impossible, the plane was already far away, with a long journey ahead of it, and if it was brought back now it would have to be refueled and all sorts of formal arrangements would have to be made which would upset the whole timetable. Dovrat eventually had to go back to Buenos Aires—but not without promising Lazar that when he got to Israel he would demand an inquiry into the inconvenience and humiliation he had been subjected to.

Dovrat couldn't have known that desperate but unsuccessful attempts had been made that evening to locate him in Buenos Aires and tell him to come to the airport earlier. Years later I had the opportunity of apologizing for the unpleasantness he had been caused.

———

Shortly before we left Buenos Aires we received clearance to fly through Brazilian air space and make a transit landing at Recife, but the incident at the Recife airport was still fresh in the crew's memory and they refused categorically to suffer the airport controller's rudeness again. For security reasons, too, we were not prepared to risk an intermediate stop in the Western Hemisphere and the two captains consequently decided to make every effort to fly the Britannia nonstop to Dakar, in West Africa. It was a difficult and strenuous undertaking, and in the pilots' cabin the atmosphere was charged with tension. Not so the service crew—they were distinctly relieved that the clandestine part of the operation was successfully over.

Eichmann awoke out of his semisleep several minutes before take-off, after the engines had already been started. His first question was whether it was a four-engine plane. From his tone it was obvious that the question wasn't so much technical as it was motivated by plain concern for his own safety—he wanted to make sure he was being taken to Israel in an aircraft capable of making such a long journey. I couldn't help thinking of the millions he had arranged to transport in packed, airtight cattle cars, without food, drink, or sanitary facilities.

Immediately after take-off the doctor examined him again and found his condition satisfactory in every way; he would certainly be able to take the long flight without any special treatment. He recovered quickly from the drug, and as soon as he felt better he asked for a cigarette. His opaque goggles, which had been replaced as soon as the drug wore off, prevented him from seeing the people around him, but he was alive to what was happening on the plane. He listened to the regular throb of the engines and remarked, "It's a very smooth flight. You've got good pilots." He was, to be sure, a seasoned traveler: during the war he had covered the length and breadth of Europe—by train, car, and plane—directing his vast manhunt.

The copilot, Gad Nishri, came to shake hands with me and congratulated me on the operation. He asked, "What about Martin Bormann and Josef Mengele?" I told him that had it been possible to start the operation several weeks earlier Mengele might also have been on the plane.

Dan Avner came to ask permission to tell the crew who the stranger was. I told him it would be better to wait until we were farther away from Argentina's shores, but he was persistent. He appealed to me again and again, until I couldn't resist him any longer. He gathered the crew and said, "You have been accorded a great privilege. You are taking part in an operation of supreme national importance to the Jewish people. The man with us on the plane is Adolf Eichmann."

His words created a buzz of excitement. Most of the crew didn't need explanations about the part Eichmann had played in the annihilation of European Jew-

ry; some of them had experienced personally the horror of the years when this man was in command of
the "Final Solution."

Zvi Gutman was busy in the cockpit when Dan
made the announcement about the passenger. Back in
the cabin, he noticed the excitement of the other crew
members and gathered immediately that this was connected in some way with the air of mystery that had
surrounded the flight.

Then he saw Dan and, with sudden urgency, as if
he just couldn't wait a second longer, asked, "Dan,
who's that man in dark glasses?"

Dan looked at him for a moment and said, "What,
don't you know? That's Eichmann!"

The next few minutes are still a little confused in
Zvi's memory. Suddenly he was running to the forward
galley, and there he stood and sobbed his heart out.
Dan stayed with him, talking to him, but Zvi didn't
hear a word. His sobs seemed to take on an existence
of their own, no longer subject to his will or his natural
sense of shame. He wept for a long time.

Afterward he turned to go into the first-class section,
but they stopped him and said he wasn't allowed any
closer to Eichmann. Later he would be given permission, when he had calmed down a little, but now, in
his present agitated state, definitely not.

Zvi regained control of himself. The tears had dried
on his cheeks, and he was finally permitted to go up
close to Eichmann. When Zvi saw the man sitting next
to Eichmann offer him a cigarette, his self-control broke
for an instant and he said, "You give *him* cigarettes!
He gave *us* gas!"

Eichmann turned around when he heard the voice,
but the goggles prevented him from seeing who had
spoken. Zvi felt he was disturbing the men guarding
the prisoner so he went away.

Later he came back and sat down. Right opposite
Eichmann he sat, his eyes glued to the murderer's face.
But Zvi wasn't seeing Eichmann. He was seeing a com-
pletely different sight. He was seeing his little brother
Zadok dragged along by a German soldier. He was so

little, Zadok, all of six years old. A six-year-old was a sure candidate for death those days, because he belonged to an inferior stock, because he couldn't be of use in one of the factories producing arms and equipment for the German army. A Jewish boy of six had no prospects: he was too little to live but big enough to die.

Zvi was bigger, so he lived. He was big enough to fool the Germans into thinking he was a man. So Zadok was now a heap of ash and he, Zvi, was head mechanic for a big airline, the man who got ready the plane that was bringing Eichmann to the State of Israel.

It was purely by chance that he was sitting here while Zadok and his mother and the rest of his brothers were gone. It wasn't even a miracle. Just blind chance, an oversight on the part of the angel of death.

How many times had he cheated death? At least ten. The first time was in the days of the great pillage, when Germans of the *Volksdeutsche* came looking for the treasures of the Jews and he was alone in the house. He was eleven then, and he knew that his uncle kept some of his merchandise in the attic, but he made up his mind not to talk. He would die but he wouldn't talk. And a German flung him to the ground and pinned him down under his great weight and held a dagger to his throat. He screamed then, and cried, and begged, but he didn't talk. Then he lost consciousness and the German threw him down the stairs. And he remained alive.

Then there were two German "actions" at Belzice, Zvi's home town in Poland. Twice the Germans came at dawn, in a tumult of cries and shots, and dragged men, women, and children out of their houses, the first time to take them outside the town and mow them down with bullets, and the second time to transport them to the death camp at Treblinka. He and his family had the two hideouts his father and grandfather had constructed, one in the celler and the other behind a false wall in one of the rooms. And he remained alive.

The Germans established a ghetto in the town, in the section close to the synagogue, and there they also brought Jews they had collected from elsewhere. Inside the ghetto they carried out the third "action." After the whole family had gone into the hideout, the little brother was missing. Zvi ran to get him to the cellar but didn't manage to get inside himself; he ran out of the town and hid in a tobacco field for half the day. As he left the field, one of the local inhabitants caught him, saw he was a Jew, and handed him over.

At the railway station he saw some of his relatives and joined them. The Jews were standing in a long line in the front of the station, a line about a quarter of a mile long. At the head of the line someone was screaming—there where the first ones were being loaded onto the train—screaming that there was chlorine in the carriages. Not many Germans were about, and most of the guards were local police, some on horseback. At a certain moment their terror subsided and the Jews in the death line started running, escaping, scattering in all directions. Zvi ran with a cousin of his to a nearby wheat field. The whole day they ran and hid, ran and hid. In the evening they came to a village where they knew some of the farmers. They stood on the outskirts for a long time, hesitating. Eventually they smothered their fears and went to one of the farmers to ask for bread and milk. He threw them a piece of coarse bread and told them to get out immediately, he wasn't looking for trouble.

Where to now? They decided to go back to the town, first to the synagogue to see if anybody was still there. Yes, a few Jews had come out of their hiding places as night fell. Germans were patrolling the streets with their local henchmen, announcing through loudspeakers that the Jews had nothing to fear, the "action" was over and they could come out now. It wasn't until very late at night that Zvi and his cousin dared steal into the family hideout.

But how long could they stay? There was reason to fear that the Poles would hand over the Jews still hidden in the town, and Zvi's father decided it was time they got away. He led the family on a night journey, with several other relatives, to the home of a Polish farmer in one of the villages, a man to whom he had previously entrusted furniture and other articles of value. The farmer was panic-stricken, but his wife wouldn't let him send them away. The ten Jews dug a hiding place in the straw of the barn and covered it over with dung. For several weeks they stayed, until winter came. The farmer told them that people were beginning to get suspicious because of the large quantities of bread he was buying, and he demanded that they leave his farm. At night they dug a new hole under the threshing shed, and at dawn left their first hiding place. But instead of going into the camouflaged hole, they hid in the snow nearby. Soon a large group of farmers came with pitchforks and scythes, stabbing and punching at the hay strewn above their hideout, and then set the threshing shed on fire. Zvi and his family had cheated death once again.

From then all they could do was roam the fields and forests and steal food to keep alive. When they heard that there was still a ghetto in their town they put all their effort into getting back inside it. But the ghetto was a trap. One morning at dawn the Germans surrounded it. They collected all the old women and children in one party, and the young women in another. Zvi wanted to remain with the men, but he was too small and they pushed him out of the group. He hid in a public toilet and then came out again. This time he stood on a large stone in the middle of the men, and the Germans were fooled and let him be. Fifty men were led away and the rest herded into the synagogue. In the evening shots were heard, then bloodcurdling screams. The fifty men came back very late and told them they had been forced to dig a mass grave for the women and children.

The next morning the men were marched to a work camp in the vicinity, some of them pushing carts with tools in them. As he was walking along with the rest of the prisoners, Zvi saw his little brother Zadok sitting in a cart. The boy told him that while the big slaughter was going on he hid behind a pile of stones, and afterward, when he saw them taking the Jews out

of the town, he joined the marchers. Zvi took his
hand and held on tight. On the way they found their
father, who was also one of the marchers. When they
reached the camp, commanded by a man named
Feiges, a muster was called and all the children and
old men were taken out of the line. Zadok hid in the
camp lavatory, but the Germans found him, and Zvi
and his father saw a German dragging little Zadok into
the group sentenced to death. They were led outside
the camp to be executed, all the old people and the
children, and a Jewish work party was sent to bury
them.

The rest were pushed into huts. Later they were
sent out to work in different factories. Zvi worked at
a plant manufacturing airplane parts. He saw his father at night, when the two surviving members of the
family lay on a straw pallet and were glad that at
least they were together. An uncle of Zvi's was in the
same camp, but he was shot down in an escape attempt. And then there was the time when several prisoners were caught stealing food, and the camp
commander Feiges gouged out their eyes with a wood-
en peg while all the Jews in the camp had to stand and
watch.

If Feiges thought that his brutal act would be a deterrent to the rest of the prisoners, he soon found out
his mistake. A few days later several youngsters broke
into the SS guardroom, took all the arms, and ran away.
The guards went on a rampage, beating and killing
the other prisoners. The dreaded parade was called and
Zvi was one of those sentenced to die. All that night,
and until the following afternoon, Zvi and the other
condemned men lay outside on the ground, waiting
for death. Then the guards appeared and announced
that they would kill every alternate man. A new muster was formed and Zvi was reprieved once more.
The Germans repeated the process the next day, and
again Zvi was spared. About a hundred were ultimately shot.

A year and a half passed, and all the prisoners were

transferred to Maidanek, where Zvi worked as a mechanic in the SS garage. Maidanek was one of the places where they brought Jews from other countries to be liquidated. Russian prisoners were also there, in an adjoining camp. As the approach of the Russian army became imminent, all the Russian prisoners were killed, and several hundred Jews whose names appeared on a list prepared in advance were shot. The rest were evacuated by train or on foot to Auschwitz. Many died on the cruel march and many were sentenced to death during the selection on their arrival at the camp. Zvi was sent with the condemned, but at the last minute a man came along looking for workmen, and when he saw Zvi he said a young fellow like that could still be useful to them. He took him out of the line of walking dead and sent him to have a shower and get a striped uniform. That was when they tattooed the number on his arm, the number he bears to this day: 18466. Then he was transported with the other workmen to Gleiwitz, where they were given soup and bread. And Zvi was given something else, a present from heaven—his father, whom the luck of the draw had also brought there.

When the Russians crossed the Visla, and Gleiwitz was under bombardment from the air, the camp was evacuated; the prisoners were marched to another camp in Upper Silesia. They hadn't been there half a day when the Gleiwitz camp commander arrived to take back some of "his" prisoners. Most of them were pleased and went with him—to continue their sufferings. Zvi and his father stayed where they were. As the Russians drew nearer, the Germans manning the watchtowers began firing incendiary bullets into the wooden huts. Many of the occupants burned to death. Zvi and his father found shelter in an abandoned warehouse made of concrete and didn't burn.

Several days later they learned that the Germans had deserted the camp, so they set off toward the forest, where they ran into a Russian patrol and were told to keep going in the same direction. A few miles farther on they met more Russians, among them an officer who addressed them in Yiddish. Then Zvi and his father knew they had defeated death.

Zvi sat opposite Eichmann and relived the years of blood and bereavement. He didn't speak. He just remembered, and the remembering squeezed mute tears from his eyes.

No one bothered him. All understood they must leave him alone. A long while later he got up, wiped away the tears, and stood for a minute next to the murderer, his eyes shining. The people watching even thought they saw a bewildered little smile playing on his lips.

At last he walked out of the first-class compartment. And from that moment on he displayed no further interest in Eichmann.

———

I put off my visit to the first-class section until the crew's interest in Eichmann had subsided a little. One reason for this was the atmosphere of tranquillity in the empty tourist cabin during those first few hours. The second reason was my desire to avoid attracting the attention of the men who didn't know what I was doing there.

When I finally went forward, I saw Eichmann sitting upright, evidently wide awake, in the seat next to the window. He couldn't see me, of course, but he could feel someone looking at him and twisted uncomfortably in his seat.

The doctor told me that Eichman was very well indeed and had completely recovered from the drug. He was still cooperating with his guards, the doctor said, and presumably he would continue to do so throughout the flight. We decided that if there was no change in his behavior we wouldn't drug him again. We arranged with the plane's officers that the crew wouldn't leave the aircraft when we landed at Dakar, but that if the authorities insisted that the plane be empty during refueling—a standard requirement—the doctor would tell them that on no account must the sick member of the crew be moved, that he and two others would stay to look after him.

I told Eichmann's guards not to put too much trust in his good behavior. They must keep constant watch that he did not get hold of anything he could use for a suicide attempt. The men guarding Eichmann during the flight were Ezra Eshet, Zev Keren, Yoel Goren, Elisha Naor, and Yoram Golan. Eichmann's food was prepared according to the doctor's specifications, so that he could be drugged if necessary without injuring his health.

During the first part of the journey Gad Nishri also helped to attend to Eichmann. To set a good example for the rest of the crew he was ready to help with even the less pleasant tasks. He never ceased marveling at Eichmann's healthy appetite. Gad himself couldn't eat a thing from the moment Eichmann was brought on board.

---

I talked with my own men only when none of the crew were around. Otherwise I pretended not to know them.

It was, on the whole, an easy flight for the passengers, but the crew had their work cut out for them. In order to reduce fuel consumption they tried to fly at the highest possible altitude. Many times they had to dodge the clouds floating in the tropical skies at the most convenient flight altitude. There was a stage when they were very gloomy about the fuel supply and were considering the possibility of landing at Freetown, Sierra Leone, instead of Dakar. The idea didn't appeal to us very much, from the perspective of security. I preferred Senegal to Sierra Leone. Apart from that, we couldn't fly from Freetown to Lydda without another intermediate landing. In fact, even the direct flight from Dakar to Tel Aviv involved serious problems, but we hoped to be able to overcome them. In the end, after a precise computation of all the data, the pilots decided to continue on to Dakar, and we arrived safely after a flight lasting thirteen hours and six minutes.

We continued to be apprehensive as we touched down, though for a different reason. We didn't know what sort of reception awaited us. For all we knew, there may have been a last-minute alarm at Buenos Aires, and perhaps a warning had already been cabled to Dakar to check the identity of all the passengers. True, we were confident of our ability to pass inspection —our precautions in this regard were very thorough —but another ordeal at the end of a tough operation was hardly a happy prospect.

But our fears proved to be groundless. Our reception at the airport was perfectly routine. Wherever we went the personnel were friendly, and our request that the passengers be allowed to remain on the plane during refueling was granted without hesitation.

Zvi was one of the few who alighted. Technical service and refueling were carried out under his supervision. On his instructions, a little more than the standard amount of fuel was squeezed into the tanks.

Leo Barkai, the steward, also left the plane to buy provisions and supplies. He tried to get his shopping done as quickly as possible to advance the time of take-off. The pilots went up to the control tower to arrange the flight plan.

All the others stayed on the plane. The men in first class were told to pretend to sleep again. This time I joined them, to keep an eye on the situation in case of an official inspection.

Eichmann didn't go to sleep, but he behaved impeccably. He sat in absolute silence as two Frenchmen walked past him, made a cursory inspection of the first-class toilets, and went back the way they had come. They were from the airport health department and were the only government officials who boarded the plane.

An hour later the doors were closed, the engines were started, and the aircraft moved down the runway. And then we were over Dakar, our nose pointed toward Tel Aviv.

# 28

The plane climbed to a great height. In their quest to do the seemingly impossible—fly a Britannia nonstop from Dakar to Lydda—the captains had two needs: altitude and a favorable wind.

The bulletins from the pilots' cabin were good; the weather was turning out just as they wished and there was every prospect of a tail wind. During this part of the journey Nishri piloted the plane while Meged took a rest. I slept most of the time, so I didn't know until later about the improvement that had taken place. At the beginning of this stage of the flight the pilots still had in mind a possible refueling at Rome or Cyprus, but as we passed over the Straits of Gibraltar the tail wind grew stronger and there was no further doubt that the fuel in our tanks would be enough to take us to Lydda.

It was dawn when I woke up. We were flying over the Mediterranean, rapidly approaching the shores of Israel. The tail wind had blown all night and the outlook remained favorable.

I washed, shaved, and changed my clothes, and felt more refreshed than I had felt for a long time. I gave the men their instructions for the final phase of the operation. As soon as the plane landed, I told them, Eichmann would be handed over to the operations group who would in turn deliver him to the legal authorities of the state. At that point our mission would be accomplished. I took the opportunity during those last few moments to thank my companions for their devotion and resourcefulness at every stage of the operation, which applied equally to all the members of the task force.

Israel's coastline was already visible through the windows, and no more heart-warming sight could be imagined. The aircraft had covered the immense distance between Dakar and Lydda in eleven and a half hours. As the wheels touched down on the runway a load lifted from my shoulders. I went into the cockpit, shook hands with the captains and their aides, and thanked them and the crew for their zealous assistance, for the quick and easy flight, and for their cordiality to me and my men.

Before alighting, I went back into the first-class compartment. I thought Eichmann was looking paler than before. He sensed the activity and bustle around him, and his whole body was shaking.

I said good-by to his escorts, including the doctor, and told them to hand Eichmann over to Hillel Ankor, who, I noticed, was already standing beside the plane.

It was Sunday, May 22, 1960, and I had been absent from Israel for twenty-three days.

———

Hillel Ankor drove to the airport with several men. He had been advised by the airline that the plane was due to arrive that morning, but until he heard the good news from me he wasn't sure if Eichmann was really on it. I instructed him to receive Eichmann into his custody, to take care that strict secrecy was preserved, and not to give his prisoner any chance of attempting suicide. I told him he must keep Eichmann under safe arrest until I let him know when to hand him over to the Inspector-General of Police.

I telephoned my wife to tell her I had just arrived and hoped to be home in the afternoon. She didn't sound surprised and didn't ask where I had been.

I then called the two men who would be responsible

for guarding and protecting Eichmann until he was put into the hands of the police. I warned them to pay strict attention to every detail of transporting and guarding him. I asked what arrangements they had made for his temporary imprisonment; what they told me sounded satisfactory. Finally, I re-emphasized that they were personally answerable for the prisoner's safety.

They drove Eichmann to his secret place of temporary imprisonment, where he was to stay until he could be handed over to the police. They decided not to reveal the prisoner's true identity to the men appointed to guard him. They were well aware that they could rely completely on the guards' efficiency and dedication, but they were wary of the reaction, for the guards themselves were survivors of the death camps. The story they told was that their prisoner was a dangerous spy and must be closely watched. This precaution had to be taken, particularly since they would be taking turns at guard duty inside the cell twenty-four hours a day.

When the identity of the "spy" was eventually disclosed to them, they felt cheated.

———

It was nine-fifteen when I completed all the arrangements at the airport. It was now time to go to Jerusalem to inform the Prime Minister that Eichmann was in Israel. I told Yaki, who had been waiting for me at the airport for three-quarters of an hour, that he must get me to the Prime Minister's office in Jerusalem by ten o'clock, when the Cabinet met for its weekly session. I was afraid that if I arrived late and the meeting had already started, I wouldn't be able to call Ben-Gurion out without attracting the attention of too many people.

All the way there I kept urging Yaki to drive faster, faster—and he delivered me to Ben-Gurion's office at ten minutes to ten. The Prime Minister's Political Secretary, Yitzhak Navon, needed no preambles or explanations—he realized I wouldn't be disturbing the

Prime Minister a few minutes before a Cabinet meeting if it weren't urgent and important. Within a few seconds I was sitting in Ben-Gurion's office. He was surprised to see me and asked when I had returned. I told him I had arrived in Israel two hours earlier and had brought him a present. He looked at me in astonishment. This was quite different from the way I usually spoke to him.

I laughed, and said, "I have brought Adolf Eichmann with me. For two hours now he has been on Israeli soil, and if you authorize it he will be handed over to the Israeli police."

He didn't reply at once. Though he had been told that Eichmann had been traced, he hadn't, it seemed, quite grasped the full significance of the event until that moment when I brought him the news that Eichmann was in Israel.

"Is his identity no longer in doubt?" he asked.

"There is no doubt," I said. His family had also been identified with complete certainty. His sons still called themselves Eichmann. There were various identifying marks on his body which proved undeniably that he was Eichmann. And when he was interrogated he mentioned certain things that only Eichmann could have known.

The Prime Minister was convinced. Nevertheless, he requested that before any official steps were taken the prisoner should be identified by one or two people who had previously known Eichmann. He authorized me to deliver the prisoner into the hands of the Inspector-General of Police, and—immediately after the identification—to have him brought before a judge for the warrant of detention to be issued.

From the Prime Minister's office I went to see my daughter. Yaki called her away from her work, and soon we were standing and talking outside.

She asked a little agitatedly, "Where were you?"

My answer was, "Somewhere," and she didn't ask any more.

————

Yaki was uncharacteristically excited on the drive back to Tel Aviv and never stopped asking questions. What he wanted to know most of all was what would happen when the secret was made public.

He drove me to my office, and a little later Ankor arrived to report on Eichmann's transfer to his temporary place of imprisonment. The task force doctor stayed with him until he was taken into the cell, examined him again, and pronounced him fit. Ankor checked the guard and security arrangements and found everything in order. I told him to go to the Inspector-General of Police, Yosef Nahmias, and inform him that Eichmann was in our hands and that, on instructions from the Prime Minister, he was to be handed over to the police to be taken before a judge for the warrant of detention.

Nahmias was stunned. He summoned the head of the Police Administration Department and asked Ankor to repeat what he had said. It was finally decided that the next morning Ankor would pick Nahmias up and drive him to the temporary jail; they would take with them a judge to issue the warrant of detention on the spot. That way both secrecy and security could be preserved.

———

Haggai was in Haifa that morning, appearing as a witness in District Court. He returned to Tel Aviv in the afternoon and came straight to my office. I had in the meantime received a message from the Prime Minister that he wanted to announce the criminal's capture to the Knesset as soon as a positive identification had been made, so my conversation with Haggai turned on two topics: the text of the Prime Minister's statement in the Knesset and someone to make the identification.

Haggai suggested Moshe Agami of Kfar Giladi, who had been the Jewish Agency representative in Vienna and had met Eichmann in 1938. Benno Cohen's name was also mentioned again. We decided to get both of them in to identify Eichmann, Agami first. It had to be done rapidly, since there were by now quite a few people who knew about Eichmann's capture and arrival in Israel, and the news was no doubt spreading in ever-widening circles.

Haggai was prepared to go to Kfar Giladi, but was only too happy when he heard that Moshe Agami was in Tel Aviv that day. He arranged to meet him right away at Café Lidiya in Masaryk Square. There he told him the story of our operation and about the necessity for a personal identification of Eichmann. Agami was tremendously excited. At Haggai's request, he described the circumstances of his two meetings with Eichmann.

Both meetings took place in October 1938, when, as the Jewish Agency representative in Vienna, he went to see Eichmann about the organization for the training of Jewish youth in preparation for emigration to Israel. Eichmann's offices at the time were in the Rothschild mansion. When Agami was taken into his office, a fairly long room, Eichmann received him with unconcealed arrogance. He was dressed in SS uniform and made Agami stand at attention three or four yards away from him. He asked him who he was and demanded that the training program be handed to him within forty-eight hours. The interview lasted five or ten minutes. Two days later Agami brought him the program and Eichmann warned him that he must stick to preparatory training and not indulge in anything else. He concluded by ordering him to report regularly to an SS officer whose name—as far as he could remember—was Gunther.

Since Agami might not be able to identify Eichmann after so many years, Haggai suggested that he talk about the two meetings and, during the course of the conversation, deliberately distort some of the names they had mentioned at the time, in the hope that Eichmann would correct him.

Haggai then drove Agami to the temporary prison, where he was first given the opportunity of observing Eichmann through a small peephole in the door. Agami said he couldn't identify the man that way. Then he was taken into the room and joined soon afterward by Haggai. This time Eichmann wasn't wearing glasses.

Agami introduced himself as Moshe Auerbach—his former name—and asked Eichmann if he remembered him as the Jewish Agency representative who had come to his office in 1938. Eichmann said that without his glasses he couldn't recognize anybody. When his glasses were brought to him, he stared at Agami and eventually said he didn't remember him. Then they spoke about the Vienna of 1938 and their two meetings, and Agami—following Haggai's suggestion—garbled the names of some of the people Eichmann had known at the time. Eichmann not only corrected him but, as they went on talking, even reminded him of some of the details of the meetings.

Now there was no further doubt in Agami's mind that the man before him was Adolf Eichmann—no other person could have known what they talked about when they were alone in 1938.

Haggai telephoned me forthwith at my home to give me the positive results of the identification. He also tried to get hold of Benno Cohen but couldn't reach him that day.

That evening I advised the Prime Minister that one of the people who had known Eichmann before the war had identified him.

---

We had another debt of honor to pay before the official announcement was made of Eichmann's capture and transfer to Israel. Since February 1960 Fritz Bauer had been told nothing about the progress of our operation. He had on many occasions questioned his Israeli contact, Reuven Harpaz, about developments, but Reuven could tell him nothing.

Now I asked that a cable be sent immediately to Cologne, telling Reuven to await an urgent message from Ankor the next morning, May 23. I wanted Bauer to learn about Eichmann's capture before the rest of the world heard it from the lips of the Prime Minister of Israel. Yet I was afraid to send the message any earlier than two hours ahead of the official announcement, for fear that the news might leak.

When the Prime Minister received the results of the

identification, he decided to make his announcement in the Knesset the following day, at four in the afternoon. The second cable to Cologne was sent the night before.

When the first cable came Reuven realized that the message for Bauer concerned Eichmann and that we must have succeeded in capturing him. He immediately got in touch with Bauer and asked if they could meet in the city the following morning. Bauer was all keyed up and wanted to know what was happening, but Reuven would say nothing except that he thought he might have some good news for him.

Ankor's cable arrived at nine-fifteen in the morning. It said that Eichmann was in Israel and that Harpaz must tell Bauer about it at two o'clock sharp. By the time Reuven deciphered the message it was already nine-forty-five, and he telephoned Bauer at once and made an appointment to meet him at a restaurant at one o'clock. He went straight out to his car and drove at a good speed toward the center of the city. As he entered the city limits, he had a blowout and the car went into a skid—only by a miracle was a serious accident averted. Reuven was struggling to change the tire, but fortunately for him a passing Dutch motorist stopped and helped him.

It was one-thirty before he reached the restaurant. Bauer had worked himself up into a fever of anticipation mingled with anxiety about Reuven's tardiness. Reuven didn't even wash his hands, filthy as they were from changing the tire. He hurried straight to Bauer's table and burst out with the news that Eichmann had been caught and in a few hours the Prime Minister would be announcing it in the Knesset.

With tears in his eyes, Bauer flung his arms around Reuven and kissed him. He asked him what he would drink in honor of the occasion and was most disappointed when he received the typical Israeli reply: soda. A few minutes later he excused himself, saying he had a telephone call to make. He explained that he considered it his duty to pass on the good news to the man he had confided in from the start. Reuven begged him to be careful not to mention names on the telephone until the official Israeli announcement was made.

# 29

The rear party of the task force was out of Argentina before Ben-Gurion's official announcement gave the Argentine authorities their first intimation of what had happened. As soon as our plane took off, Gabi and Ehud drove back to *Tira*. Dina and Eli had been waiting there, growing more and more impatient as the minutes ticked by—it was two in the morning before they got back, four hours after the Eichmann convoy had left the safe house.

Gabi and Ehud gave their friends a full report on the final stage of the operation, and all four of them settled back to enjoy the wonderful feeling of relief: at last they were rid of the oppressive burden of taking care of Eichmann. They discussed Yitzhak's adventure with much laughter and cheer, and decided that the way he boarded the plane almost straight from the taxi fitted in perfectly with the image he had created while in Argentina: the spoiled rich man's son, with unlimited money to spend, always renting villas and cars, treated with such deference that even the plane wouldn't leave until he turned up.

They got up early in the morning to finish their final assignments. It was only now, as they carried out their last inspection of the villa to make sure they had forgotten nothing, that they realized just how much they had been longing for this moment.

When *Tira* was completely cleared they drove to Buenos Aires, to the safe house *Ramim,* where Shalom

Dani and Menashe were staying. Rafael Arnon, who
had been held there the day before, was given back
his papers in the middle of the night—now restored
to their original state by Shalom—and had left Argentina very early in the morning. Menashe was due to
leave that night and during the day had to turn in the
keys to all the apartments and houses they had rented.
Dina and Shalom booked seats on a plane to Montevideo the following morning, May 22.

Gabi, Ehud, and Eli bought train tickets to Chile.
Gabi and Ehud didn't want to travel by air, as they
had been seen a lot at the airport during the last few
days. Getting berths in a sleeping compartment, they
soon found out, was a matter of luck, since bookings
were usually made two months in advance. However,
the travel agent told Ehud to try at the railway station because there were sometimes last-minute cancel-
lations. Ehud was, that way, fortunate enough to get
three berths for the forty-hour journey.

It had been weeks since any of them had eaten a
meal under pleasant and comfortable conditions, so
they decided to celebrate the tough assignment and
their farewell from Argentina with a lavish meal at a
good restaurant. The waiters didn't know why the
party was in such high spirits but they were also soon
infected by the merriment and put themselves out to
please their customers. The only thing that upset them
was that the lady wouldn't touch any of the delicacies
they heaped on the table. They didn't know, of
course, that she observed kashruth.

Menashe left after dinner and the next day, May 22,
the rest of the party split up. Gabi, Ehud, and Eli set
out in the afternoon on their long journey across South
America, and in the evening Dina and Shalom left
for Montevideo.

---

When the three train "tourists" reached Mendoza,
the border station between Argentina and Chile, they
felt twinges of apprehension about possible complications. For more than a day and night they had been
cut off from all communication with the outside

world. They hadn't read a newspaper or listened to the radio. They had no idea of what had happened in the meantime, and for all they knew trouble might await them at the border station. But their fears were not realized, the border inspection was completely routine.

They arrived in Santiago late at night. They remembered that they had an acquaintance there, an Israeli woman who was doing temporary work in Santiago. Despite the late hour, they telephoned her and arranged to meet her in the morning. They concocted a story for her: they were on a tour of South America and thought they couldn't possibly leave the enchanting continent without going as far as the Pacific Coast. They spent the next day touring the city with her, intending to go to Valparaiso the day after. But they read in the morning papers that a severe earthquake had caused havoc in southern Chile, about three hundred fifty miles from the capital, and they were afraid that anyone at home who knew where they were would be worried about them. They wanted to send a cable that they were safe, but it wasn't easy to get away from their charming escort even for a few minutes. At last Ehud found an excuse to slip out, and he sent a cable to a private address saying that there was no cause for worry and that if no flights were available they might have to stay in Chile until the end of the week. He signed it with a name known only to the members of the task force.

Later, on a bus, Ehud happened to glance over the shoulder of the passenger on the seat in front of him and saw the name EICHMANN blazoned in enormous letters across the front page of a newspaper. As soon as the driver made a stop, Ehud got off the bus and bought all the papers he could find.

He pointed to the headline and asked in a surprised voice, "What's all this about Eichmann?"

The young woman translated for them: "It says here that they've caught Eichmann."

"Who's this Eichmann?"

She explained the part Eichmann played in the extermination of the Jews in Europe and added, "Ben-

Gurion announced in the Knesset that Eichmann was discovered by the Israeli Security Services and is now in custody in Israel. Maybe you had something to do with it?" she said with a laugh.

"We wish we had," they replied in a joking chorus.

They were rather surprised that the news was published while they were still in South America. How could they go back to the Atlantic Coast now? The following morning they inquired about possible flights and they were able to get two seats on a plane to Montevideo and one to Rio; Ehud and Eli would take the first route and Gabi the second.

Ehud and Eli's plane landed at Buenos Aires for about three-quarters of an hour and they made themselves as inconspicuous as possible. They were particularly afraid that someone would recognize Ehud, who had spent so many hours at the airport prior to Eichmann's departure. Fortunately, nothing happened.

On the flight from Montevideo to Rio they were discussing in Hebrew the newspaper publicity on the Eichmann affair, when suddenly Ehud observed the name on a suitcase in the rack which apparently belonged to the passenger sitting in front of him: M. ZOREA. Their fellow passenger must be the Israeli Brigadier Zorea and he nudged Eli to keep quiet. The officer didn't seem to have overheard their conversation—at any rate, he hadn't turned to see who was speaking behind him.

They were not the only members of the task force to come across Brigadier Zorea on their journey. At São Paulo, where they were about to embark on their flight to Europe, Dina and Shalom Dani saw him as they arrived from Montevideo. Shalom wanted to go up to him and tell him he was an Israeli, but Dina was against it. However, they still managed to find an opportunity to talk to him, and Dina remarked, "Your country is in the news lately."

"What do you mean?"

"I read in the newspaper that you caught a Nazi criminal by the name of Eichmann," she said.

"Oh yes," Zorea replied, and he started telling them about the holocaust and what it meant for the Jewish people.

"I was in Europe during the war and saw what the Nazis did," Dina said.

Brigadier Zorea looked at her sympathetically. "If that's the case, you certainly understand how it was for us."

"Yes, I understand perfectly," she said. "By the way, in one of the papers it says that Eichmann was taken to Israel on the same plane that brought your delegation to Argentina. Didn't I hear that you were one of the delegates?"

"I was," he said, "and it can't be true. It's impossible that I shouldn't have known about it. But then not everything you read in the newspapers is true. I'll make inquiries and if you'll give me your address I'll let you know the results," Brigadier Zorea said jocularly.

The conversation ended at that point, because the passengers were being called to board the plane.

# 30

The day Eichmann was brought to Israel two officers from police headquarters were summoned to the Inspector-General's office: Matityahu Sela, head of the Investigation Department, and Shmuel Roth, acting head of the Criminal Branch. Nahmias was noticeably excited. He told them that Eichmann had been captured and brought to Israel, and as soon as they heard this they understood their chief's excitement and were caught up in it themselves.

There was no need to explain to Shmuel Roth the significance of the murderer's capture. Many of his family had been caught in the net Eichmann had spread all over Europe. The next morning, when he arrived at Eichmann's temporary prison in company with Judge Yedid Halevi, he was astounded by the man's colorless personality. Like so many others, he had imagined that Eichmann would look quite different.

Roth translated into German the judge's questions about the prisoner's identity.

He answered unhesitatingly, "I am Adolf Eichmann."

The judge then read out the warrant of detention.

The police were particularly interested in having a second identification of Eichmann because there were no fingerprints on record from the period when he was an SS officer. Accordingly, Benno Cohen was requested to go and see the prisoner.

Cohen drove to Camp Iyar—the prison where Eichmann was now installed—accompanied by Police Officer Efraim Hofstaetter, who had been appointed Deputy Chief of Bureau 06, the special office set up by the Inspector-General of Police to prepare the brief for the prosecution against Eichmann. Hofstaetter was happy to be involved at the end of the operation he had joined in March 1958. On the way, Benno Cohen told him that he saw Eichmann for the first time when he appeared at a meeting of Zionist workers in Berlin before the war. Hofstaetter asked him to talk to Eichmann about that meeting and to muddle up the names of the people he mentioned, with the object of getting Eichmann to point out his mistakes.

As they walked into the cell Eichmann turned white with terror—he thought they were going to take him out to be executed. Hofstaetter asked Benno Cohen if he recognized the prisoner. He said he didn't. Pointing to Cohen, Hofstaetter asked Eichmann in German if he knew him. Eichmann made the same complaint as on the previous occasion—they had taken away his glasses—and then he peered at Cohen from close up and said he didn't know him.

Hofstaetter then introduced Cohen to the prisoner: "This is Mr. Benno Cohen."

"The name doesn't mean anything to me," Eichmann replied.

Hofstaetter went on to ask, "Do you remember the Palestine Office in Berlin?"

"Of course, I remember it very well."

"And you still don't remember Mr. Cohen?"

"No."

As he heard Eichmann speak, it all came back. Now Benno Cohen remembered the voice and accent. When Hofstaetter turned back to him and asked if he could identify the man facing him, Cohen was able to reply with confidence, "Yes, I know him. He is the Gestapo officer Adolf Eichmann."

Eichmann nodded, and Hofstaetter asked him, "Do you remember that in the spring of 1939 you called a meeting of representatives of Jewish organizations at Prinzalbrechtstrasse in Berlin?"

"I don't recall such a meeting because I only arrived in Berlin in October 1939." But a few seconds later he added, "But it's possible that I happened to be in Berlin for meetings several times before then."

Benno Cohen broke into the conversation, saying, "At the meeting we're referring to there were present Dr. Paul Epstein, head of the Jewish community, Dr. Lilienfeld, Heinrich Stahl, and Otto Hirsch."

"Otto Hirsch?" Eichmann interrupted. "Yes, that's the man who spoke Swabian and kept raising his voice."

Benno Cohen asked him what had happened to Paul Epstein.

Eichmann turned red and replied, "Terrible . . . they shot him. But that was after I gave up my job there, when I was in Hungary."

Benno Cohen continued talking, listing the names of Zionist workers in Berlin, and Eichmann responded to his questions and remarks like an expert on the subject. Cohen mentioned the name of the Zionist Dr. Frieden.

Eichmann corrected him. "The name isn't Frieden but Prinz." Then he launched into details about a Zionist meeting that took place in Berlin in the thirties, on the occasion of Dr. Prinz's leaving Germany. Eichmann was sent to supervise the meeting on behalf of the Gestapo.

Cohen asked him if he remembered the name of the man who preceded him in the office of Gestapo supervisor of Jewish affairs, saying, "I think his name was Kuhlmann or Kotschmann . . ."

Eichmann corrected him immediately. "Excuse me, sir, you're apparently referring to Kochmann, fat like this, and short . . ."

By the end of the conversation Benno Cohen could confirm that he no longer had any doubt that the man he was talking to was Adolf Eichmann, the Gestapo officer with whom he had dealings in Berlin during the

thirties, before he emigrated to Israel. He identified
him with absolute assurance, on the strength of his
appearance, his voice, his way of speaking, and the details he remembered about events known to both of
them.

———

On May 23 I again went to Jerusalem. The Prime
Minister was about to assemble the Cabinet ministers
to inform them of the capture of Eichmann. Shortly
afterward he would be making it public in an announcement to the Knesset. I arrived at the Prime
Minister's office at three o'clock. After a short discussion in the Cabinet, I went with Ben-Gurion to the
Knesset building.

The session was opened, as usual, at four o'clock in
the afternoon. Half an hour earlier a rumor had started
circulating through the capital to the effect that the
Prime Minister was going to make an important statement in the Knesset, and there was an atmosphere of
suspense in the House, from the benches of the Knesset
members to the rows of spectators in the gallery.

It was one of the rare times that I appeared in
public. A couple of minutes before the Prime Minister requested the Speaker's permission to take the
floor, I walked in and took a seat in the section reserved
for nonmembers, behind the Cabinet table.

In a voice full of emotion with a note of solemnity
Ben-Gurion read out his statement:

I have to announce in the Knesset that a short
time ago one of the greatest of Nazi criminals
was found by the Israeli Security Services: Adolf
Eichmann, who was responsible, together with the
Nazi leaders, for what they called the "Final
Solution of the Jewish Problem"—that is, the extermination of six million Jews of Europe.

Adolf Eichmann is already under arrest in Is-
rael, and he will shortly be brought to trial in
Israel under the Nazis and Nazi Collaborators
(Punishment) Law of 1950.

The Prime Minister's announcement came as a complete surprise to the Knesset members. It had appeared that the government was reacting apathetically to the recurrent reports that Eichmann was alive; no one in the Knesset had known that volunteers from Israel were in action, making their effort to bring him to judgment.

The news flashed from the Knesset to the entire nation of Israel, to the tortured who had survived the murder factory, to the bereaved who had lost so many dear ones. This reconfirmation of the rule of law heartened them and renewed their faith in justice.

And the news reached the far corners of the earth, imbuing all decent people with a feeling of respect; and it carried with it a clear warning to the murderers of the Jewish people, hiding in their holes, who thought that the years would whiten their sins and silence the cry of the blood they had shed, and that none would come any more to make them face judgment for the millions they had slain in their criminal frenzy.

# *Index*

321

# "HITLER'S WAR"

From the German point of view and secret Nazi documents never before revealed to the public, here is the whole gigantic drama of the most crucial days of World War II. Bantam now presents the books that individually capture the major personalities and events of the war.

| | | | |
|---|---|---|---|
| ☐ | CRACK OF DOOM by Willi Heinrich | 8041 | $1.25 |
| ☐ | THE MURDERERS AMONG US by Simon Wiesenthal | 7593 | $1.25 |
| ☐ | THE GAME OF THE FOXES by Ladislas Farago | 7477 | $1.95 |
| ☐ | PICTORIAL HISTORY OF THE THIRD REICH by Neuman & Koppel | 6705 | $1.25 |
| ☐ | EYEWITNESS HISTORY OF WW II: VICTORY by Abraham Rothberg | 5903 | $1.25 |
| ☐ | EYEWITNESS HISTORY OF WW II: SIEGE by Abraham Rothberg | 5901 | $1.25 |
| ☐ | EYEWITNESS HISTORY OF WW II: COUNTER-ATTACK by Abraham Rothberg | 5902 | $1.25 |
| ☐ | EYEWITNESS HISTORY OF WW II: BLITZKRIEG by Abraham Rothberg | 5900 | $1.25 |
| ☐ | THE LAST 100 DAYS by John Toland | 5812 | $1.65 |

Buy them at your local bookstore or use this handy coupon: